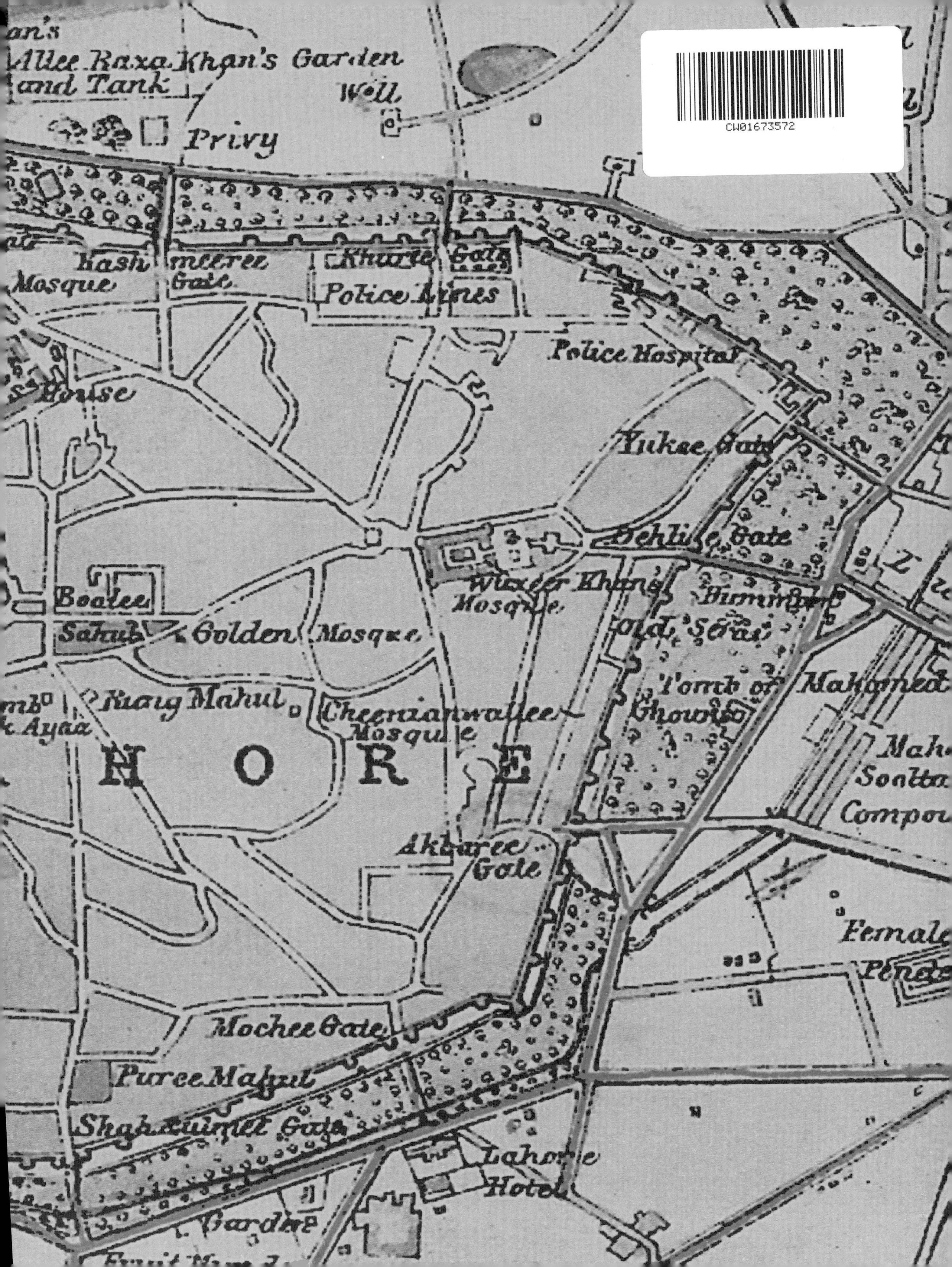
Allee Raza Khan's Garden
and Tank
Well
Privy
Mosque
Police Lines
Police Hospital
Golden Mosque
Cheenianwallee
Mosque
H O R E
Akbaree
Gate
Mochee Gate
Tomb of Mahomed
Lahore
Hotel
Female

LAHORE RECOLLECTED

AN ALBUM

10-2-07
Mian Amer Mahmood
ZILA NAZIM
City Distt. Govt. LHR

OTHER BOOKS BY F. S. AIJAZUDDIN

PAHARI PAINTINGS AND SIKH PORTRAITS IN THE LAHORE MUSEUM

SIKH PORTRAITS BY EUROPEAN ARTISTS

AITCHISON COLLEGE ; THE FIRST HUNDRED YEARS 1886-1986

LAHORE: ILLUSTRATED VIEWS OF THE 19TH CENTURY

HISTORICAL IMAGES OF PAKISTAN

THE ARMLESS QUEEN AND OTHER ESSAYS

RARE MAPS OF PAKISTAN

FROM A HEAD, THROUGH A HEAD TO A HEAD
The Secret channel between the U.S. and China through Pakistan

THE BARK OF A PEN
A Miscellany of Articles and Speeches

THE WHITE HOUSE & PAKISTAN
Secret Declassified Documents 1969-1974

LAHORE RECOLLECTED

AN ALBUM

BY

F. S. AIJAZUDDIN

SANG-E-MEEL PUBLISHERS
LAHORE
2004

For

HABIB FIDA ALI and NAYYAR ALI DADA

Two inspired architects,
who have contributed, each in his own inimitable way,
to the architectural identity of modern Lahore

954.9143 Aijazuddin, F. S.
Lahore Recollected / F. S. Aijazuddin.-
Lahore: Sang-e-Meel Publications, 2004.
236p. : Photos.
1. Lahore History. 2. Pakistan
History, Culture. I. Title.

First Edition : 2003
2nd Printing : 2004
Published by
Niaz Ahmad
Sang-e-Meel Publications,
LAHORE (PAKISTAN)

Printed at:
MAHMOOD KAMBOH PRINTER,
LAHORE.

ISBN 969-35-1453-X

SANG-E-MEEL PUBLICATIONS
Chowk Urdu Bazar Lahore. Pakistan. Phone 7667970
Phones: 7220100 - 7228143 **Fax:** 7245101
http://www.sang-e-meel.com e-mail: smp@sang-e-meel.com
25 Shahrah-e-Pakistan (Lower Mall), P.O. Box 997 Lahore-54000 PAKISTAN

CONTENTS

PREFACE

The city of Lahore will never run out of biographers. It will always, even after it has crumbled beyond habitation and become another Nineveh or Ephesus, find someone who feels inspired enough to chronicle its past and to leave for future historians a personal reconstruction however partial of its identity.

Perhaps the most pedantic of its historians to date must remain Syad Muhammad Latif, whose book *Lahore: Its History, Architectural remains and Antiquities*, published in 1892, represents an almost magisterial summation of facts known about the city up to the moment of his writing. The conscientiousness with which he marshaled those facts and the manner of his presentation was not surprising, considering his training as an Extra Judicial Assistant Commissioner in Gurdaspur. Dr M. Baqir's *Lahore: Past and Present* came sixty years later, in 1952, and although he too derived his sources from earlier accounts and guidebooks, he broadened his references to include vernacular publications about Lahore.

Since then there have been a number of other publications, each providing modern readers with a different vision of Lahore. My earlier book *Lahore: Illustrated Views of the 19th Century* for example, presented a panorama of Lahore seen through the eyes of nineteenth century visitors, primarily artists both foreign and local, both professional and amateur. I included also some work of early photographers such as Dr J. McCosh whose calotypes of the Badshahi Masjid and Maharaja Ranjit Singh's samadhi are as significant to the history of photography as the historic monuments they depict.

The only justification I can offer for compiling a second book on Lahore (beyond a filial affection for my home-city) is that during the intervening ten years since the appearance of my first book, there has been a perceptible, productive response among social historians, archivists, bureaucrats and citizens alike, a palpable and growing concern with the preservation, restoration and if nothing else documentation of Lahore's unique image. Another unexpected audience that has developed since the appearance of my earlier book is one of individual collectors, many of whom have been fortunate in acquiring early prints, watercolours and lithographs of Lahore, as my wife Shahnaz and I had done when we began collecting more than twenty-five years ago.

Prominent amongst them, and certainly the most forthcoming, has been Mr Robert Scoales, a retired librarian who despite being a Scot lives in Ealing (U.K.), and whenever he is in Lahore, takes rooms (usually No. 3) in the Orient Hotel on McLeod Road. From there, dressed in the superficial camouflage of a white shalwar-kameez, he makes forays into the streets and alleys of Lahore, looking out for anything that will enhance his already formidable knowledge about the architecture and topography of Lahore. If there is a letterbox still in use that carries the initials 'VR', of Queen Victoria before she was declared Queen Empress in 1877, Bob is sure to stumble across it. (He did. It stands in the street adjacent to King Edward Medical College.) He scours the footpaths and bookshops in search of unusual books or ephemera about old Lahore. And when he returns to Ealing, he continues his search, scanning the catalogues of specialist bookshops and postcard fairs for any material about Lahore. Bob has not only assembled an enviable collection of such valuable material but also generously agreed to its use in this publication. He carried much of it over on successive visits to be examined by me and to be scanned for this publication. For his unstinting largesse and warm friendship, I offer my deepest thanks, akin to the intensity of a dedication.

To Omar Khan, my thanks for timely information regarding the dating of certain photographs by Burke, Bremner and Bourne.

Let me also express gratitude to Mian Attique Ahmad who curated with me a memorable exhibition of Old Lahore at the Lahore Museum in March this year, to Mr Tariq Mahmood for editorial and other assistance, to Mr Khurram of RN Scanner Process House, and to Mr Zulfiqar Ahmed and Mr Suleman Qaiser for the layout and design. To Mr Niaz Ahmad of Sang-e-Meel Publications, I am especially grateful for his insistence that I should attempt another book on Lahore, his encouragement when I toyed with the idea, and then his patience while I took my own time to assemble this book.

To my wife Shahnaz, my love as always, and for my son Komail, a promise that the next book will definitely not be on Lahore.

F. S. AIJAZUDDIN
October 2002

INTRODUCTION

Had Lahore been accepted by the rest of the world as the epicentre of the universe - which native born Lahoris are convinced it is anyway - it would have conformed to the Big Bang theory, for from the moment of its first creation before recorded time, it has continued to explode, scattering its parts in every direction. The mohallas of its inner core - the Black Hole of the ancient walled city - have replicated themselves into one contiguous constellation of sprawling urban suburbs.

Over the same period of its evolution, its population too has multiplied, from 128,000 in 1871 to 2.2 million in 1972, and to an estimated 7.2 million in 2002, a human swarm spreading over and ravaging the surrounding countryside. Housing colonies and factories have replaced agricultural fields, streets without pavements have dehydrated nourishing watercourses, and houses have been grouted in the cavities left by uprooted nesting trees. A forest covering 1963 acres of woodland became a Model Town.

Lahore is now home to over 7 million people, spread over a physical area of 1770 kilometres. They live as they have done for centuries, an aggregation of loosely connected communities, coexisting within a generic, amorphous identity. Since the earliest of times, that pattern has remained unchanged. Only its extent has. 'Lahore is a city that perhaps can be described more appropriately as a federation of neighbourhoods, markets and special districts, each highly individual in character. Functionally as well as architecturally, these neighbourhoods reflect consecutive historical stages of the city's growth,' Mohammad Qadeer, a modern author on Lahore, has written. 'The Walled City was shaped by the Mogul social system. It evolved as a mosaic of socially cohesive and functionally specialized neighbourhoods.'[1]

He has compared the military-social order under the Mughals with its modern social counterpart, suggesting that while the former 'resembled European feudalism', the latter was based 'on territorial communal principles'. According to Qadeer, 'Cities were divided into quarters or districts, each inhabited by a tribe or clan or a guild fraternity under the patronage of a noble family. These neighbourhoods were villages of a kind wherein rich and poor were knit together through customary obligations and privileges. There were also commercial districts and market bazaar specializing in commodities such as jewels and spices. Lahore was also organized along these lines. Within the walls of Lahore there were, originally, nine such quarters and, according to an estimate, 27 quarters of varying sizes constituted suburbs towards the east-southeast of the city.'[2]

Those insular concentrations continue even today, as will be borne out by anyone who wants to buy for example an electrical appliance. The customer will be referred first and instinctively to Hall Road. Similarly, for kitchen utensils, one is directed towards Bhanda bazaar within the congested Shahalami Market, for bamboo ladders to Bansa bazaar, for woolen shawls to Kashmiri bazaar, for old clothes to Landa bazaar, and for paper to Kaghzi bazaar. The concept of 'stop and shop' under one roof has yet to develop into the norm. A medieval trader-controlled market is transforming but only very gradually into one that is more consumer-responsive. Meanwhile, until the customer finally becomes king, the trader continues to behave like a robber-baron.

At the macro level, the development of Lahore as a metropolis has necessarily always reflected the impulses and whims of its rulers. Under the Mughals, it functioned as a fortified outpost. Lahoris, benefiting from imperial patronage, lived within the safety of the congested walled city. For want of space, they built their recreational gardens outside the city walls, and their mausoleums in the open scrub-land that surrounded the city. The successors to the Mughals often local governors liberated from the onerous control from a distant and unsympathetic Delhi reduced the city once however briefly an imperial capital - to their own provincial level. At the end of the 18th century, the rapacious Bhangi sardars who periodically

1. Qadeer (1983), p. 81.
2. Qadeer (1983), p. 72.

scoured the countryside and shared their spoils in unequal portions, divided the city, and it was only in the gnarled hands of a diminutive political entrepreneur Ranjit Singh that Lahore became once again the capital of a kingdom. Taking control of it in 1809, the Sukerchakia misl leader who became a raja and from that a Maharaja, used Lahore as both the platform from which to launch his predatory ambitions and flaunted it as his prize, a monumental symbol of his success.

The defeat of the Sikhs in 1849, a decade after the death of Maharaja Ranjit Singh, and the subsequent annexation by the British altered both the pattern of governance and the geography of Lahore. Development of the city was no longer the elliptical consequence of an arbitrary or individual decision; it became a formalised responsibility, executed within the framework of a linear imperial plan. The rhythm of Lahore's life as a colonial governorship was calibrated for the next century or so to the pulsations emanating from the imperial capital of Calcutta (now Kolkata), and after 1911 from Delhi.

It could be argued that Lahore to a great extent still continues to live in the nineteenth century. It does so physically in the sense that it still uses buildings such as the Secretariat, the GPO, and Lawrence Hall built by far-sighted 19th century British administrators, town planners and architects, but it does so also subconsciously by using that ninety-eight year period of British rule as a reference point in its search for a modern identity. It has erased from its collective memory any trace of a period of inter-communal coexistence between Muslims, Hindus, Sikhs, Christians and Parsees. Any residual reminders from buildings such as Dyal Singh or Lakshmi mansions, or beneficences such as the Dyal Singh Library or the Sir Ganga Ram or Gulab Devi hospitals have lost any acknowledgment of their founders. It is not accidental perhaps that each of these buildings mentioned is protected by an indestructible legal trust. Those which were not, like the Jain mandir in Old Anarkali or the Hindu temple near Shahalmi market or the samadhi of Maharaja Sher Singh near Shah Bilawal behind the University of Engineering and Technology, became derelict and were finally destroyed, ostensibly in retaliation for desecration in 1992 of the Babri Masjid in Ayodhya.

A second generation of Pakistanis and even more so its successor - the third generation - does not remember a time when the Muslim population of the Punjab was an economic minority. According to the Census of 1941, out of a total population of Punjabi Muslims, almost one - third comprised artisans, craftsmen and agricultural labour. The Hindus dominated the non-agricultural commercial occupations such as trading and money-lending, and the Sikhs agriculture. Dr M. S. Randhawa, who served as the Resettlement Commissioner on the Indian side after the partition of the Punjab in the crimson autumn of 1947, has provided a first hand account of the trauma involved for the departing Hindus and Sikhs: 'Hindus were the owners of nearly all commercial buildings of any importance in Lahore, and banking, insurance and industry owed their progress to their enterprise. The educational institutions of the Hindus, the D.A.V. College, Sanatan Dharam College, and a Medical College were all at Lahore.' [3]

As a Punjabi Sikh himself, he felt the impact of partition even more deeply: 'Central Punjab is the cradle of Sikhism. The founder of the Sikh faith, Guru Nanak, was born in Talwandi, now called Nankana Sahib, in Sheikhupura District. Nankana Sahib...is as sacred to them as Rome is to the Roman Catholics.' The departing Sikhs left behind not only the very crucible of their religion but also the product of their industriousness the fertile agricultural colonies of Lyallpur (Faisalabad), Montgomery (Sahiwal) and Sargodha, in which the non-Muslim population in each (a major component of whom were Sikhs) was never less than 30%. Probably the most telling statistic of that period of communal exchange, when entire villages migrated and had to be relocated on opposite sides of the fresh, still bleeding border, was that the total non-Muslim population of West Punjab in 1941 was 4.351 million, outnumbering but only marginally the total Muslim population of East Punjab of 4.286 million. Their migration was an exodus of Biblical proportions, with the twist that in this 20th century Exodus both the Israelites and the Egyptians left their homes and crossed a Red Sea of blood in the hope of the Promised Land.

3. Randhawa, M.S., *Out of the Ashes*, (Bombay, 1954), p.5.

The effect of this evacuation on Lahore was dramatic. Almost 40 % of its non-Muslim population, i.e. Hindus, Sikhs and Christians, quit their homes precipitately, leaving a physical and social vacuum, to be filled by Muslim evacuees and freebooters. In Model Town, the experimental housing scheme developed in the 1920s to foster communal co-existence and symbolically a microcosm of Lahore itself, almost half of the residents left in 1947, its mandir and gurdwara abandoned. Only the mosque flourished.

The often uneasy coalition between these pre-1947 communities has been replaced in today's Lahore by an amalgam of industry, trade, commerce, services, health and education, a mixture of vibrant private enterprise and ponderous government diktat, by individual endeavour retarded by official apathy. It is an administrator's nightmare and an entrepreneur's dream. It has grown into a city that acknowledges no boundaries, neither within itself nor outside itself. Lahore no longer feels the need to be: it is.

No one visiting Lahore leaves without a tour of its sights, and as every such journey needs some form of locomotion, the reader is invited to choose his or her favourite style of transport from the 19th century palanquin or *palki* to the bullock cart, the horse-drawn 'Tums-Tums' and 'Ekkas', the *tongas* and the Hackney carriages, the bicycle and the vintage motor car - all of which have been plying the streets of Lahore over the past hundred years, and some do so even today.

Browsing through this album, they can follow a physical tour through the city, starting from the royal necropolis containing the tombs of Jahangir, his wife Nur Jahan and her brother Asaf Khan (A 1-10), located at Shahdara on the western bank of the river Ravi. Crossing the swaying but serviceable bridge of boats, one would first encounter the city walls (B 1-11). Behind and within them lay the Citadel of Lahore or Fort Complex (C 1-19), the Inner City (D 1-9) and its teeming often malodorous bazaars (E 1-5), no different from any medieval city that had yet to discover public sanitation.

Quitting the old city from the western exit that was once the site of Taxali gate, the tour will continue along the Lower Mall (F 1-17) as far as Chaburji, rejoin the Mall at the Town Hall (G 1-28), and then continue in an eastwardly direction towards Charing Cross (H 1-4) and the Upper Mall (I 1-9) and the bureaucratic enclave known as GOR I, an abbreviation for Gazetted Officers' Residences (J 1-5). Charing Cross (now Faisal Square) as its name implied stood at a crossroads. Montgomery Road lay due north, Egerton Road north-east, and Cooper Road diagonally northwest. To the south was Queen's Road (K 1-3) Empress Road, would bring one to the Railway Station and the Railway Workshops (M 1-4). The extremities of Lahore in those early days would have been the Military Cantonment (N 1-9), the symbol of British military occupation of Lahore until 1947, the newest of Lahore's suburbs Model Town established in the 1920s (O 1-11), and the Shalimar Gardens (P 1-6), a symbol of Mughal self-indulgence, that cooling those who sought relief from the city's claustrophobic interiors, and a respite for those travellers who needed to rest after the rigours of an overland journey on indistinct roads before entering the city.

Many of the images recollected in this album of Lahore were published during the early twentieth century as souvenir postcards. Their value lies less in any inscriptions they carry (most of them are in fact blank) but in the historicity of their illustrations. They recall a by-gone Lahore, a city that is rapidly fading from conscious memory and in certain cases from sight itself, as old buildings are demolished to yield place to newer ones. Other pictorial material has been obtained from the well-documented annual Reports of the Buildings and Road Department of the Government of the Punjab, published in a consistent format but with varying levels of detail since the 1870s. These contain valuable material information about the construction of various public buildings, supported by contemporary photographs taken during their construction. Important supplements have been the indispensable Lahore District Gazetteers (*si monumentum requiris* of the British Raj, consult any Gazetteer), many guidebooks and a few all-too-rare trade directories of Lahore that provide often fascinating data on the citizenry of that time.

To encourage researchers to explore on their own into the changing topography of Lahore, details from two maps of Lahore - sixty years apart in time - have been included here. The first is a map, published in August 1867 by the Surveyor General of India from Calcutta (now Kolkata) under the title: *Plan of the City & Environs of Lahore shewing the Civil Station of Anarkullee, and the Cantonment of Meean Meer, 1867.* It was lithographed by H.A.D. Lawrence. The second, titled *Guide Map of Lahore*, also published by the Survey of India, was issued sixty years later, in 1927. If one picture is equal to a thousand words, a map often speaks volumes. If photographs provide one dimension, and topographical maps another, and a contemporary description the vital third dimension, taken together these three make possible a more composite reconstruction of the city of Lahore during the intervening period.

Readers are invited therefore to climb into whichever mode of transport takes their fancy, to embark and disembark wherever they decide, at any spot, at any monument, and on any page of this album, and to admire the Lahore that once was and occasionally still is.

NOTE

To maintain a correlation between the references to various roads in Lahore, the original names have been retained, wherever appropriate. The renaming of roads in Lahore has been confusing at times, for the same names have been applied to different roads at different times for example, before 1876, the Mall was known as Lawrence Road, after which the latter name shifted to the road that later became Queen's Road. Then it referred to the road that ran on the south side of Lawrence Gardens. Lawrence Road has now become Liaquat Ali Khan Road and Queen's Road has changed its name but not its gender to Fatima Jinnah Road.

In September 1981, the Lahore Municipal Corporation notified the new names for Lahore's major roads. Subsequently other changes were made. The former and new names are:

Abbot Road	= Iftikhar Hussain Mamdot Road
Beadon Road	= Maulana Mohammad Ali Jauhar Road
Brandreth Road	= Sardar Abdur Rab Nishtar Road
Charing Cross	= Faisal Square
Cooper Road	= Khwaja Nazimuddin Road
Durand Road	= Sir Syed Muhammad Khan Road
Egerton Road	= Khalifa Shujauddin Road
Empress Road	= Shahrahi-i-Bin Badees
Fane Road	= Justice Kayani Road
Ferozepur Road	= Shahrah-i-Roomi
Hall Road	= Bahadur Yar Jung Road
Jail Road	= Ghous ul Azam Road
Lawrence Road	= Liaquat Ali Khan Road
McLeod Road	= Maulana Zafar Ali Khan Road
Maclagan Road	= Jamaluddin Afghani Road
The Mall	= Shahrah-i-Quaid-e-Azam
Nabha Road	= Sir Muhammad Shah Road
Nicholson Road	= Bakht Khan Road
Queen's Road	= Fatima Jinnah Road
Race Course Road	= Hussain Shaheed Suhrawardy Road
Temple Road	= Hamid Nizami Road

The Lahore Cantonment had similarly renamed roads within its jurisdiction, and then simplified them even further. For example, from Muradabad Road, Shara-i-Zahoor-ul-Islam has become Zahoor Afridi Road. Fortunately, Sadar Bazar remains unchanged as Sadar Bazar both in function and in name.

All bibliographical references have been simplified to the surname of the author, the year of publication and the page or illustration number. Items from the Robert Scoales collection have been marked with the prefix 'RS'.

Fig 1. A night journey by palanquin or *palki,* February 1842. Lithograph by Lehnert after a sketch by Prince Alexis Soltykoff (Paris, 1850).

Fig 2.
A bullock cart.
Postcard, c. 1900.

Fig 3. A bicycle with carrier boxes, near Bakra mandi or the open air Goat bazaar, held in the open area outside Bhati Gate, Lahore. Photograph, c. 1920.

Fig. 4. A Tum Tum, Lahore. Postcard, c. 1900.

According to Hobson Jobson, the word 'Tum Tum' was derived from 'Tandem', an English cart drawn by a single horse.

Fig 5. Ekka carriage. Postcard, c. 1900. A small carriage drawn by a single horse, used from the time man decided to ride behind a horse rather than astride it. The Greek Arrian wrote that 'to be drawn by a single horse is considered no distinction.' (Quoted in Hobson-Johnson, p.336.)

Fig. 6. A 2nd class Hackney carriage, near Nila Gumbad, Anarkali. Postcard, 1900. The church in the background is the Holy Trinity Church, then Anglican and now the Church of Pakistan. Its foundation stone was laid by Sir Robert Egerton (Lieutenant Governor of the Punjab, 1878-1882) on 22 March 1881.

Fig. 7. A Tonga. Postcard, c. 1900. A light two - wheeled horse drawn carriage, in which its passengers sat back to back. The word tonga is said to have been derived from the Sanskrit 'tamanga' or platform.

Fig 8. The cover of a tourist brochure containing small views of Lahore, c. 1920. The vehicle shown is a brougham landauette.

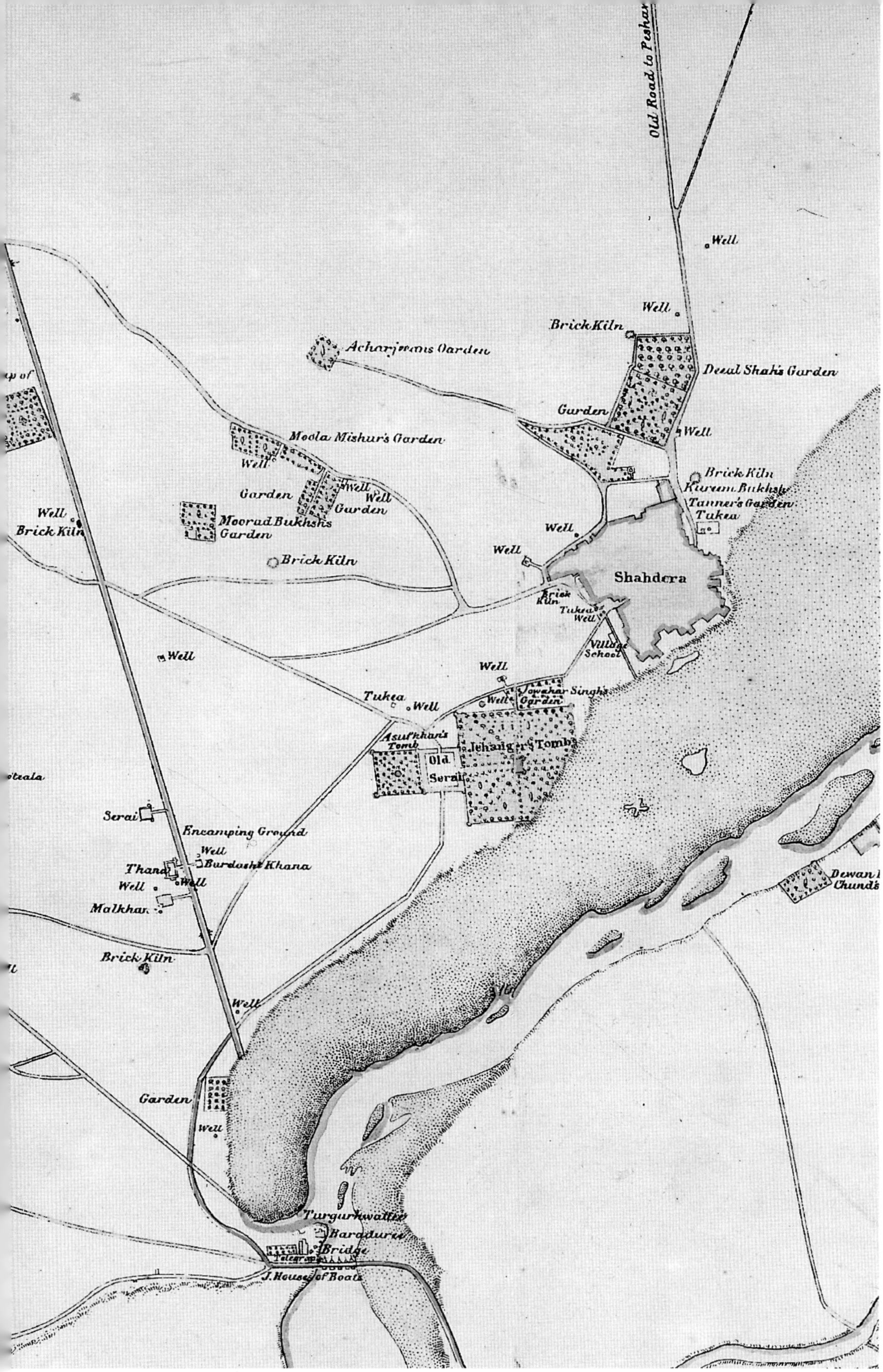

Old Road to Peshawar
Well
Well
Brick Kiln
Acharjeeans Garden
Deeal Shah's Garden
Garden
Well
Moola Mishur's Garden
Well
Brick Kiln
Kureem Bukhsh
Tanner's Garden
Tukea
Well
Garden
Well
Well
Garden
Moorad Bukhsh's Garden
Well
Brick Kiln
Brick Kiln
Well
Shahdera
Brick Kiln
Tukea
Well
Village School
Well
Well
Tukea
Well
Well
Jowahar Singh's Garden
Asuf Khan's Tomb
Old Serai
Jehangir's Tomb
Serai
Encamping Ground
Well
Thana
Burdasht Khana
Well
Well
Malkhana
Dewan
Chund's
Brick Kiln
Well
Garden
Well
Turgurhwallee
Baraduree
Bridge
Telegraph
J. House of Boats

SHAHDARA

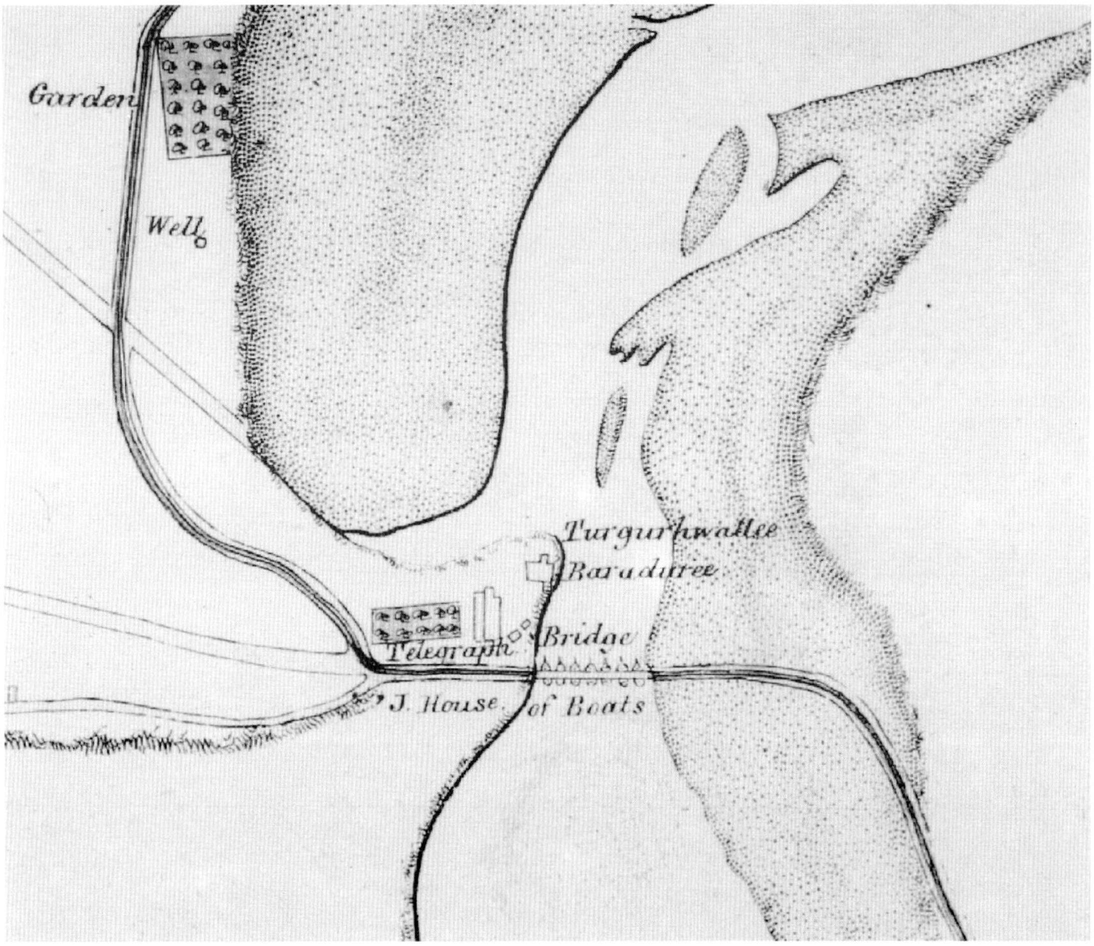

(a) Detail from 1867 map.

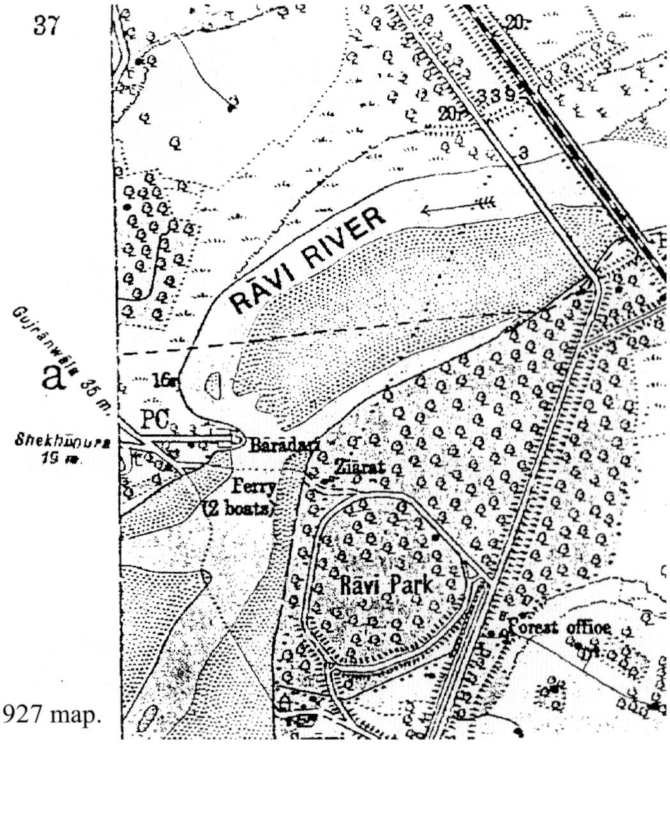

(b) Detail from 1927 map.

SHAHDARA

Had the city of Lahore been located in ancient Egypt, it might have been Luxor on the river Nile, with the village of Shahdara its Thebes, the royal necropolis, for at Shahdara, on the opposite bank to the living city, lay the tombs of an emperor Jahangir, his empress the gifted but grasping Nur Jahan, and a kingmaker, her brother Asaf Khan who managed to outwit her to secure the Mughal throne for Shah Jahan, the rightful heir and fortuitously his son-in-law. The tombs of all three - once related in life and now as close to each other in death - are within walking distance of one other on the right bank of the river Ravi.

The Emperor Jahangir died in 1627 and willed that he should be buried in a garden belonging to his wife Nur Jahan. His tomb, a prelude to the dramatic crescendo that Mughal architecture was to attain subsequently during the reign of his son Shah Jahan, took ten years to complete and cost ten lakhs of rupees. Anyone with experience of builders, ancient or modern, will readily understand the inordinate length of time and the high cost. Such extravagance in both time and money, though, was perhaps inherent in such a grand scheme that covered nearly sixty acres and envisaged an open serai bordered with cubicles for travellers, and the emperor's final resting place, guarded by four minarets set as sentinels at each corner of the marble and red sandstone edifice.

The mosque opposite the entrance to the tomb might have been the original limit of the tomb. Upon the death of Asaf Khan, Jahangir's brother-in-law, in 1641, his tomb was built in an area behind the mosque by the loyal Shah Jahan. The more modest tomb of the empress Nur Jahan was constructed outside, within sight of but not within the royal complex itself.

The 1867 map of the Shahdara area might almost have been commissioned by Shah Jahan for it ignores Nur Jahan's tomb altogether, showing only the garden surrounding Jahangir mausoleum and the damage caused by the inconsiderate Ravi to its southeastern corner. Goulding mentions that 'the Emperor's tomb has always been in danger of erosion by river action, and it appears from old records that this danger was so imminent in 1854 that a special grant of Rs 6,000 was sanctioned by the Chief Commissioner for the construction of protective works for the tomb and the well-known Baradari lower down the river.'[1]

Repairs and reconstruction of the necropolis became a recurring obligation as time and the river's depredations took their toll. The Buildings and Roads Department report, for example of 1905-6, records that 'the tile floors of the upper and lower platforms on the west side of Jehangir's tomb were restored, and the minarets which had been badly shaken by the earthquake were rebuilt.'

The location of the mausoleum and the restful ambience of its gardens made it a favourite picnic spot for Lahorites over weekends. The following description sent by Alfred W. Stratton, a Canadian by birth, who succeeded the explorer Aurel Stein as the Registrar of Punjab University and concurrently Principal of the Oriental College, Lahore, in December 1899 is typical. In a letter dated 26 January 1900, Stratton wrote: 'Mr Stein, my predecessor, is visiting Lahore, and gave a breakfast there, with tea before we came away. We were there from eleven till half-past four, ten of us in all.' Stratton describes the building as ' a great square building on a high platform, with four high towers, a floor of red and buff-coloured marbles, walls of red (Agra) sandstone with patterns on white marble and black slate, tracery everywhere, and everywhere the flower designs the Muhammadans knew so well how to make. All about a great garden: not far off the Ravi in sight, and the quaint bridge of boats we crossed by. Our table was spread on the floor

1. Goulding (1924), p.7.

under one of the arches looking out on the garden. We sat on cushions, and the servants bent low to serve us. Coming back I had the most enjoyable ride on my bicycle, and made the whole distance in twenty-five minutes. It must be about five miles.'[1]

Four months later, in April, Stratton returned to Shahdara, again as a guest of Dr Stein's, this time for dinner: 'Last night when I came in, as soon as I could get a cup of tea I dressed and drove out to Shahdara to a dinner-party of Dr. Stein's. The moon rose about half-past eight, and the sky was cloudless. Our dinner-party was on the centre of the roof of Jahangir's tomb. The table-cloth was spread on the roof, and we sat on cushions, three on each side. At some distance from us on the roof was another party with table and chairs. I doubt whether they were more comfortable, and we were certainly more in harmony with the traditions of that place[.] The lamps perhaps added depth of colour to the roses scattered everywhere over the large cloth, and made us conscious of the palms and lilies, and screened us from the other party. Yet even without them, the moon was bright enough, I fancy, and gave a softer light than any shaded candles. I sat between Mrs Arnold [wife of Professor Thomas Arnold] and a very pretty girl who talked well of superstitions, and books, and camels, and elephants, and India, and Norway.'

'After dinner we went to the top of one of the minarets. The depth of colour that we saw in the blossoms, white, and yellow, blue and shades of pink and red, easily distinguishable as we walked through the garden to our carriages, was surprising. There is a far greater mass of light here by day than in the west, but by night the light is simply glorious. It seems to me that the moon is less of a silver and more of a golden moon than at home'.[2]

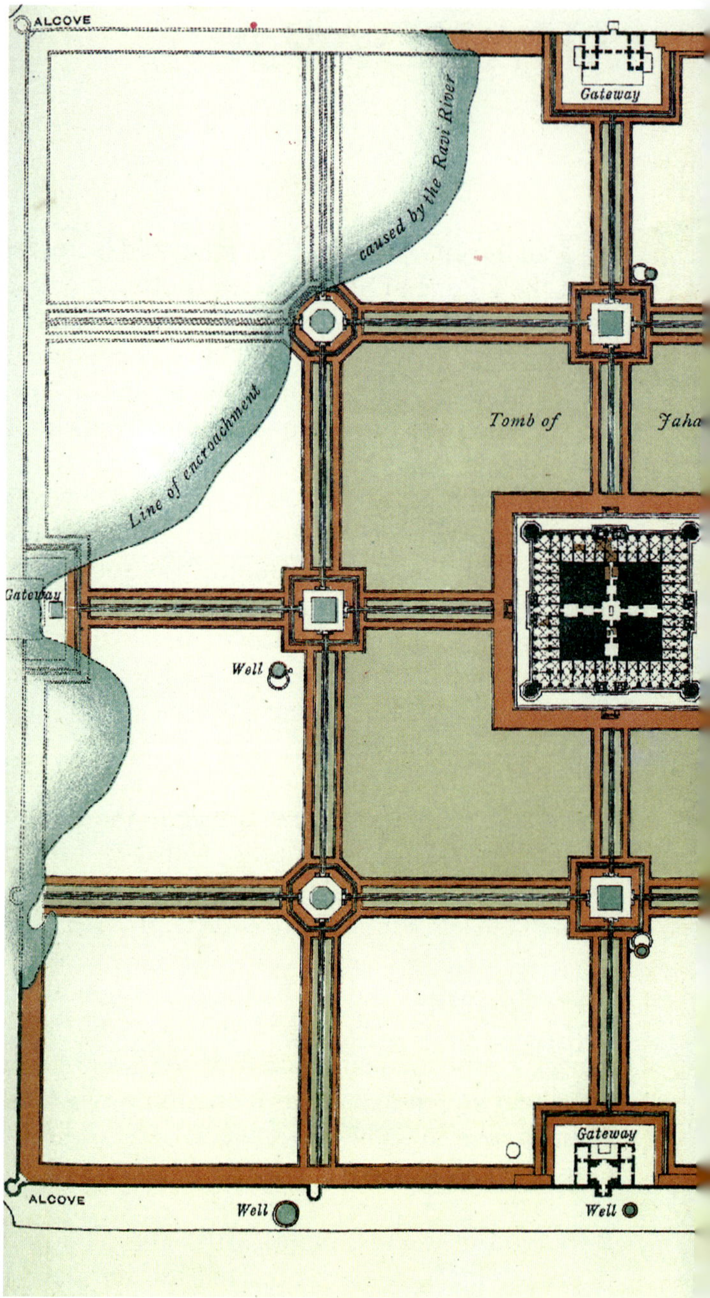

A 1. PLAN OF JAHANGIR'S TOMB, SHAHDARA

Lithograph, published in W. Griggs, *India: Photographs and Drawings of Historical Buildings* (London, 1896), no. 68.

1. Stratton (1908), pp.106-7.
2. Stratton (1908), pp. 162-3.

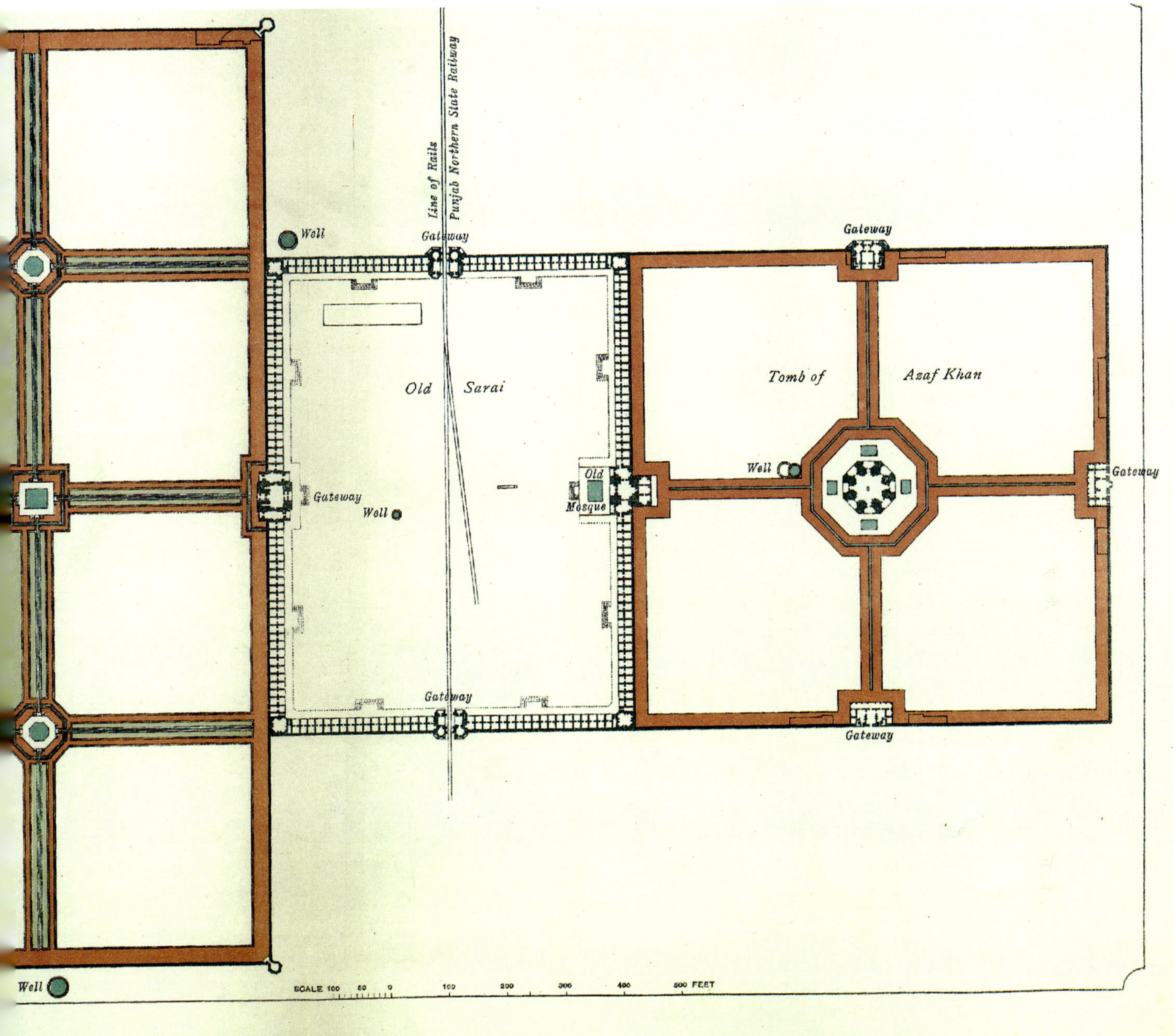

68.—TOMB OF JAHANGIR AT SHAHDARA NEAR LAHORE.

A 1. PLAN OF JAHANGIR'S TOMB, SHAHDARA

The geometrical symmetry so beloved of Mughal architects and landscapists - of the mausoleum complex containing the tombs of Jahangir and Asaf Khan is clearly visible in this plan. The erosion by 1896 appears to have been considerable, and as if nature had not inflicted its worst on the complex, the Punjab Northern State Railway added its insult to nature's injury by constructing a line of rails across the Old Serai (now known incorrectly as the Akbari Serai). 'This court has been occupied by workmen and railway officials,' wrote E.B. Eastwick, adding laconically, 'who have not improved it.' [Eastwick (1883), p.199.]

The relative space occupied by the emperor and his grandee is reflected in the area occupied by each. The middle courtyard or old serai, surrounded on all four sides by chambers, served as a staging post for travelers.

A 2. THE MINARETS OF JAHANGIR'S TOMB

A 2. THE MINARETS OF JAHANGIR'S TOMB

Lithograph, by J.D. Harding after a sketch by Charles S. Hardinge, done at Lahore in 1846. Published in C.S. Hardinge, *Recollections of India* (London, 1847), pl. 10.

Charles Hardinge accompanied his father Sir Henry Hardinge (then Governor-General) to Lahore after the defeat of the Sikh Durbar during the First Sikh War in 1845-6. He took time off to sketch some of its prominent monuments and although his drawings were perhaps more indicative than architecturally accurate, any deficiency in his compositions were compensated by the skilful and often over-imaginative talent of his lithographer in London J.D. Harding, who for local atmosphere populated the foreground with figures such the blind story teller, camel driver and the behishti or water seller dispensing water from his distinctive container made of animal hide.

A 3. THE GATEWAY INTO THE TOMB OF JAHANGIR

A3. THE GATEWAY INTO THE TOMB OF JAHANGIR

Photographic postcard, c. 1920. (RS/H)

The elevated red sandstone gateway connecting the serai with the emperor's takht-gah served both as an entrance and as an introduction to the architectural scheme a dramatic contrast of white marble decorative motifs set in red sandstone - seen to greater effect in the mausoleum building itself. E.B. Eastwick admired the gateway as being a 'very handsome archway' and described it as being 'of white and red sandstone about 50 feet high [with] 4 or 5 rooms in it which have at times been occupied by the Babus in connection with the railway.' [Eastwick (1883), p.199.]

A 4. THE TOMB OF ASAF KHAN

A 4. THE TOMB OF ASAF KHAN

Photo postcard, c. 1920. (RS/109)

What the tomb robbers perpetrated on the tombs of the pharaohs at Thebes, the Bhangi Sikh sardars in the late 18th century and after them the builders under Maharaja Ranjit Singh inflicted particularly on the tombs of Asaf Khan and of his sister Nur Jahan. They removed the precious marble facings and decorative pietra dura, leaving a shell of exposed brick.

Asaf Khan died in 1641 and his tomb, sumptuous by the standards of his time, was built by his son-in-law and sovereign Shah Jahan at a cost of three lakhs of rupees. The tomb took four years to complete. Its naked dome is visible behind the white facade of the mosque and the gateway in the middle foreground.

This particular photograph was taken from the roof of Jahangir's mausoleum.

A 5. JAHANGIR'S MAUSOLEUM SEEN FROM THE GATEWAY

A 5. JAHANGIR'S MAUSOLEUM SEEN FROM THE GATEWAY

Photograph by W. Baker, c. 1864. (Courtesy: British Library.)

Baker's photograph shows the lush and verdant overgrowth that has overtaken the ordered garden laid out at the time of the tomb's original construction. Trees jostle for supremacy in the quadrangles on either side of the brick walkway leading to the central raised fountain.

William Baker, a British Sergeant belonging to the 87th regiment, took up photography commercially after quitting military service in 1861. He worked in partnership with the more talented and prolific John Burke until his final retirement in 1873.

A 6 (a & b). TWO PHOTOGRAPHS OF THE ARCADE AND MINARETS OF JAHANGIR'S TOMB

Photo postcards, c. 1920-30. (RS/3 & RS/156)

A 6 (a). 'Shah Dera is a splendid ruin, its beauty consisting not so much in the plan or arrangement of the building, as in the details,' the Austrian visitor Baron Charles Hugel wrote after his tour of the monument on 11 January 1836. 'Marbles and precious stones are there in profusion. The chief building, placed in a fine garden, forms a square with a beautiful minaret at each corner; these are covered with pietra dura, and appear from a distance as though painted in a variety of colours; they should be seen very near, for the colours have a very poor effect when viewed from any point distant enough to embrace a proper view of the gigantic edifice itself. The ground floor consists of an arcade, raised on several steps, and a lofty terrace, whence, towards the west, the highly ornamental entrance leads to the small vaulted chamber, the tomb of Jehanghir, which is very similar to that in the Taj Mahal at Agra. The light falls on it from above.' [This was to conform to Jahangir's instruction that his grace was to be remain open to the skies so that the blessings of the Almighty could rain down upon it.]

A 6 (b). 'There is nothing of the same kind in India more elegant, than the terrace which runs round the roof of the building, formed entirely of pietra dura, and having an open balustrade of marble. I ascended one of the minarets, to gain a view of the long-desired Lahor, which has a goodly appearance from this distance, with its high walls and stately minarets and houses. In the foreground, are the buildings belonging to Shah Dera, which extend down to the Ravi; then comes the river; next, a long line of fields, intermixed with groups of trees, now clad in their fresh livery of spring; beyond these are the handsome edifices built by Jehangir in Lahor.'

A 6 (a). THE ARCADE AND MINARETS OF JAHANGIR'S TOMB

A 6 (b). MINARETS OF JAHANGIR'S TOMB

A 7 (i - vi). ARCHITECTURAL DETAILS FROM JAHANGIR'S MAUSOLEUM

Published in W. Griggs, *India: Photographs and Drawings of Historical Buildings* (London, 1896), nos. 70- 75.

70.—SHAHDARA, NEAR LAHORE. Tomb of Jahangir.
Details of marble and stone on outer face.

A 7 (i). Details of marble and stone on outer face (no.70).

A 7(ii). Details of marble and stone on outer face, and details of door (no.71).

A 7(iii). Details of fresco and mosaic (no.72).

A 7(iv). Coloured tile mosaic on walls (no.73).

A 7(v). Coloured tile mosaics on walls (no. 74).

A 7(vi). Details of panel walls (no.75).

A 8. THE CENOTAPH OF THE EMPEROR JAHANGIR

A 8. THE CENOTAPH OF THE EMPEROR JAHANGIR

Watercolour by William Simpson, March 1860. (Courtesy: Mr Paul Theroux.)

The marble cenotaph, intricately inlaid with semi-precious stones, marked the place below which lay the actual grave of the emperor Jahangir lay. On its sides are the ninety-nine attributes of God, with an invocation to God on the headstone, and at the foot, an inscription in Arabic that translated reads : 'The illuminated resting place of His Majesty, the asylum of pardon, Nuruddin Muhammad Jahangir, AH 1037 [1627AD]'.

A 9. THE TOMB OF EMPRESS NUR JAHAN

A 9. THE TOMB OF EMPRESS NUR JAHAN

Photo postcard, c. 1900. (RS/94)

Nur Jahan's relevance to the course of Mughal history effectively ended when she made an abortive bid to secure the throne for Prince Shahryar, her son-in-law, and was outwitted by Shah Jahan, Asaf Khan's son-in-law. The neglect she endured during her widowhood until her death in 1645 was perpetuated when the grand tomb she had constructed for herself gradually over the centuries fell into disrepair. Unattended and forgotten, it became an easy prey for marauders who found other uses for its precious inlaid marble. It is said that much of the marble that adorns the Golden Temple at Amritsar came from the facings of the tomb of Nur Jahan.[Latif (1892), p.109, fn.]

The omission of Nur Jahan's tomb from the map of 1867 (see page 17) is a reminder of the extent to which the monument to the once powerful Mughal empress who had the unique distinction of having a coin issued bearing her name had slipped into merciless oblivion.

The tomb, like that of her husband, was designed as a square built on a raised platform, with the actual grave in a basement beneath the central upper chamber where a marble cenotaph as ornate as that of her husband once stood. Her daughter Ladli Begum is buried beside her.

A 10. BRIDGE OF BOATS

A 10. BRIDGE OF BOATS

Photograph, published in J.H. Furneaux, *Glimpses of India* (Bombay, 1895), p. 322.

Until the mid 19th century, the only way to cross the Ravi would have been by ferry. William Moorcroft, making that crossing on 15 May 1820, wrote: 'The road [to Shahdara] is intersected by three different branches of the Ravi, separated in the dry weather by intervals of half a mile; but in the rainy season the two most easterly branches are united, and form an expansive and rapid stream. The water is always thick and muddy, and abound with fish, which had been taken under the Raja's [Ranjit Singh's] protection. In some moment of whim he had issued an order prohibiting fishermen to ply their trade upon the Ravi. The first two branches are fordable, but the third, which is the principal one, has a ferry.'

In the 1867 map, the bridge of boats connects the two banks of the Ravi at the site of Mirza Kamran's baradari, identified on the map as 'Turgurwallee Baraduree', an identification echoed by Latif in his illustration of it as 'Baradari of Mirza Kamran or Targarh.' From the map it would appear that the baradari stood on the right bank of the river, rather than being marooned as it is today on an island between the branches of the river.

Goulding, for one, mourned the replacement of the boat bridge by the new road bridge: 'The dismantling of the boat-bridge a few years ago, in consequence of the construction of the new roadway alongside the railway bridge, has removed a familiar and picturesque feature of the old landscape and the old Baradari is no longer on the main line of traffic.' The Baradari had been 'used in the sixties as a residence for the European Superintendent in charge of the bridge of boats'.

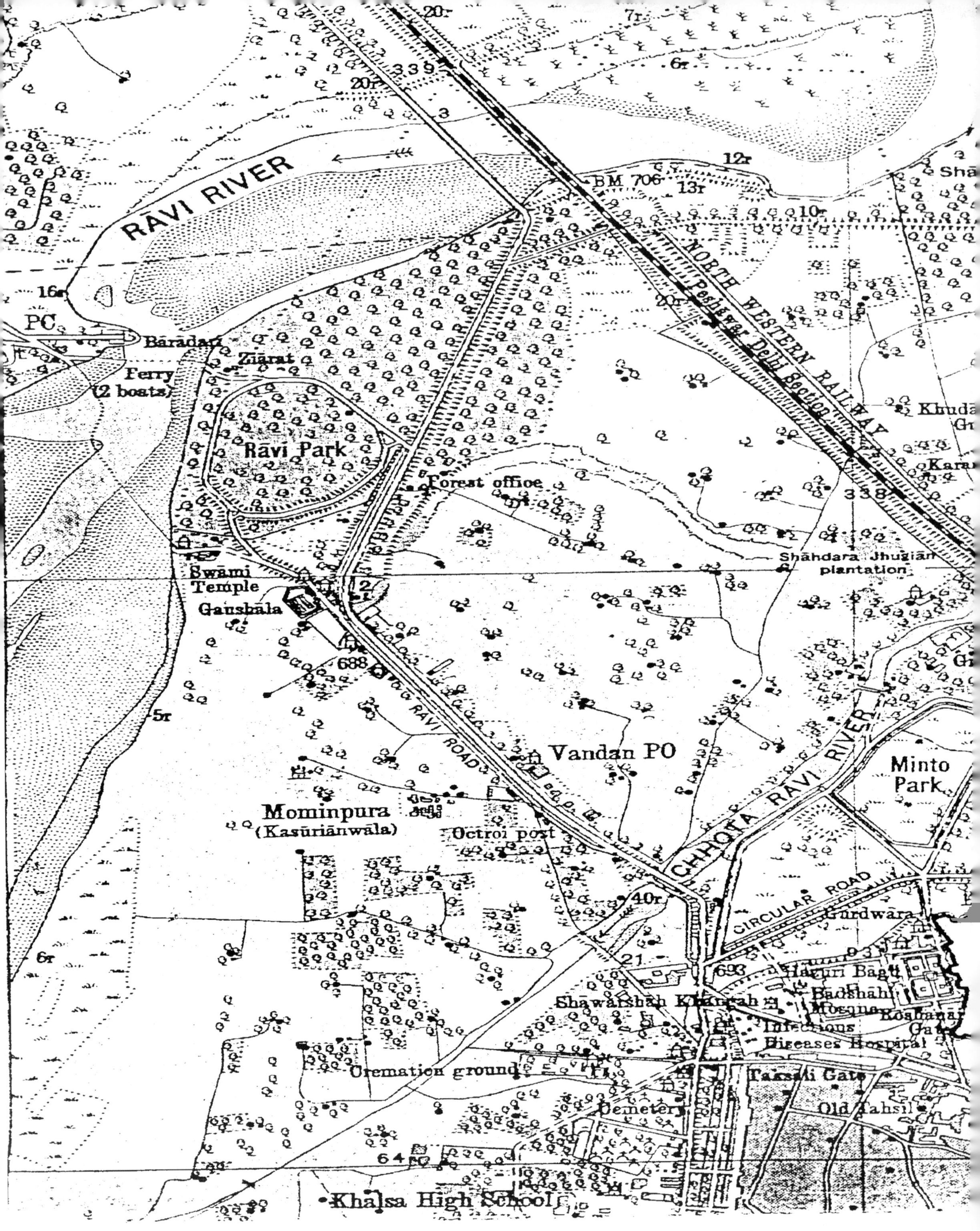

Detail from 1927 map.

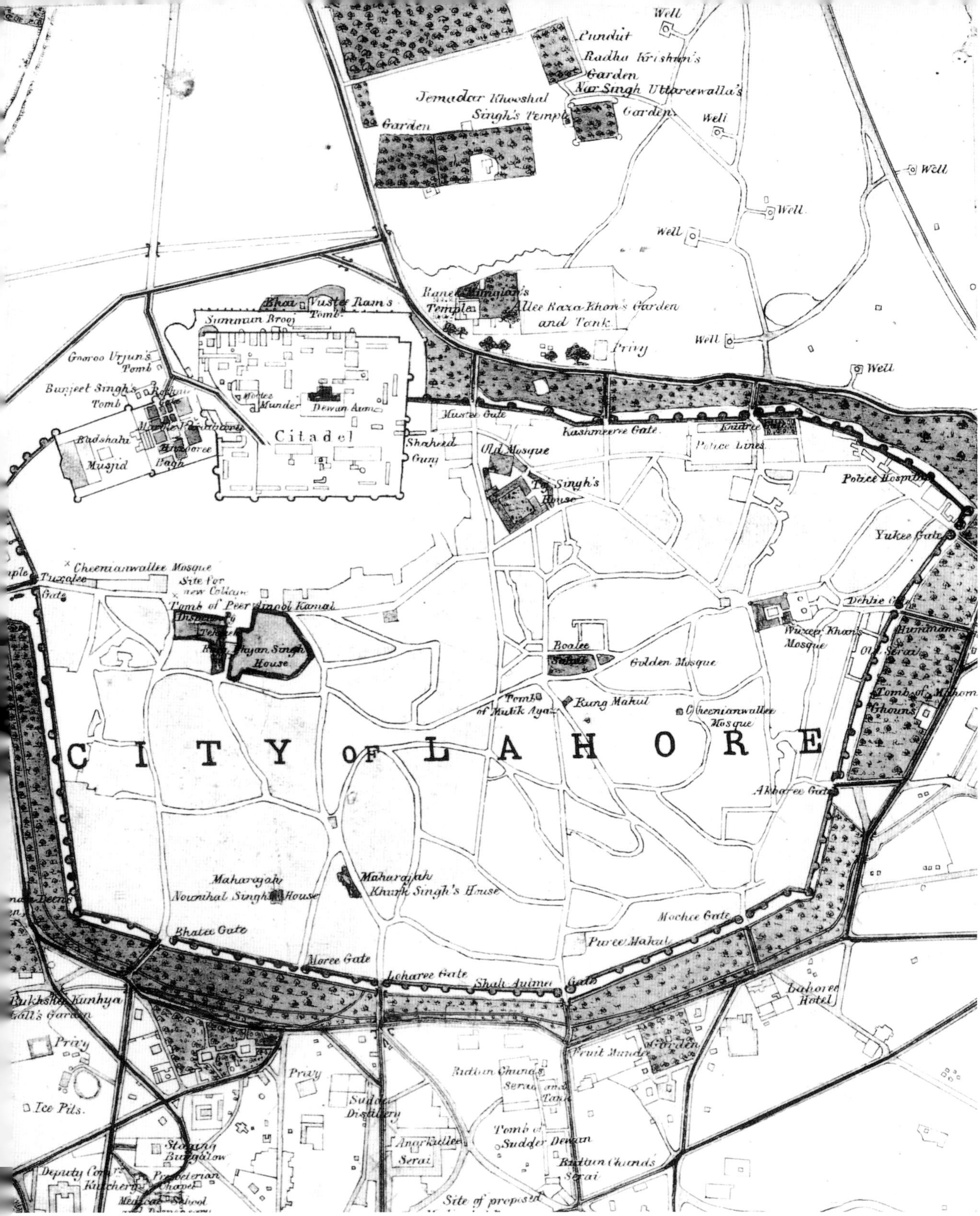

Detail of the Walled City from 1867 Map.

THE WALLED CITY

B 1. A PANORAMA OF THE WALLED CITY OF LAHORE

Lithograph by W. and N. Hanhart, from a drawing done by a local artist, Lahore 1842. Published in Honigberger, Dr. M. H., *Thirty-five Years in the East* (London, 1852), pl. XV.

The dramatic view that would have caught the attention of every visitor who approached Lahore from the northwest was depicted in this sketch of the city walls. Rising above them are the upper storeys of the fort and to its right, the red sandstone minarets and white marble domes of Aurangzeb's mosque.

The open area in the foreground was cleared for use by Ranjit Singh as a parade ground and subsequently by the occupying British as Lahore's first racecourse. On the right is the branch of the river Ravi that flowed during the monsoons near the Fort walls.

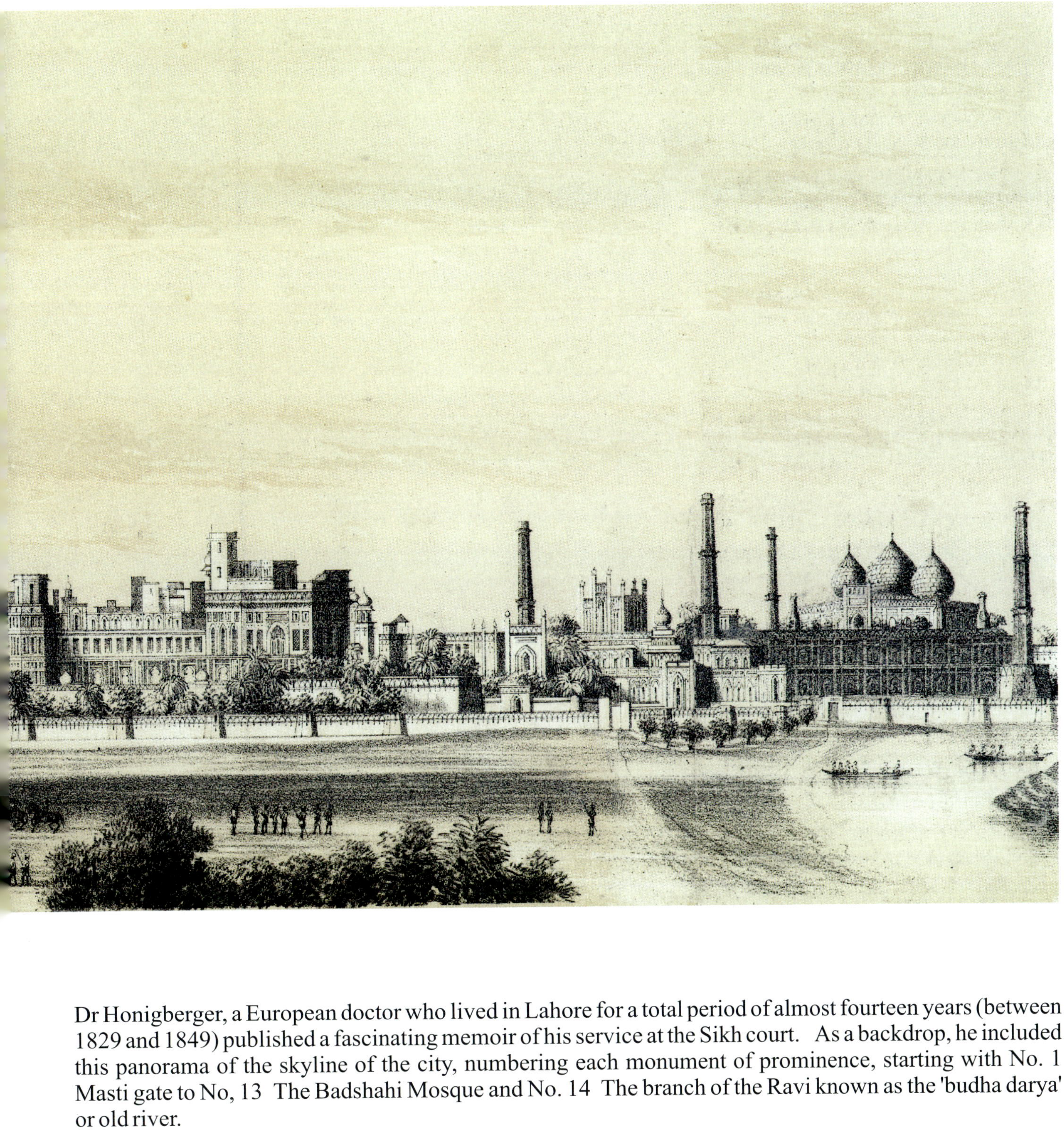

Dr Honigberger, a European doctor who lived in Lahore for a total period of almost fourteen years (between 1829 and 1849) published a fascinating memoir of his service at the Sikh court. As a backdrop, he included this panorama of the skyline of the city, numbering each monument of prominence, starting with No. 1 Masti gate to No, 13 The Badshahi Mosque and No. 14 The branch of the Ravi known as the 'budha darya' or old river.

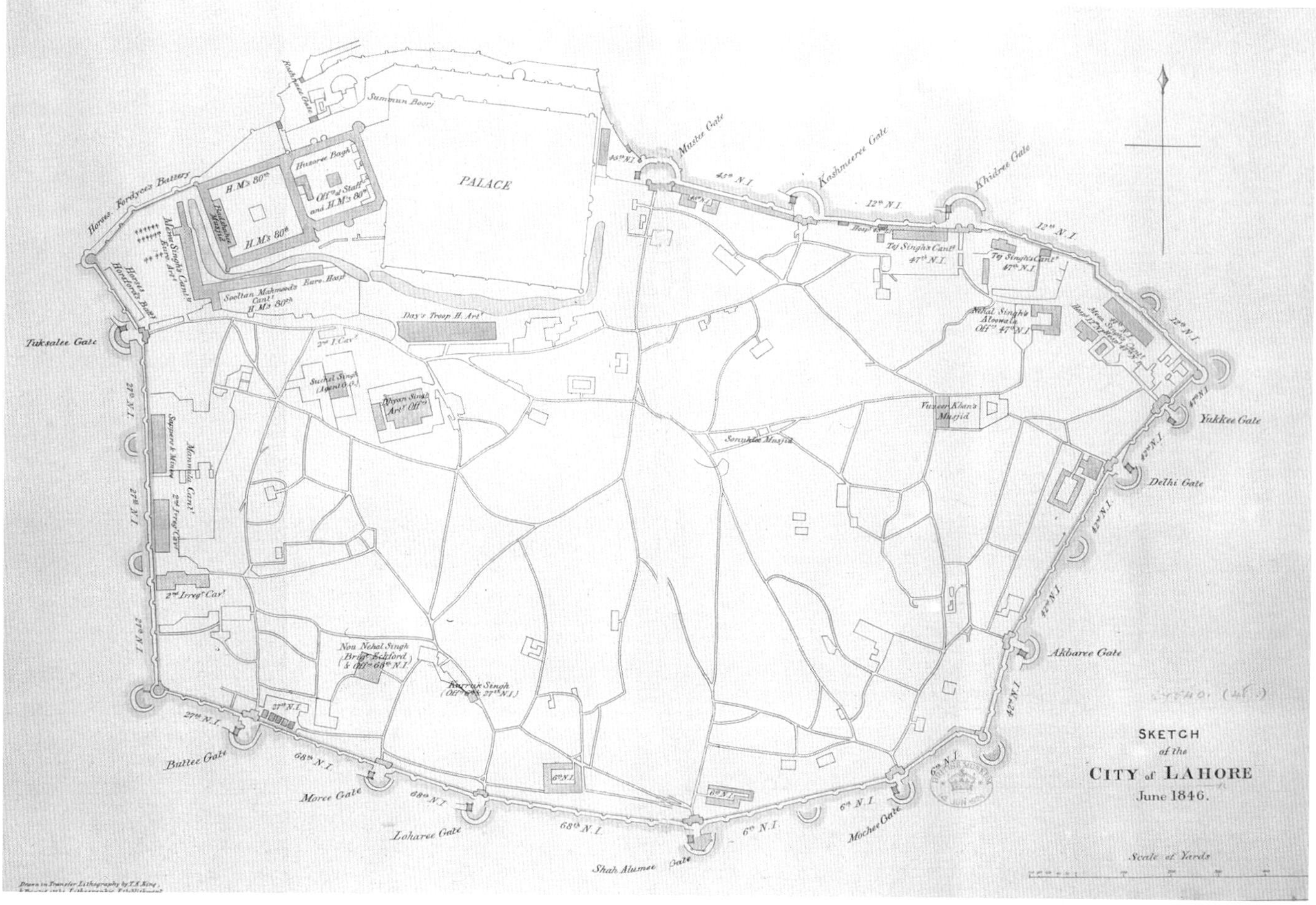

B 2(a). MAP OF THE WALLED CITY OF LAHORE, June 1846.

B 2(a). MAP OF THE WALLED CITY OF LAHORE, June 1846.

Drawn by T. King, and printed at the Lithographic establishment of the Quarter Master General's Office, Horse Guards, London, 1847. (Courtesy: British Library.)

Following the defeat of the Sikh Khalsa army during the First Sikh War over the winter of 1845-6, a treaty was negotiated at Lahore and signed on 9 March 1846. A supplement signed a few days later, on 11 March, which at the request of the Lahore Durbar, provided for the continued presence of British troops until the end of the year. This unusual request was 'to give the govt. time to reorganize the army. Otherwise, they were convinced the disbanded soldiery would return, pillage the town, murder the prince [Maharaja Dhuleep Singh] & throw the whole country in confusion.' [Quoted in Singh, B.S. (ed.), *The Letters of the first Viscount Hardinge of Lahore to Lady Hardinge and Sir Walter and Lady James 1844-1847* (London, 1986), no. 81, p.158.]

The deployment of the garrison within and below the walls of the old city are shown on this map, drawn by T. King and published in London in 1847, a year after the war ended. It shows that Her Majesty's 80th Regiment that had fought in the battles of Mudki, Ferozeshah and Sobraon, were quartered within the Badshahi Masjid and the Hazuri Bagh. The Agent of the Governor-General was housed in Raja Suchet Singh's haveli, and the various Native Infantry divisions between the city gates.

Nothing bears out Thornton's subsequent and often-repeated delineation of the city of Lahore than this map. He describes it as 'an irregular trapezium with its longest side looking northward. Its extreme length is one mile and a quarter; its extreme breadth, including the citadel, a little more than three quarters of a mile. The south, west, and east sides are surrounded by a brick wall, which was formerly 30 feet high, but which has been reduced to about 15 feet for sanitary purposes. The north side, looking over the Ravi towards Shahdara, is occupied by the palace, the Jama Masjid, Ranjit Singh's tomb [samadhi], and adjoining buildings.' He continues: 'Outside the wall was formerly a deep moat, but since the extension of the Bari Doab Canal to Lahore, this moat, which had outlived its military purpose and was merely an offensive ditch, has been filled in, and, with the aid of a branch-cutting from the canal, the space reclaimed has been laid out as a garden by the municipality.' [Thornton (1876), p.45.]

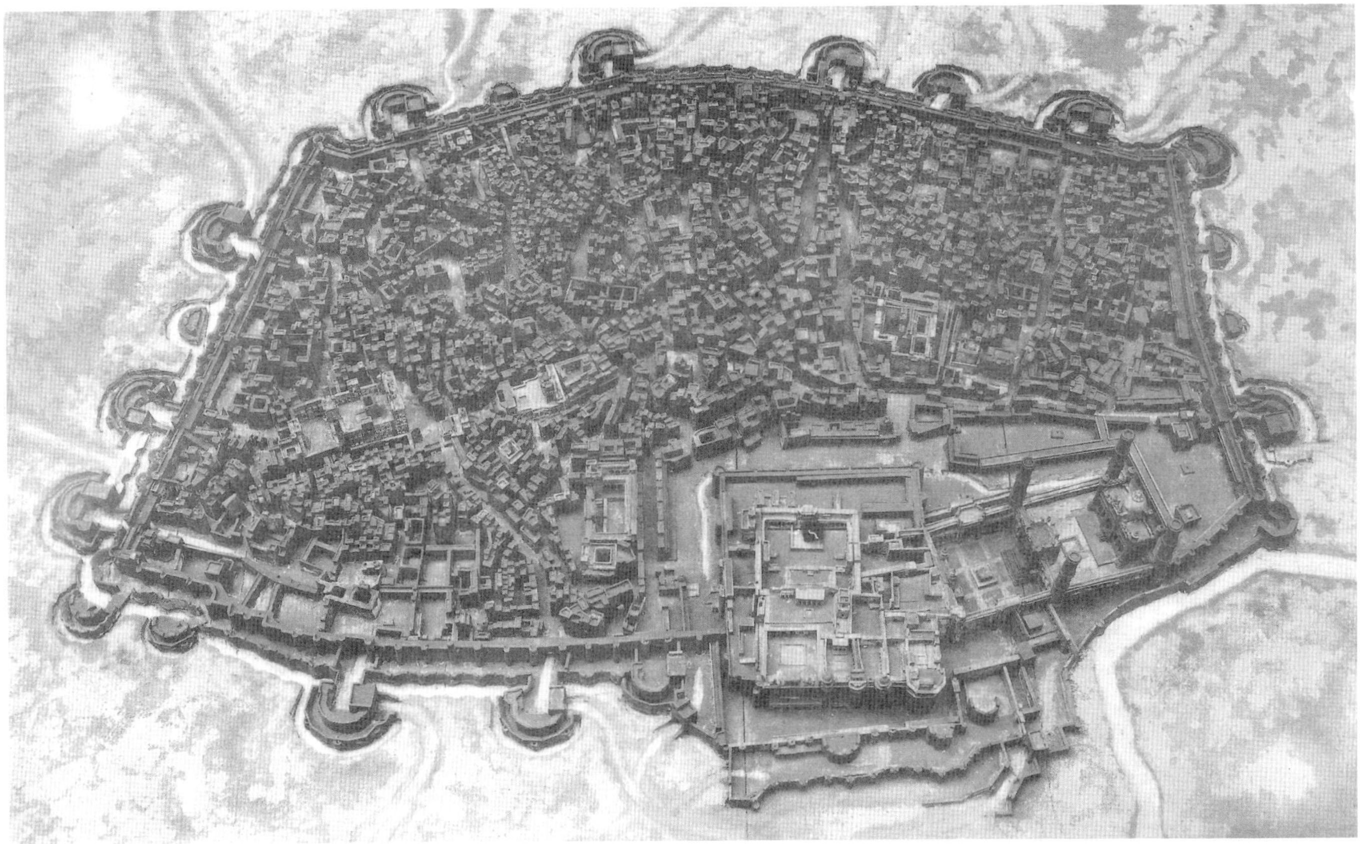

B 2 (b). A MODEL OF THE WALLED CITY

B 2 (b). A MODEL OF THE WALLED CITY

A wooden model of the walled city, c. 1925.

This wooden model was built to scale and kept at the Victoria and Albert Museum, London, for a number of years before it was destroyed. The model gives a bird's-eye view of the city seen from the north. Prominently visible from the right are the Badshahi mosque and the Fort. The rectangular building east of the fort is probably the haveli of Raja Dhyan Singh, the Dogra chief minister to Maharaja Ranjit Singh, while further eastwards is the mosque of Nawab Wazir Khan.

The twelve gates in clockwise order are: Roshnai Gate, Masti or Masjidi gate, Kashmiri gate, Khizri gate, Yakki gate, Delhi gate, Akbari gate, Mochi gate, Shah Alami gate, Lahori gate, Bhati gate, and Taxali gate. Mori gate located between Lahori and Bhati gate did not merit being classified as a gate as it was the conduit for the disposal of the considerable refuse that accumulated daily within the congested old city.

B 3. A SIKH PARTY ENTERING ONE OF THE CITY GATES

B 3. A SIKH PARTY ENTERING ONE OF THE CITY GATES

Lithograph based on a sketch by Prince Alexei Soltykoff, March 1842, titled: *Une Rue de Lahore* [A road of Lahore].

Prince Alexei Soltykoff, a Russian noble, visited Lahore in 1842 during the reign of Maharaja Sher Singh. His memoirs were published in Paris in 1848 as *Letters sur l'Inde and Voyages dans l'Inde, pendant les annees 1841-46*, in which this particular lithograph appeared.

Lahore made a less than favourable impression on Soltykoff, who complained: 'One can only traverse the crooked lanes of the city on an elephant with great difficulty and they are so narrow that one brushes against the walls the whole time, in imminent danger of being crushed by the fall of one of these hovels, whose four or five storeys seems to tremble under the weight of their balconies and their inmates. The so-called triumphal gates, by which one passes from one quarter of the city to another, are in an equally alarming state of disrepair.' [Garrett (1935), p.100.]

B 4. MASTI GATE

B 4. MASTI GATE

Photo postcard, c. 1920. (RS/100)

Identified imaginatively on the photograph as the 'Slaughter Gate', this gate is in fact the Masti gate or Masjidi gate, built by Akbar c. 1566. It took its name from the nearby mosque built in 1614 by the empress Maryam Zamani, the mother of Jahangir. According to Waliullah Khan (1961), 'the Fort of Akbar's period had only two gates, one on the east (Masjidi gate) and the other on the west which was later replaced by the Alamgiri gate.' [Khan (1961), p.16.]

B 5 (a). DELHI GATE

B 5 (a & b). DELHI GATE

B 5(a). Photograph, c. 1920.

Of the two gates of old Lahore that have lost their identity completely - Taxali because it was demolished and Delhi gate which was restored in what Thornton complained was 'a quasi-classical and incongruous style' both continue to be used as thoroughfares into the walled city. Thornton mentions specifically 'some old hammams or hot air baths, parts of which have been removed by the municipality to clear the way for the new honorary magistrate's katchery, which is in the wing of the gate itself. These hammams were of exceedingly massive construction. They were formerly very numerous in Lahore and the suburbs'. [Thornton (1876), p.47.]

B 5(b). Photo postcard, c. 1920. (RS/38)

B 6. MOCHI GATE

Sketch by R.C.W. Reveley Mitford, and published in *Orient & Occident* (W. H. Allen, London, 1888).

A rather fanciful sketch of Mochi gate, combining a number of typically 'oriental' features.

B 5 (b). DELHI GATE

B 6. MOCHI GATE

B 7 (a). SHAHALMI GATE

B 7 (b). SHAHALMI GATE

B 7 (a & b). SHAHALMI GATE

The Shahalami gate was named after Moazzam Shah, the second son of Aurangzeb, who fought his younger brother Azim for the crown after their father's death in 1707. Taking the royal title of Qutbuddin Shah Alam, he ruled for five years before dying in Lahore in February 1712.

B 7(a). Photo postcard, c.1920. (RS/37)

B 7(b). Photograph, c.1920.

B 8. RATAN CHAND'S TANK

B 8. RATAN CHAND'S TANK

Photo postcard, c.1910. Photo by Bremner. (RS/9A)

Outside Shahalami gate was located the serai, water tank and Shivala constructed by Dewan Ratan Chand Dhariwala, probably on the site of the garden that had been awarded to him by the British in 1849. As a boy, Ratan Chand had been a favourite of Maharaja Ranjit Singh, and when he reached manhood he was known at court as Ratan Chand 'dhariwala' to distinguish from another younger Ratan Chand. He served as the Postmaster General in1846, was appointed Honorary Magistrate of Lahore in 1862 and became a member of the Municipal Committee. Described by Latif as 'one of the most active and intelligent of Honorary Magistrates', he was also a liberal donor to civic causes, for which he was rewarded with the title of Dewan in January 1865. Dewan Ratan Chand died in 1872.

B 9. LAHORI GATE

B 9. LAHORI GATE

Sketch by B. Blascheck, n.d. (probably 1930).

This printed sketch is from an album of eight illustrations of Lahore, published by B Blascheck. No further information is available about the artist, not even from the sparse notes accompanying each plate. The text for *No. 3 The Lohari Gate* read: 'The Lohari Gate was one of the thirteen entrances into the city when it was surrounded by the wall which was only recently removed. Here at any time of the day the incongruous jumble of modern Indian life can be seen; the unceasing traffic of past and present, bullock carts, coolies, motors and bicycles pass to the accompaniment of the very oriental noises and smells without which no bazaar is complete.'

B 10. BHATI GATE

B 10. BHATI GATE

Photo postcard, c.1920. (RS/35)

One of the southern gates of the old city, Bhati gate took its name, according to Latif, from the Bhatias, 'an ancient Rajput tribe who inhabited these quarters in old times.'

B 11. TAXALI GATE

B 11. TAXALI GATE

Watercolour by William Simpson, 1864. (Courtesy: British Library.)

One of Lahore's early sacrifices to the demands of modernity, Taxali gate - the only gate on the western side of the old city - was dismantled completely. No trace of it remains except the name and its association with the site of the old Mughal mint.

This watercolour was completed by Simpson in 1864 from a sketch he had made of the gate during his visit to Lahore in March 1860.

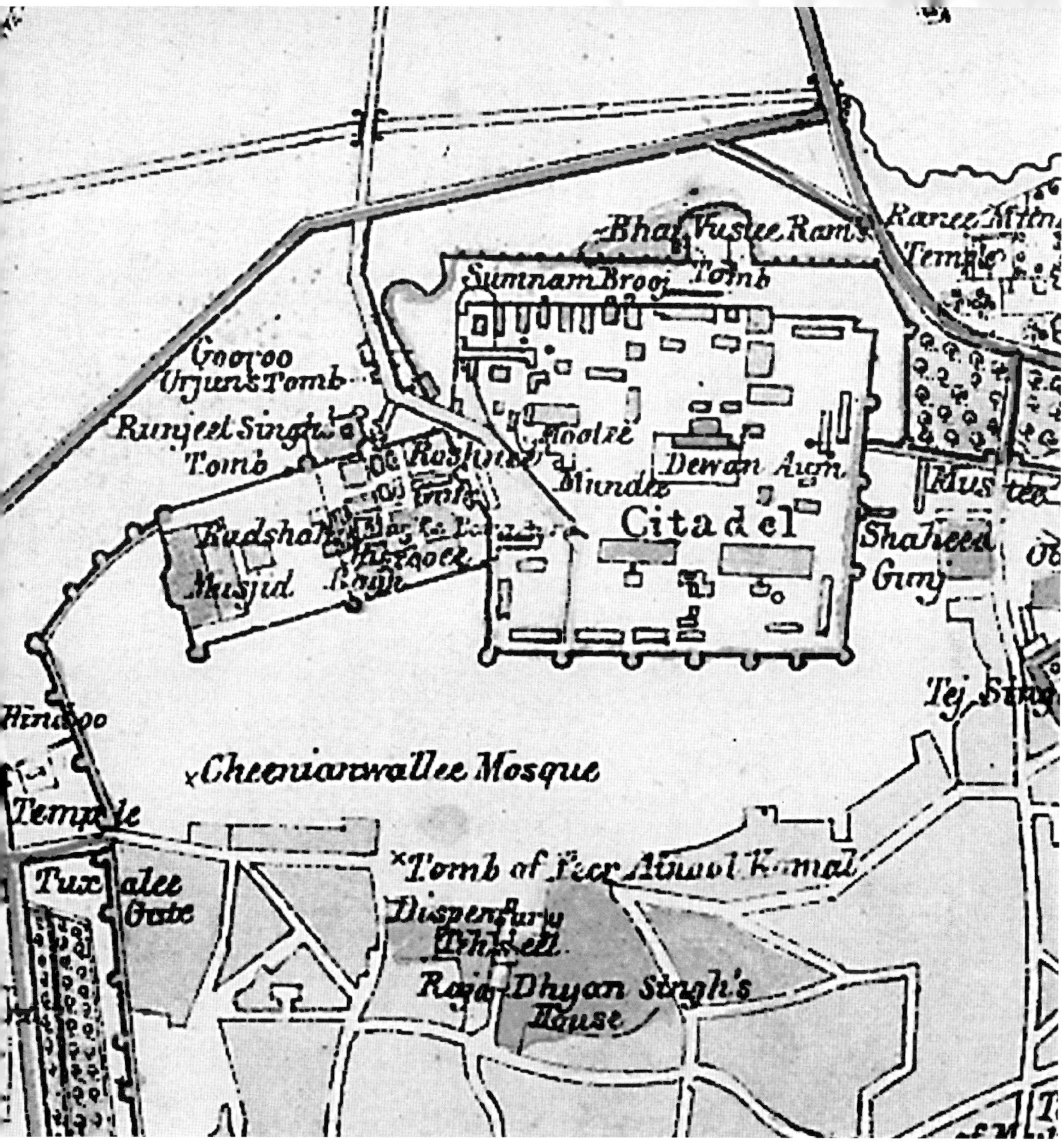

Detail from 1867 map.

THE CITADEL OF LAHORE

THE CITADEL OF LAHORE

It is inevitable that by its very location, on the safe left bank of the river Ravi, a fortification of some significance must have existed on the site of the present Lahore Fort. The earliest verifiable reference available is of the demolition, on the orders of the emperor Akbar, of the mud brick fort and its replacement by one constructed from burnt bricks. The most easterly side of the fort is attributable to Akbar's reign. Jahangir, his successor, gave the functional buildings an imperial character. He had a quadrangle built, known today by his name, in 1617-8, at the centre of which was a square fountain surrounded by marbled walkways. The rooms overlooking the quadrangle had facings of sandstone, their roof supported by eaves of carved elephants and other animals.

Shah Jahan expanded the fort, adding halls of public and private audience, sleeping chambers cooled by gurgling fountains, rooms and offices for the attendant courtiers, and the exquisite but underrated Moti Masjid, as white and as pure as the matched pearl rosary that remained his favorite during his incarceration at Agra until Aurangzeb ruthlessly snatched it from him, as he had already his throne. Fortunately Shah Jahan did not live to see the Sikhs convert his pristine mosque (the Moti Masjid) into a treasury and the British then use his marble-columned Diwan-i-Khas as a garrison church. 'The open archways were closed with canvas and the pierced marble screens and fountain were filled with concrete.' [Vogel (1911), p.50.] The Summan Burj was perhaps one of the few buildings ordered by Shah Jahan that retained its original character and purpose. Attempts were made to modify sections of it, and additions were made without concern for its architectural identity, particularly on the roof of the Sheesh Mahal during the reign of Ranjit Singh and his successors.

Aurangzeb's contribution to the Citadel of Lahore-the majestic mosque, completed in 1673-4 acts as a counterpoint to the secular preoccupations of his predecessors. It stands independent and at an eminence, separated from the fort by the neutrality of the Hazuri Bagh.

A crucial and valuable clue to the geography of the Lahore Fort is available through the foresight of Fakir Qamruddin, who provided the British in 1883 with a detailed map, complete with annotations of the uses to which various buildings had been put during the Sikh period and the specific spots where dramatic events to which he had been a witness had occurred.

Access to the Fort would have been through the Alamgiri gate, facing the Hazuri Bagh. A visitor would have passed the cook houses (used in the 1970s as a prison for political prisoners) before entering the large Diwan-i-Am garden, where the emperor appeared in public audience, visible to the nobles ranged before him at descending levels according to status and rank.

The small building in the foreground in that garden may have been the one that Eastwick mentions in this telling reminder on the mortality of Caesars and Emperors: 'In this Diwan-i-Am, or Hall of Audience, the Emperor daily sat in state; and as he took his seat the musicians stationed in the naqar khanah opposite struck up a martial strain, while a glittering pageant of men, horses, and elephants...passed in review before him; but meanwhile there issued from an empty tomb immediately in front, which has now disappeared , the voice of a mulla reminding the Shah-in-Shah from time to time that he too must die like other men.' [Thornton (1876), pp.54-55.]

The Toshakhana or treasury of the Sikhs can be located in the foreground. It was here that Misr Makraj, Ranjit Singh's trusted treasurer, kept the Koh-i-Nur and other precious jewels. After the conquest of the

Punjab in 1849 and occupation of the Lahore Fort, the contents of the Toshakhana were also surrendered to the British and given into the custody of Dr John Login. The list of items placed in his charge included 'The Diamond (Koh-i-Noor); The State jewels and treasures in gold, silver, and precious stones; dishes, plates, cups, cooking pots, and *ghurrahs* of gold and silver; The vast store of Cashmere shawls, *chogas*, *etc.* Runjeet's golden chair of State; his silver summer house, gold and sliver poled; tents and camp equipage of rich Cashmere; arms and armour, very magnificent; Shah Shooja's State pavilion, gorgeously embroidered; Relics of the Prophet: his shoes, walking-stick, shirt, cap, and pyjamas; his book of prayers in the Kufic character; several locks of his hair; The Kulgee "plume" of the last Guru (Govind)'.

During the British occupation, a road was made from the Hathi Pol (the private entrance to the Summan Burj apartments) up to the level of the Diwan-i-Am, cutting across the garden. The Khwabgah in Jahangir's Quadrangle is now a museum of military relics; the smaller Khwab-gah is known as the Diwan-i-Khas, with an Arzgah or Place for Petitioners two storeys below at ground level; and the Hamam-i-Badshahi can only be imagined from its foundations.

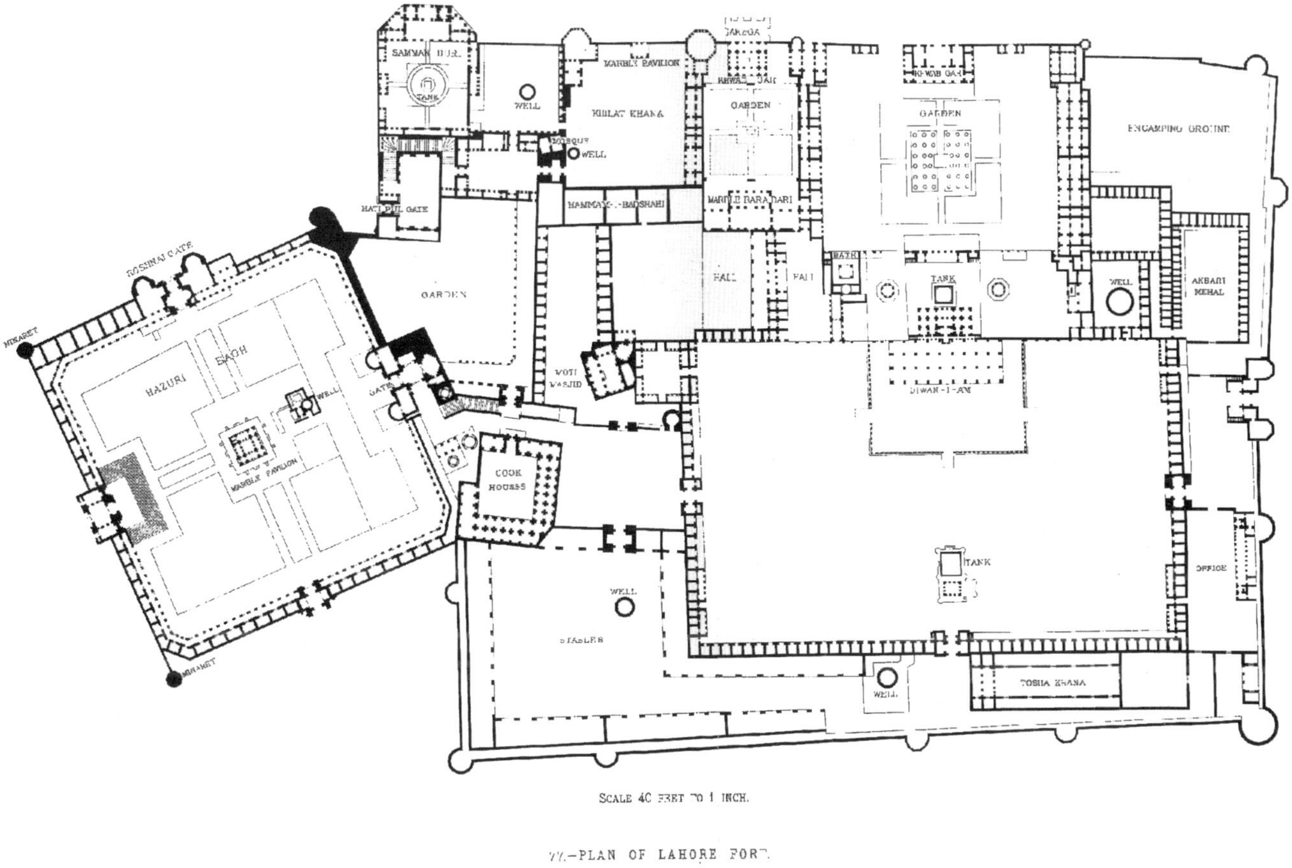

C 1. MAP OF THE LAHORE FORT

C 1. MAP OF THE LAHORE FORT

Prepared from an original compiled from data provided by Fakir Qamruddin, 1883. The map was reproduced subsequently in W. Griggs, *India: Photographs and Drawings of Historical Buildings* (London, 1896), no. 77, and again in Vogel's article *'Historical Notes on the Lahore Fort',* Journal of the Panjab Historical Society (Calcutta, 1911), Vol.1, No.1.

C 2. A PARTY OF BRITISH VISITORS IN HAZURI BAGH

C 3 (a). VIEW OF THE ALAMGIRI GATE AND THE LAHORE FORT

C 2. A PARTY OF BRITISH VISITORS IN HAZURI BAGH

Photograph, c. 1870.

Posing in the unkempt Hazuri Bagh, this group of British visitors has been photographed against the backdrop of the Alamgiri gate of the Lahore Fort. The upper storey of the marble pavilion is visible between the trees.

C 3 (a & b). TWO AERIAL VIEWS OF THE LAHORE FORT

C 3 (a). Photo postcard, c. 1930. (RS/9)

This photograph must have been taken from the southeastern minaret of the Badshahi mosque. From this elevation, the interior of the Lahore Fort is clearly visible. The main buildings identifiable from left to right are the Sheesh Mahal with its distinctive five arches and superstructures, the barracks built by the British in the area that was an open garden, and the white marble Diwan-i-Khas, also with five arches.

It is generally assumed that the two bastions flanking the Alamgiri gate entrance to the Lahore Fort were constructed at the same time as the Mosque itself, i.e. circa 1670-75. The gate was sealed and bricked up by the British and remained closed to the public until it was opened on 18 November 1949.

C 3(b). Photo postcard, c. 1930.

Turning his camera further southwards, the photographer took this view of the Lahore Fort. Again, gazing at the scene from left to right, the three white domes of the Moti Masjid are visible, behind it to the right the three storeyed building that is now the Sikh museum housing relics associated with Maharaja Ranjit Singh and the Princess Bamba collection of paintings. The Diwan-i-Am is seen at better advantage here. By this time it had ceased being used as a barrack and its upper rooms that had once 'been fitted up for a dining room' for soldiers had been vacated. In the far distance is the Masti gate, and in the middle fore-ground the numerous barracks that the British had constructed indiscriminately within the fort. 'The stern necessities of English military life,' Thornton wrote in his guidebook, 'have had no reverence for the relics of departed greatness, and there is only one part of the Fort and Palace which is not put to some practical modern use. This is the Saman Burj.'

C 3(b). VIEW OF THE LAHORE FORT

C 4. THE MARBLE KACHERI

C 4. THE MARBLE KACHERI

Photo postcard, c. 1930. (RS/21)

The *kacheri* was an addendum to the Sheesh Mahal or royal private apartments. It was used by Maharaja Ranjit Singh who rarely, if ever, sat in the Mughal jharoka in the Diwan-i-Am, redolent as it would of have been of imperial power.

The European painter August Schoefft made this building the backdrop for his huge canvas *Der Hof von Lahor* - that summarised the kinship, alliances and hostility within Ranjit Singh's glittering but irascible followers. The painting, formerly in the collection of Princess Bamba Sutherland, is now on display in the Sikh Gallery of the Lahore Fort and has been analysed in Aijazuddin (1979).

C 5. THE SHEESH MAHAL

Photo postcard, c. 1930. (RS/98)

Perhaps the most breathtaking building in the dramatic Lahore Fort must be the Sheesh Mahal, named after the shimmering silvered mirrors set in the walls and ceiling. Built originally by Shah Jahan in 1631-32, it was the most secluded and therefore the most private of lodgings within the fort, occupied by the empress or maharani and her female attendants. The inner heights of the pillars are inset with pietra dura, and the chamber has panels on the walls containing frescoes, painted during the period of Sikh rule, depicting scenes from the Krishna Lila and the Bhagavata Purana, and a picture of Guru Govind Singh leading his forces.

C 5. THE SHEESH MAHAL

An officer in the Bengal Army left an observant account of his meeting with the Sikh Ranjit Singh in the early years of his reign: 'On the 23rd [May 1808], I waited upon the Rajah Runjit Singh, who received me very politely, in a grand, lofty, spacious saloon of the palace, all marble, and inlaid with red and other coloured stones, pretty much resembling that at Agra. It is about 100 feet in length, and is called the Aeena Muhul [or Hall of Mirrors], from the decoration of its roof by small square-shaped piece of glass, at which the raja informed me the Singhs [Sikhs] used to amuse themselves by firing with their matchlocks, and would soon have destroyed it totally, had he not put a stop to their amusement, by making it his chief place of abode. In front of this saloon there was a fountain playing, and in the centre of it, is his hot weather sleeping room, tattied in; his wives and other ladies occupying the greater part of the palace, which is very spacious, and all built of marble.' [Anon., 'A Tour of Lahore in 1808, by an Officer of the Bengal Army', *Punjab Past and Present*, Vol. 1, Part 1 (Patiala, 1967), p. 129.]

The small building on the far right was the hammam or washroom converted for the use of his son Maharaja Sher Singh in the early 1840s. The formal surrender of the Sikh Kingdom in 1849 took place in the Sheesh Mahal, and in the 1850s the Nawab of Bahawalpur, then a state prisoner, was incarcerated here. Such is the fortune of kings and nawabs that less than ten years later, his successor was having a large house built for himself in Lahore.

C 6. THE INTERIOR OF THE SHEESH MAHAL

C 6. THE INTERIOR OF THE SHEESH MAHAL

Photo postcard by Bliss & Tilden, c.1930. (RS/19)

The ornate roof consisted of small painted panels of wood, secured together in a repetitive design. Thornton writing in 1876 describes the process: 'Small pieces of wood of suitable geometrical forms, frequently hexagonal, are cut out and painted separately. They are afterwards joined together on the ceiling, and the process is by no means so slow and costly as the finished result would lead one to imagine.' [Thornton (1876), pp.57-58.]

By 1905-6, the Government was informed that 'the preservation of the ornamental roof of the Shish Mahal, which is threatened with destruction on account of the rotting of the old massive beams, has unfortunately been found impracticable. The breaking up of the ceiling continues, and all it is possible to do is to prop up the beams from below. To entirely restore the roof, even if workmen could be found to do such work now, would be too costly.'

C 7. THE VIEW FROM THE SHEESH MAHAL

C 7. THE VIEW FROM THE SHEESH MAHAL

Photo postcard, c. 1930. (RS/17)

C 8. THE NAULAKHA PAVILION

C 8. THE NAULAKHA PAVILION

Photo postcard, c.1930.

The Naulakha pavilion built by Shah Jahan in 1632-33 remains an architectural enigma, its curved stone slabs seeming to defy gravity. It stands on the northwestern side of the courtyard and has marble screens and traces of pietra dura

C 9. THE ARMOURY

C 9. THE ARMOURY

Photo postcard, c.1930. (RS/22)

'Opposite the Shish Mahal, in an arcade closed in with glazed windows and doors, is the Armoury, which contains a heterogeneous assortment of weapons and uniform worn by the Sikh army [...including] modern muskets and rifles the cuirasses emblazoned with the Gallic cock which the "French guard" of Ranjit Singh wore in emulation of French cuirassiers. The silver-plated helmets and breastplates of the Italian and French officers employed by the Sikh ruler and here shown.' [Thornton (1876), p. 58.]

C 10. SOME SIKH GUNS ON DISPLAY

C 10. SOME SIKH GUNS ON DISPLAY

Photo postcard, c.1930. (RS/23)

'Among the guns are examples of *zamburahs*, small-bore iron cannons mounted on the wooden saddles of camels, and heavy matchlocks, supported on two legs in front like the arquebus of medieval Europe. Larger than these are the Jazail- huge musket barrels, roughly mounted, and used like the Chinese jingal, which they much resemble, in protecting forts. The curious light guns mounted on apparently inefficient wheels or castors were invented by Gulab Singh for hill warfare, and were drawn by a man or a goat.' [Thornton (1876), p.58.]

C 11. THE BARRACKS WITHIN THE LAHORE FORT

C 11. THE BARRACKS WITHIN THE LAHORE FORT

Photo postcard, c. 1920.

One of the many permanent barracks constructed by the British forces during their occupation of the Lahore Fort.

C 12. THE VIEW FROM THE ROOF OF THE SHEESH MAHAL

C 12. THE VIEW FROM THE ROOF OF THE SHEESH MAHAL

Photograph by Samuel Bourne, c.1864 (no. 416).

Almost every guidebook advocated that every visitor should climb up to the roof to obtain of a view if not of parading troops, as Ranjit Singh did, then of the surrounding buildings and 'the varied bustle and life of the Fort and City.'

Samuel Bourne, one of the pioneers in early Victorian photography, positioned his camera to take the widest picture of the panoramic view at his feet while he stood on the roof of the Sheesh Mahal.

In the immediate foreground on the left is the Armoury within the Sheesh Mahal, behind it in the distance the upper storey of the Hazuri Bagh pavilion, the lofty entrance to the Badshahi Masjid, and the Mosque itself. The white domed samadhi of Maharaja Ranjit Singh dominates the right side, obstructing the Roshnai gate entrance to the Hazuri Bagh.

C 13. ANOTHER VIEW FROM THE SHEESH MAHAL ROOF

C 14. THE HAZURI BAGH PAVILION

C 13. ANOTHER VIEW FROM THE SHEESH MAHAL ROOF

Photo postcard by H.A. Mirza & Sons, Delhi, c. 1930. (RS/14)

The building in the foreground is the Guard Room built by the British in 1863 near the entrance to the Lahore Fort. This entrance provided access to the Summun Burj and the royal apartments.

C 14. THE HAZURI BAGH PAVILION

Photo postcard, c. 1930. (RS/10A)

Assembled rather than built for Maharaja Ranjit Singh from decorated marble slabs purloined it was said from Mughal tombs, the baradari provided a cool refuge to the maharaja from the summer heat.

By the 1860s, the area around the pavilion was 'very much neglected and …a mass of jungle.' In 1913-14, it was leveled and grassed, raised pathways laid, and trees planted to give it the ordered appearance it today enjoys. The cost of this work amounted to Rs 23,427.

The Lahore guide of 1932 informed its users that 'the magnificent Baradari has been ruined by lightning shock. The main building is still intact, but it has become very shaky and it will not be able to stand any more shocks however slight. It would cost about Rs 1,00,000 to reconstruct and repair this splendid structure. On account of the present financial stringency, it would take some time before the work of reconstruction would be taken in hand.' Since then the baradari has remained topless.

C 15. THE INTERIOR OF THE BADSHAHI MOSQUE

Photo postcard by Herman Dass & Sons, Umballa, c. 1930. (RS/26)

The façade of the Badshahi Mosque with its white marble inlay set into the red sandstone is seen to best effect in this photograph, taken from the middle tier of the southeastern minaret of the mosque.

The outer domes are in a sense false domes for they cover the inner domes which are truly hemispherical.

C 15. THE INTERIOR OF THE BADSHAHI MOSQUE

C 16. VIEW OF RANJIT SINGH'S SAMADHI AND BADAMI BAGH

C 16. VIEW OF RANJIT SINGH'S SAMADHI AND BADAMI BAGH

Photo postcard, c. 1930. (RS/5)

The spiked masts in the middle ground are those of a wireless station located near the Lahore Fort. The pencilled inscription on the reverse of this photograph reads: 'This is the county just outside the Fort Lahore an the photo is taken from the tower similar to that shown on the left. You can see the six poles of the Wireless Station, where we used to do guard [duty] when at the Fort. The view is practically the same as you get from the Fort walls at the side'.

C 17. A VIEW OF THE OLD CITY

Photo postcard, c. 1930.

C 18. A PANORAMIC VIEW OF THE OLD CITY

Photo postcard, c. 1930. (RS/4)

Almost as interesting as the picture on this postcard is the inscription on its reverse. Sent on the 4 April 1941, it read: 'Left Karachi at 8.20 [p.m.] and travelled comfortably in air-conditioned train to Lahore. Ripe cornfields, woods, flat country. Arr. Lahore 6 p.m. Wide roads, trees, grass, flowers particularly roses everywhere. Faletti's Hotel cool, shut up, dull, comfortable. Gardens with flowers and birds. Visited Museum with its Kipling association. Drove round fort with fat Fakir Mohammed's taxi. Rested p.m. After tea drove by canal to Shalimar Gardens. Were reminded of Versailles, Durban, and Kashmir. Lovely trees and grass, roses, hoopoes, mango-trees, fountains, pavilions. Very tired but not too dirty. Went cinema to see *The Great Dictator* [Charlie Chaplin's satire on Hitler, released in 1940].'

C 17. A VIEW OF THE OLD CITY

C 18. A PANORAMIC VIEW OF THE OLD CITY

C 19. AN AERIAL VIEW OF THE LAHORE FORT, HAZURI BAGH AND BADSHAHI MOSQUE COMPLEX.

Photograph, c. 1920.

Photographed from the air in the 1920s, this view of the northern ramparts of Lahore's majestic fort echoes Honigberger's panorama (see B 1). Particularly distinguishable are (from left to right) Masti gate, the Diwan-i-Am with an unfenced expanse of open land between the fort and the perimeters of the old city, the triple domes of Shah Jahan's private Moti masjid, the larger domes of Aurangzeb's grander Badshahi masjid, and the on the far right the Summan Burj and behind it the samadhi of Maharaja Ranjit Singh. In the far distance are the wooded area and fields that have since become the suburbs of Mominpura and Qila Lachman Singh.

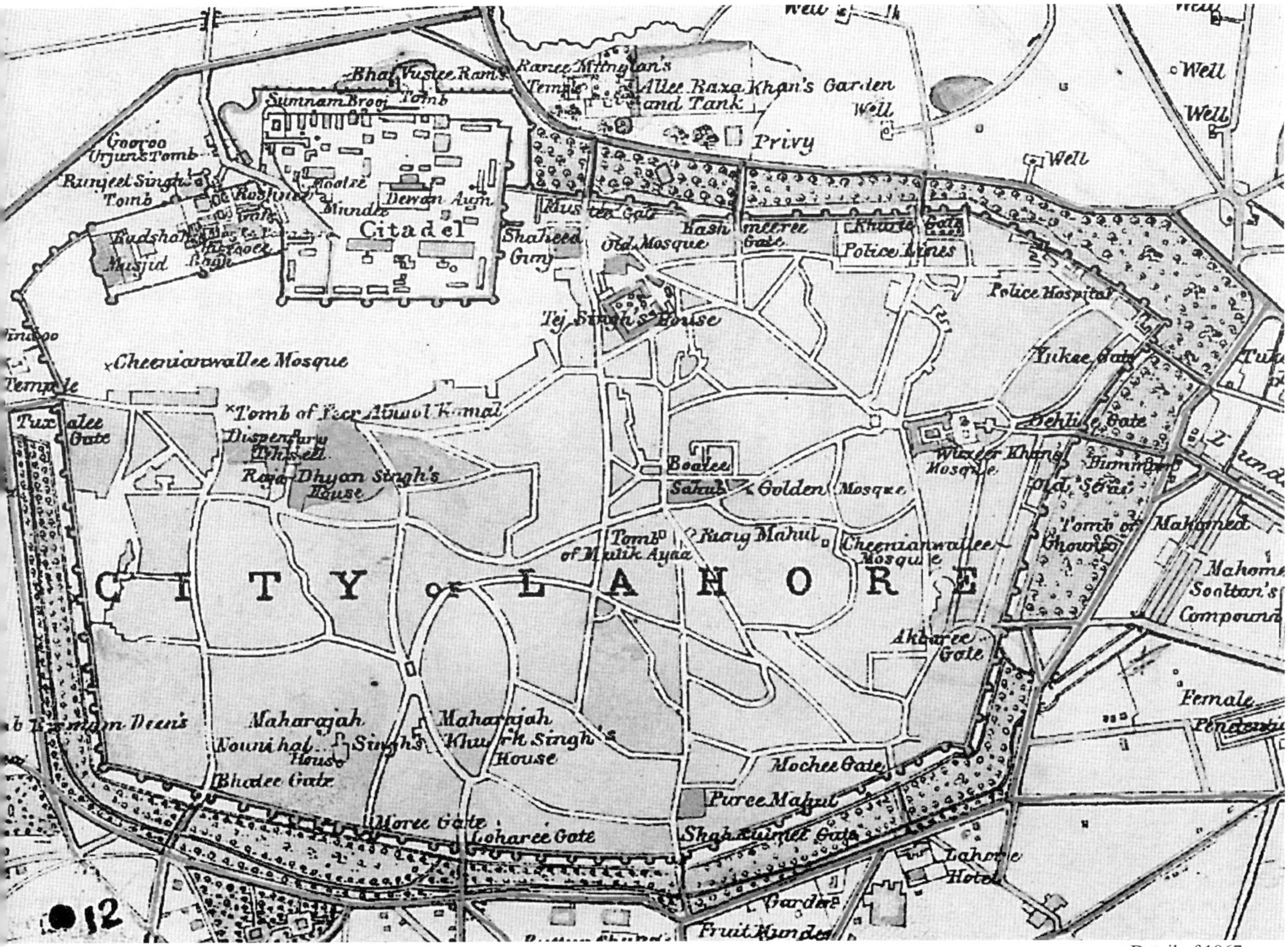

Detail of 1867 map.

THE INNER CITY

D 1. THE GOLDEN MOSQUE

D 1. THE GOLDEN MOSQUE

Photo postcard, c. 1930. (RS/29)

The Sonehri Masjid or Golden Mosque took its name from the gilt gold domes. Built in 1753, it seems almost a private mosque in what soon developed into a crowded public marketplace. Thornton mentions that 'behind the mosque is a baoli or large well, with steps descending to the water's edge. The well is said to have been dig by Arjun, the fifth Sikh Guru; the superstructure was built by Ranjit Singh.' [Thornton (1876), p.49.] The Dabbi bazaar led into the Kashmiri bazaar (for all kinds of shawls) and the Sarafa or gold bazaar.

D 2. A STEREOSCOPIC VIEW OF A LAHORE BAZAAR

Stereoscopic photograph by James Ricalton, 1888. (RS/L)

'Modern buildings, however fine, need not engage our attention in India,' an intrepid American school-teacher-cum-traveller James Ricalton (1844-1929) wrote in his photographic travelogue of the visit he made to Lahore in 1906. 'We are in search of scenes peculiar to the country, therefore I have chosen a native thoroughfare in the native quarter [...] And here in the heart of Lahore we look down into a typical street, in a typical town. The street is narrow, dingy, not too clean [...] At this moment the street below is not so full of

D 2. A STEREOSCOPIC VIEW OF A LAHORE BAZAAR

life as at an earlier hour. To catch an instantaneous stereograph of moving figures in this dark street requires a strong light from a meridian sun, and at midday most people retire to shady nooks; those we see are of the middle and lower class.'

After spending the rest of the paragraph describing the 'very active and garrulous pilferers the black rooks that abounded in the bazaar he continued: 'Have you noticed the oriel windows? They are common in every street, and some are very beautiful, and those are of a common order. We can only see the towers of the Vazir Khan's mosque [.] Do you observe there are no sidewalks in that street; that in place of a sidewalk there is an open sewer; and do you notice, over the sewer just below, a small bedstead and another similar one on the roof of the second building on the left? Those are frames on which to sleep and are called charpoys. A bedstead like the one on the roof costs about fifty cents.' [Lucas (1990), p. 67.]

In his monograph on the work of James Ricalton, Christopher Lucas described the use of stereoscopes in early photography: 'Stereoscopic photography also played an important role alongside the more conventional monocular format in chronicling the sights of nineteenth century India. Stereoscopy, the art of creating full three-dimensional relief by pairing two slightly dissimilar pictures and fusing them optically to recreate binocular vision appeared early in the formative years of photography. Its practical invention is usually credited to an Englishman, Sir David Brewster (1781-1868), who made several significant improvements on a device developed some years previously by Sir Charles Wheatstone (1802-1875). The result in 1850 was the appearance of the world's first hand-held stereoscope.'

'Thanks to Brewster's optical instrument and its successors [...], it was now possible to view a double photograph or paired set of prints in such a way that a convincing illusion of depth was created. Instead of perceiving an image confined to a flat plane, as it would ordinarily appear, to the observer's eye the subject now seemed to leap off the page and take on solid form.' [Lucas (1990), pp. 24-25.]

D 3. GATEWAY TO WAZIR KHAN'S MOSQUE

Chromolithograph, from a drawing by Amir Buksh, and published in W. Griggs, *Journal of Indian Art* No. 19 (July 1887).

No monument in the old inner city encapsulates all the elements of the spirit and the talent of Lahore as uniquely as does the Mosque of Wazir Khan. Founded in 1634 through a bequest by Nawab Ilmuddin Khan (a grandee of Shah Jahan's, and also known as Wazir Khan), the mosque represents not only his viceregal largesse but the generosity of every anonymous artisan who contributed his skill - whether it was in construction, tile making and design, or wall painting - to make the mosque a spiritual and an aesthetic experience.

The heavily decorated entrance prepares the visitor for the consummate workmanship inside. Not surprisingly, every generation of students in Lahore's art schools has sharpened its vision by studying and copying the details that are to be found on its façade, its minarets and within the chamber itself. The drawing from which this chromolithograph was prepared had been made by Amir Buksh, a teacher at the Mayo School of Arts (now the National College of Arts). It was part of a series documenting the monument for its students and for posterity an open-minded attitude at various with some of the later craftsmen assigned for the work of renovation. In his article, F.H. Andrews, former Principal of the Mayo School of Arts, admired the tile work as being 'extremely fine, particularly when the bright mustard yellow is not too lavishly used', but complained that 'the secret of the art is said to have died with an aged karigar, Muhammad Baksh, who expired at Lahore in 1876 under the weight of ninety-seven years, having never in all that time consented to take a pupil.'

D 4.

D 4. THE INNER SIDE OF THE ENTRANCE TO WAZIR KHAN'S MOSQUE

Chromolithograph by W.Griggs, from a drawing by Sher Muhammad. Published in *The Journal of Indian Art,* No. 19, (July 1887).

Andrews's published notes on the mosque read: 'The material used in the construction of the Mosque is a small tile-like brick universally used by the Moghuls when stone was unobtainable or too costly. The only stone used in the building is used for brackets and some of the fretwork (*pinjra*). The walls were coated with plaster (*chunam*) and faced with a finely-soften quality of the same material tooled to a marble-like surface and coloured. All the external plasterwork was coloured a rich Indian red, in true fresco, and the surface afterwards picked out with white lines in the similitude of the small bricks beneath. The extreme severity of the lines of the building is relieved by the division of the surfaces into slightly sunk rectangular panels, alternately vertical and horizontal, the vertical panels having usually an inner panel with arched head or the more florid cusped *mihrab*. These panels, where they are exposed to the weather, are generally filled with a peculiar inlaid *faience* pottery called *kashi*, the effect of which must have been very fine when the setting of deep red plaster of the walls was intact.'

D 5.

D 5. THE INNER FACADE OF THE MOSQUE OF WAZIR KHAN

Watercolour by Muhammad Din, c.1880.

'The facade of the sanctuary is practically covered with *kashi* and is divided into the usual oblong panels. A beautiful border is carried rectangularly round the centre archway, and inscriptions in Persian characters occur in an outer border, in a long panel over the archway, and in horizontal panels long the upper portions of the lower walls to right and left. The spandrels are filled in with extremely fine designs.'

'With the *minars*, however, the facade of the sanctuary, and the entrance gateway, where a very small portion of the surface was left for plaster, the effect of the gorgeous colours against the soft blue of a Punjab sky, and saturated with brilliant sunlight and glowing purple shadow, is indescribably rich and jewel-like.' (Andrews, quoted in Chaghatai (1975), p.13.)

D 6. FRESCO DECORATION IN THE MOSQUE OF WAZIR KHAN

Chromolithograph by W. Griggs from a drawing by Mohammed Din, Allah-ud-din and Amir Baksh, c. 1880. Published in *The Journal of Indian Art,* No. 19, (July 1887).

D 6. FRESCO DECORATION IN THE MOSQUE OF WAZIR KHAN

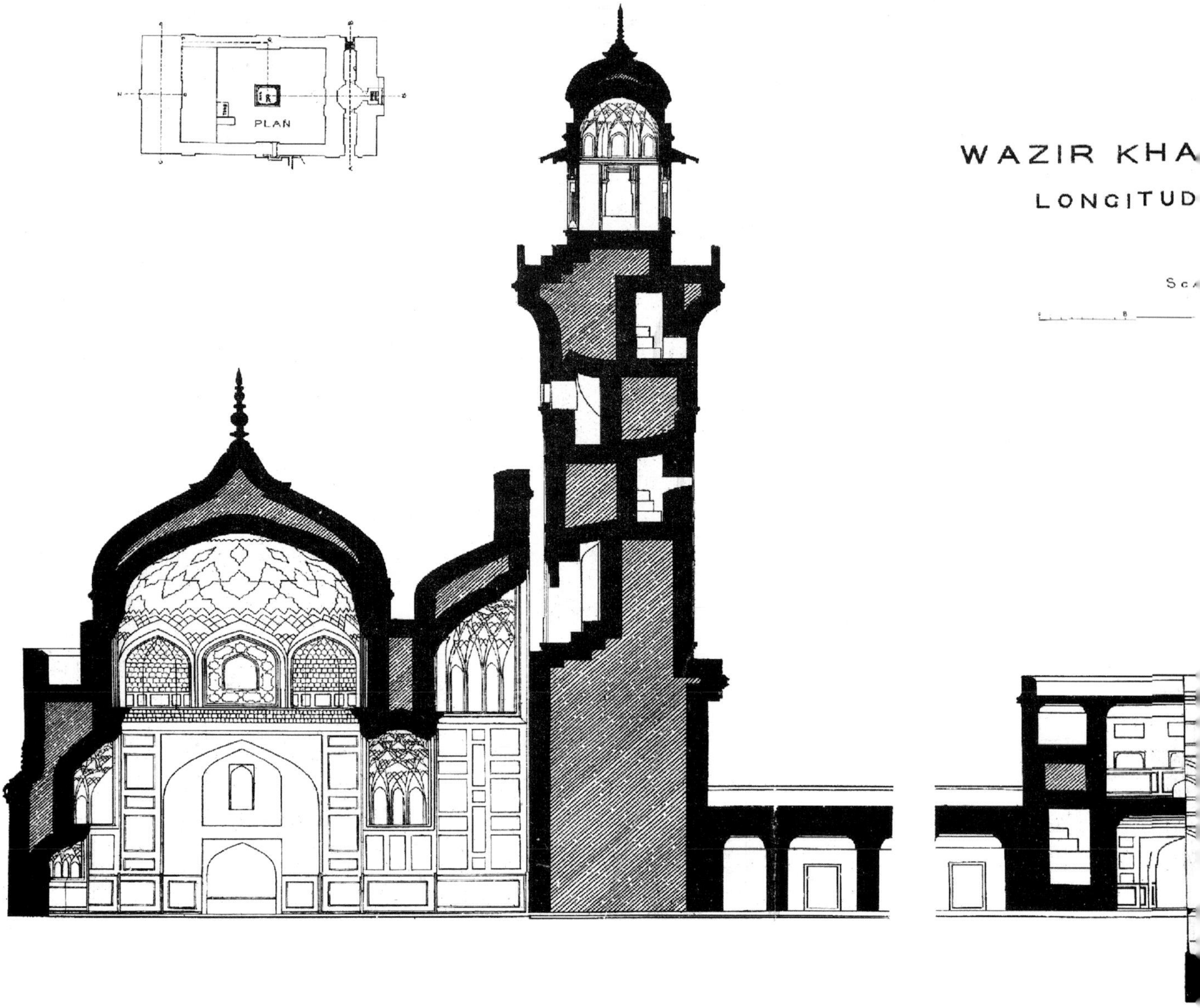

D 7. A CROSS-SECTION OF WAZIR KHAN'S MOSQUE

Drawing by Fred H. Andrews. Published in *The Journal of Indian Art,* No. 19, (July 1887).

The longtitudinal cross-section of the mosque was derived by Fred Andrews from measurements and drawings made by his students in the Mayo School of Arts, 'as part of their practical training.'

'It will be seen from the section through the sanctuary (...) that all the domes are double. This arrangement, usual with builders with many masters of the Roman Renaissance, although perhaps not quite academic, has the advantage of permitting unhampered the employment of the most harmonious forms for the interior and external aspects respectively, and probably this was the motive actuating the architect. Incidentally it also gives greater protection form the heat of the sun.'

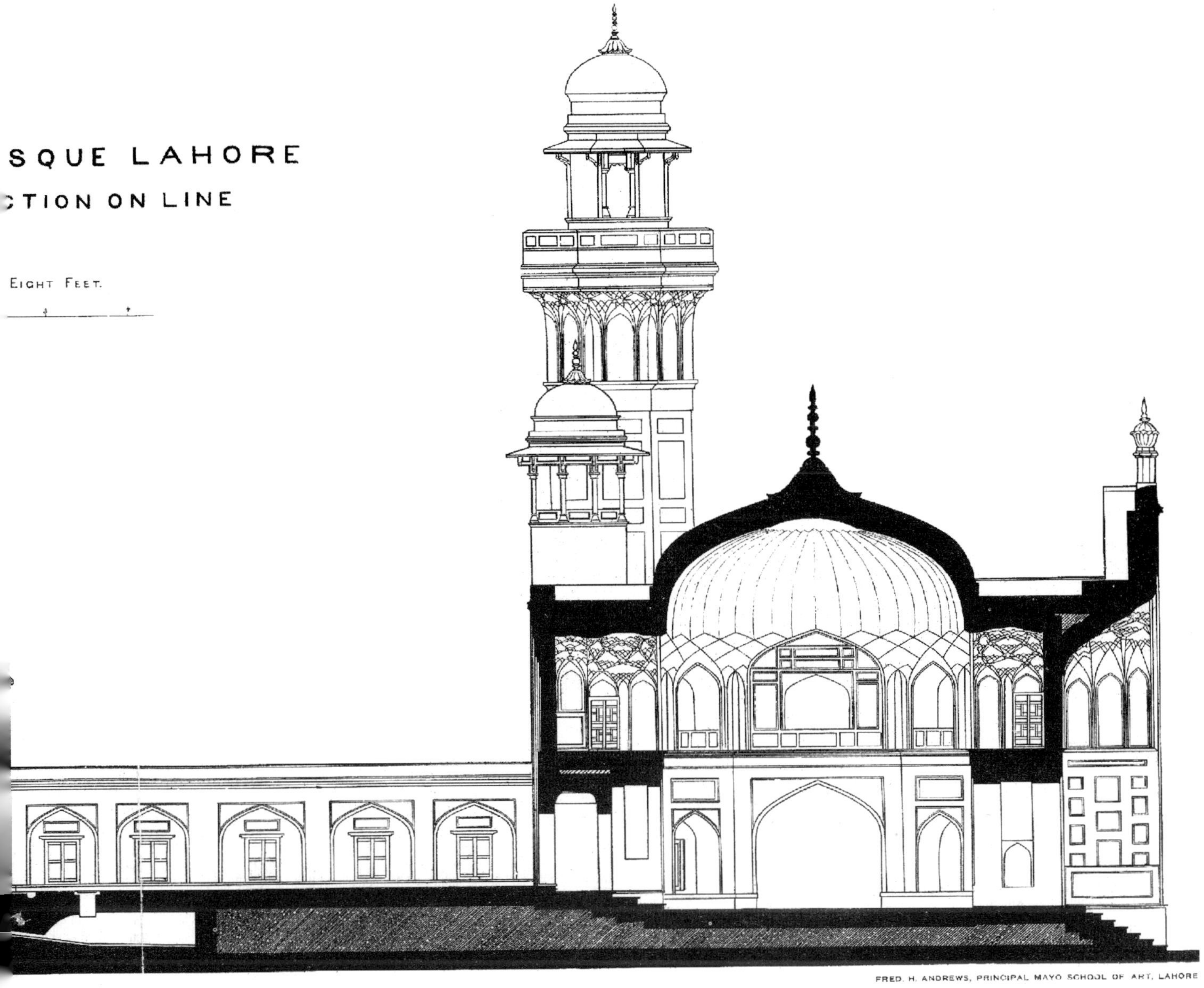

D7. A CROSS-SECTION OF WAZIR KHAN'S MOSQUE

Right and left of the façade of the sanctuary are two stately octagonal minars 100 feet in height. On the long sides of the quadrangle are ranged small *khanas* or cells, each closed by the usual Indian two-leaved door set in a slightly recessed pointed arch, of which there are thirteen on each side, forming a blind arcading, interrupted between the fifth and sixth *khanas* on each side by a pavilion rising above the general level, containing larger apartments and an upper storey reached by two flights of steps, which also give access to the roof of the arcading and pavilions. As the plan shows, these pavilions occur, in the centre of the north and south sides of the lower level of the pavement. In the pavilion on the south side is a fountain set in a circular scalloped basin, and served from the main which supplies the tank in the quadrangle. The source of the water supply is a well provided with an elevated Persian wheel placed just outside the south wall of the mosque.' (Andrews, quoted in Chaghatai (1975), p.12.)

D 8. THE SHRINE OF MIRAN BADSHAH

D 8. THE SHRINE OF MIRAN BADSHAH

Photograph, c. 1930.

Within the inner courtyard of the mosque of Wazir Khan lies the subterranean tomb of Syed Muhammad Ishaq, known as Miran Badshah, a divine from Iran who settled in Lahore during the time of the Tughlaq dynasty. The tomb therefore predates the mosque.

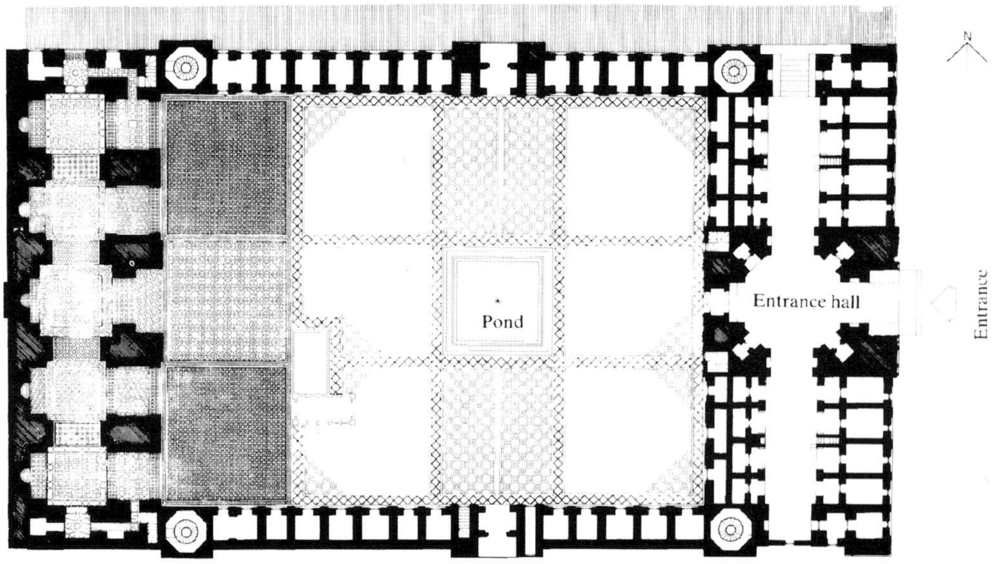

D 9. Plan and section , Masjid Wazir Khan.

THE BAZAARS OF THE INNER CITY

THE BAZAARS OF THE INNER CITY

In many small but significant ways, the rhythm of life within the teeming old city remained unchanged over the centuries. Minds did not open and therefore neither did the streets, filling up like a cove each day with an incoming tide of humanity and emptying by nightfall.

'The population of Lahore,' Thornton recorded in 1876, 'which contains 19,830 houses, is, according to the most recent census, that of February 1875, 92,035, of whom 40,777 are females; that of the suburbs, which contains 6,617 houses, is 36,406, of whom 12,785 are females. The number of English is 1,723, Punjabis are counted at 109,323, Hindustanis [i.e. natives of the North-Western Provinces, etc.] 11,334, Bengalis 729, Afghans 474, and unclassified 4,858. Of these, 1979 are agriculturalists, 17,852 are manufacturers and traders, 973 are described as professionals, 2343 are clerks, 278 are pensioners, 24,406 live by manual labour and 240 are engaged in the direction of labor. [Thornton (1876), p.12.]

G. C. Walker in an early Gazetteer of Lahore, described the conditions of domesticity within the old city in 1893-4 as: 'The streets of Lahore city are for the most part narrow and winding, the houses, though lofty and to all appearances well built from the outside yet inside are much cramped for space and ill-ventilated. They generally consist of three or four stories high; built of burnt bricks laid in mortar. Very few have even a courtyard in front. On the basement floor is a small dark room, in which the women of the house spend most of their day, spinning, cleaning cotton, or working at their needles. Next to this room is a small cell, perhaps 5 or 6 feet square, in which the grain is soaked for cooking, generally by an old woman who has no other means of earning her livelihood. On the floor above is a small room used as a kitchen, from which, perhaps a window opens out into a narrow alley outside, or a sky-light lets in light from above. Adjoining it are two small rooms (*kothies*) of which one is used for a general store-room and the other as a depositary for the family valuables. The third floor generally has three sleeping rooms, all are very small and ill-ventilated and hemmed in on three sides by the walls of adjoining houses. In these also property can be stored and if necessary food is cooked. The fourth floor contains but one small room at the back, the remainder being an open place in front of a corner of which is a small latrine. This space and the open roof above are used as a sleeping shed; the latrine is the only convenience of the sort available to all residents of the house, male or female; an open drain *(parnalah)* leads down the front wall of the house into the alley below, where it is carried off by an open saucer gutter into the main drain in the adjoining street.'

Thornton, writing some fifteen years earlier and perhaps on a fuller stomach, viewed the city more charitably: 'Within the city walls the streets are narrow and winding, but some of them, from the overhanging balconies of wood curiously carved and colored, the striped awnings over the shop-fronts, and the gay costumes of the population, are highly picturesque; while the streamers of bright colored cloths hung at intervals across from balcony to balcony prove that the wondrous dyes of Kathaea, which moved the warriors of Alexander to admiration, are not altogether things of the past.'

Stratton writing in 1900 to the young niece of his fiancée was equally forgiving, dwelling on the sounds rather than on the sounds and smells of Lahore's bazaars: 'Perhaps your Aunt Anna told you something of Lahore of the narrow streets, and the tiny shops that are all open in front, and where the shopkeeper sits on the floor and shows his wares all to the customer who stands below him in the street (bazaar), and of the dark-skinned people with their bright eyes and jet-black hair, and of the handsome turbans the men wear, and the pretty transparent veils the ladies thrown over their heads and shoulders.' [Stratton (1908), p.98.]

The Lahore Directory of 1914 measured the Old City as covering 558 acres with a resident population of 120,436. The whole city was 29 square miles in area with a population of 228,687. If one excluded the cantonment area, the area became 22 square miles and the population 210,271. 'The immigration into the city is very large, as many as 436 per mile of its inhabitants being born outside the district. The Railway affords means of living for 30,814 persons [.] Domestic service supports 26,647 persons [.] The preponderance of males over females is the consequence of the nature of this immigration and a proportion of 596 females to every 1000 males in the city is not surprising.' [Lahore Directory (1914), pp.26-27.]

Muhammad Qadeer's monograph on *Lahore: Urban Development in the Third World* describes the population explosion in Lahore during the last century: 'Lahore has grown almost 14 times in size since the beginning of the twentieth century. From a population of 202,964 in 1901, it grew to a population of 2,920,000 in 1981. These census figures generally underestimate populations, due to enumeration difficulties.' [Qadeer (1983), p.74.]

Those difficulties continue, while the population continues to grow. In 2002, it was estimated at 7.2 million.

E 1. VIEW OF THE INNER CITY

E 1. VIEW OF THE INNER CITY

Photo postcard, c.1930. (RS/33)

E 2. STREET SCENE

E 2. STREET SCENE

Photo postcard, published by the Punjab Religious Book Society, Lahore, c.1930. (RS/34)

E 3. A HOUSE IN THE INNER CITY

E 3. A HOUSE IN THE INNER CITY

Photo postcard, c.1930.

This architectural confection of a building is still standing and may be seen near the entrance of Wazir Khan's mosque. Although the façade has undergone many changes, the uppermost decoration and the semi-circular lotus shaped seat are still distinguishable.

(18)
RARRA TAILLIAN.
Cattle pressing oil on ground floor of dwelling house.

E 4. AN OIL PRESS WITHIN THE OLD CITY

Photograph, c. 1930.

An usual but interesting insight into a vertical connection between a man's livelihood and his home. The blindfolded beast is treading in circles, turning an oil press. Its dung made into cakes dries on the walls, to be used in time as fuel by the housewife looking quizzically from the open window above.

E 5. HONORARY MAGISTRATES COURT

E 5. HONORARY MAGISTRATES COURT

Photograph by A. Sache′, c. 1880.

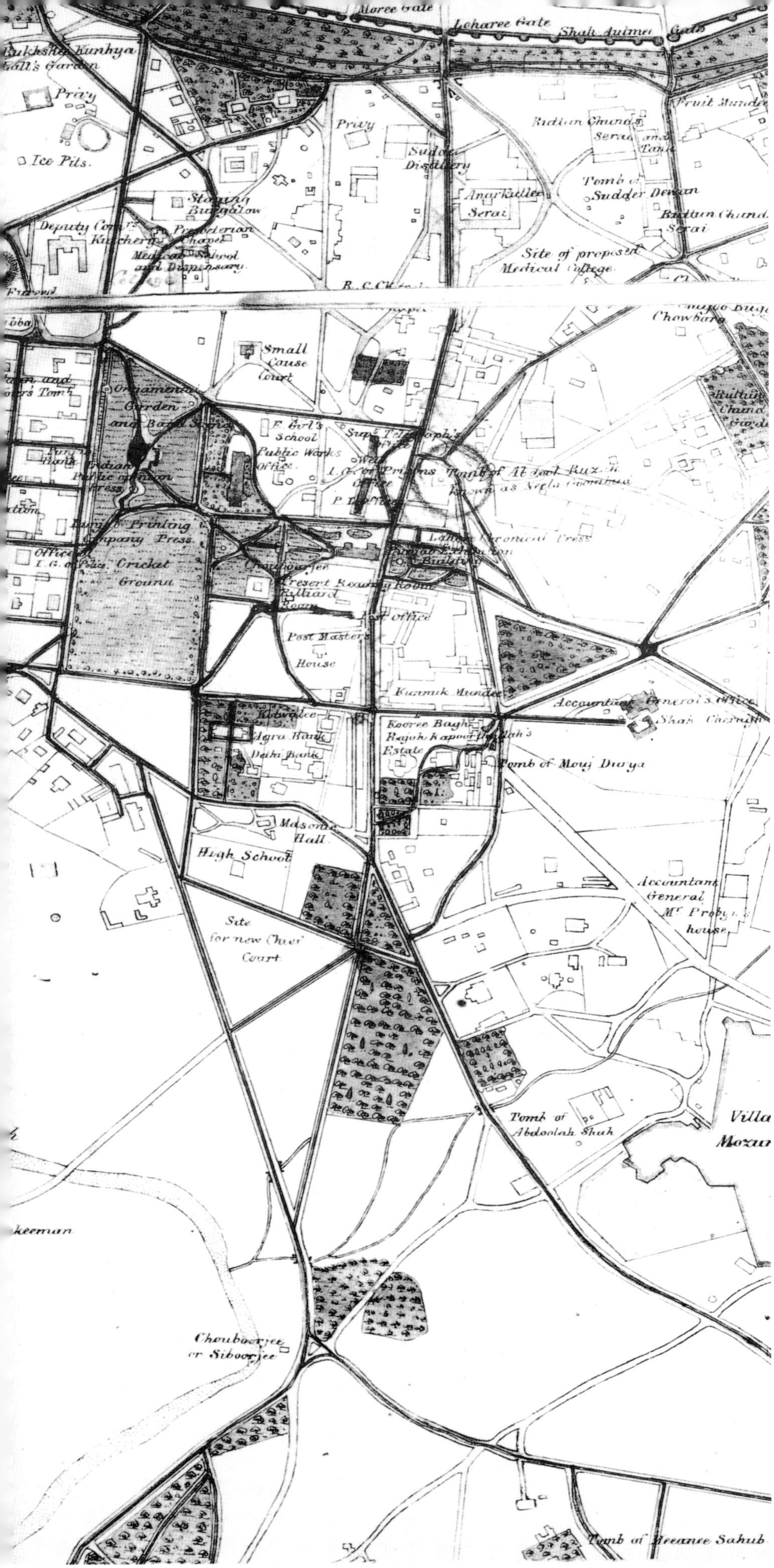

Detail from 1867 map.

THE LOWER MALL

Detail from 1927 map.

LOWER MALL

The area outside the security of the city walls was a comparative wilderness, dotted with tombs of Mughal personages and the remnants of their gardens. 'To the south of the city,' Thornton wrote in his guidebook of 1876, 'extends in a vast semicircle with a radius of some three or four miles, an uneven expanse interspersed with the crumbling remains of mosques, tombs and gateways, and huge shapeless mounds of rubbish from old brick kilns. Within the last few years an immense change has taken place in this region, which was utterly waste and desolate for a long time after the annexation in 1849. Immense quantities of old bricks have been removed and used in road-making and as ballast for the railways, and other old buildings are being used as quarries, whence the material for modern works is drawn; while the European houses and gardens in Donald Town, the metalled roads overshadowed by trees, and the vegetation consequent on the introduction of irrigation, have transformed a part of the artificial desert on this side of the city into a suburb which reminded a recent French traveler of Enghien or Passy, near Paris.' [Thornton (1876), p.2.]

The first cantonment of Lahore was located at Anarkali, south of the old city. 'The houses here,' the Lahore Gazetteer of 1883-4 recorded, 'are the oldest in the station, having been for the most part built in 1847-8, at the time the Cantonment was first formed. Here are the Secretariat, formerly the Residency, the Financial and other offices and the Chief Court.'. [Lahore Gazetteer (1883-84), p.164.]

'Originally there was only one Mall, now known as the Lower Mall,' Goulding recalled, 'extending from the Deputy Commissioner's court to the Multan Road junction. It is very probable that the new nomenclature came into general use about the time that the portion of the Civil Station between Government House and Anarkali was christened Donald Town, in commemoration of Sir Donald McLeod's Lieutenant-Governorship. One seldom, if ever, hears of Donald Town in these days, but Anarkali and Naulakha, the two original sub-divisions, are still well-defined areas.' [Goulding (1924), p.31.]

The speed with which Lahore moved into the twentieth century is reflected in a publication titled 'Lahore Directory'. Published in 1914, it begins with a history of Lahore derived from earlier guidebooks, provides biographical and other details of principal residents, and from page 133 onwards lists according to each major street the residents of Lahore and whose house or which office one was likely to encounter on the left and the ride side of each road. The list in the Directory is alphabetical starting with Abbott Road from the junction of Empress and Davis Roads. To maintain the sequence of the historical flow of Lahore's expansion eastwards away from the old city, the most appropriate place to commence might be the Lower Mall from outside Bhati Gate.

Quitting the walled city via Bhati gate, the following buildings, offices and residences would have flanked the main road:

LEFT

Vacant house of Mr Roshan Lai, Bar at Law
The Punjab Hindu Sabha
Kayastha Boarding House
Mr Roshan Lai, Bar at Law
Anarkali Police Station No.2
DAV School [1]
Government College
Gol Bagh
Fire Brigade Office
The Victoria Jubilee Hall
Municipal Office and Town Hall
Punjab Volunteers Club
Forman Christian College Ground

RIGHT

Mr J.Y. Buchanan
Mr J.E. Parkinson
Central Model School
Central Training College
District Courts
Rose Cottage
Messrs Jamsetjee's & Sons [2]
Punjab Association Club
Govt. College Boarding House
Mr H. Brandon, Pleader
District Offices and Courts, Block 11
Postal Stock Depot (Punjab/NWF Circle)
Small Cause Court
Office of Dy. Inspector General of Police, Central Range
The Secretariat Offices and Tomb of Anarkali
Mr Lionel Heath, IES [3]
DAV Boarding house for school students
Mr Wades' Boarding House
Mr. T.V. Eyre, Shorthand lecturer
Messrs H.B.L. Cooper & Co., Merchants and bankers
Jhind House [4]
West End Board and Residence
Mr Balak Ram, Bar at Law
R.B. Lala Ganga Ram, CIE
Mr C. Bevan Petman
Mr. A.H. Diack, ICS

1. Now the Government Muslim Model High School.
2. These shops were replaced by the Government College Hostel.
3. Then Principal, Mayo School of Arts.
4. Jhind House, owned and occupied for many years by a Mr A. Ludlam, Assistant Secretary to the Financial Commissioner. (Goulding (1924), p. 40.)

F 1. RAI MELA RAM'S BUILDING

F 1. RAI MELA RAM'S BUILDING

Photo postcard, c. 1930. (RS/28)

This building belonged to Mela Ram, who was according to Latif's brief biographical description 'a well known contractor of the Railway Department. He possessed much private means; died in 1890.'

By the 1920s, Rai Bahadur Mela Ram's building had been torn down. Goulding mentions two old barracks 'situated at the southern end of the road now known as the Lower Mall, which was in those early days the one and only Mall.' He says they 'were known as "Mela Ram's Barracks," having been purchased by that enterprising capitalist. Until their demolition, they were let out in suites to Government clerks and other persons of small means. One of the suites was, for a time, used as a private school for girls.' [Goulding (1924), p.22.]

The location of Mela Ram's building has been identified on the Lahore Survey map of 1921-22. as No. 41, close to the shrine of Data Ganj Baksh.

F 2. LADY WILLINGDON HOSPITAL, NEAR TAXALI GATE

F 2. LADY WILLINGDON HOSPITAL, NEAR TAXALI GATE

Photograph by Bali and Sons, 1933.

The main building of the new hospital for women was located on the Ravi road, behind the Badshahi Mosque and very close to the site of Taxali gate. Its Operation Block was opened by Lady Willingdon on 12 March 1933.

The hospital consisted of a main Block with 56 beds in four wards and eight single bed private rooms. It also had an Administration Block, Operation Block and two Labour rooms on the Ground floor and two Operating rooms on the First floor. The project cost Rs 10,76,420, of which Rs 774,211 was applied towards the cost of the buildings, gardens and roads, and the remaining Rs 302,209 was spent of the ancillary utilities, including air conditioning.

F 3. THE NEW DENTAL HOSPITAL

F 3. THE NEW DENTAL HOSPITAL

Photo, 1930.

Located near to Lady Willingdon Hospital, the new Dental Hospital was completed at a cost of Rs 126,772 and handed over on 1 March 1930. By 1933-34, only the hospital portion of the building had been put into use, and proposals were then presented to the government to put the Dental School into operation, for which a further Rs 15,000 was requested.

F 4. CENTRAL MODEL SCHOOL

F 5. GOVERNMENT COLLEGE

F 4. CENTRAL MODEL SCHOOL

Photo postcard, c. 1930. (RS/41)

The Government Central Model School, as it is now called, was established in 1883 as a both to impart education to classes at the Primary and Middle 'Anglo-Vernacular' School and to train students at the adjacent Central Training College. These older students were required to teach classes at Central Model School for a specified period every day and also at least once a week, watch more mature master teach their classes. [Latif (1890), p.319.] Today, 120 years later, the school has 5418 pupils.

F 5. GOVERNMENT COLLEGE

Photo postcard, c. 1930.

An imposing Gothic building, designed by W. Purdon (Superintending Engineer), the main building of Government College was begun in 1872 and took five years to build. The construction was done by Rai Bahadur Kanhaiya Lal at a cost of Rs 320,537.

The 1867 map of Lahore confirms that once a staging bungalow existed on the site of the mound that is now crowned by Government College. It has since been demolished.

F 6. GOVERNMENT COLLEGE HOSTEL

F 6. GOVERNMENT COLLEGE HOSTEL

Photograph, 1921.

Described as 'a handsome building', the hostel for the students of Government College was built on the site formerly occupied by the Parsi merchants Jamsetjee's & Sons. The work started in January and cost about Rs 600,000.

F 7. THE NEW VETERINARY COLLEGE

F 7. THE NEW VETERINARY COLLEGE

Photograph, 1916.

'The Punjab Veterinary College was founded in 1882 at the Lahore Veterinary School and was removed to the existing premises in 1915.' [Khosla (1932), p. 26.]

The design of the new Veterinary College west of the District Courts was a joint effort by J. Begg who designed the elevation and Basil M. Sullivan who furnished the details. The Buildings and Road Department Report for 1914-15 reads: 'The new Veterinary College and associated Buildings at Lahore, designed on the most up to date lines, were practically complete during the year and have been occupied by the Veterinary Department. Expenditure during the year was Rs. 3,24,620 out of a total of Rs. 6,64,873. This College will, it is believed, compare favourably with any other of its kind in India, and its rapid completion is due chiefly to the energy of Mr. Dorman, the Executive Engineer.'

The nearby house owned by a Mr. Cooper had been bought earlier in 1901or 1902 for the contagious diseases ward of the proposed Veterinary College.

The Main building was opened by Baron Hardinge of Penshurst, then Governor-General and Viceroy, in December 1915.

F 8. THE STAIRCASE OF THE NEW VETERINARY COLLEGE

F 8. THE STAIRCASE OF THE NEW VETERINARY COLLEGE

Photo, 1916.

The impressive wooden staircase and the marble tiled floor are still in place at the Veterinary College.

F 9. THE TOMB OF ANARKALI

F 9. THE TOMB OF ANARKALI

Sketch by James Grant, and published in Cassell's *Illustrated History of India* (London, 1876), Vol. 2, p.534.

An early sketch of the tomb of Anarkali, a favourite of Jahangir while he was still Prince Salim, the heir apparent. Anarkali paid for these dangerous affections with her life. She was sentenced to death by the emperor Akbar and ordered to be entombed alive in 1599. The tomb was completed by a grieving Jahangir in 1615.

During the early 19th century, it served as an annexe to the houses occupied by Maharaja Ranjit Singh's heir Kharak Singh and subsequently by his European mercenary General Ventura, who kept his harem of local ladies lodged in the tomb.

Anarkali's tomb was converted into the church of St. James's and remained in use until the construction of the new Cathedral on the Mall. [See G 21.]

F 10 - 14. THE TEMPORARY LEGISLATIVE COUNCIL CHAMBER AND OFFICES

As temporary accommodation for the new Legislative Assembly of the Punjab, a Council Chamber was ordered to be built in the vicinity of Anarkali's tomb. The area had once been the military station for the British garrison until it was shifted to Mian Mir.

In 1868-9, an early reference to its potential as a site for administrative offices is recorded in a report that discloses that many natural hollows at Anarkali had been filled 'as one of the works for affording employment to the famine-stricken population'.

The initial estimates for the Temporary Council Chamber were Rs 430,000. The order for its design was given in February 1920 to Mr Basil Sullivan (who had earlier done the interior of the Veterinary College), and perhaps responding to the urgency of the need, the building was completed in less than two years, by December 1920 when the new Legislative Council held its inaugural meeting in the completed building.

Additions were made from time to time. In 1932-33, for example, work worth Rs 39,000 was completed, and in the following year, to expand the capacity of the Chamber, some major modifications were made. The Buildings and Roads Report for 1933-34 disclosed: 'The work started at the end of the Spring Session and completed in September 1933, at a cost of Rs 30,800. The altered Chamber will now accommodate 200 members, in place of the provision of 96 originally existing, and increased gallery and vestibule accommodation has also been given.'

F 10. THE TEMPORARY COUNCIL CHAMBER, UNDER CONSTRUCTION

Photo, 1922.

F 10.

F 11. THE COMPLETED LEGISLATIVE COUNCIL CHAMBER

F 12. THE CHAMBER BUILDING SEEN FROM THE SOUTHWEST

F 13. THE INTERIOR OF THE COUNCIL CHAMBER

F 11. THE COMPLETED LEGISLATIVE COUNCIL CHAMBER

Photo, 1922.

These buildings are now the offices of ministers of the Punjab Government.

F 12. THE CHAMBER BUILDING SEEN FROM THE SOUTHWEST

Photo, 1922.

F 13. THE INTERIOR OF THE COUNCIL CHAMBER

Photo, 1922.

This view of the north side of the Council Chamber shows the entrance and above it the Public Gallery. The paintings flanking the doorway are copies of the coronation portraits of King George V and his consort Queen Mary, done by Sir Luke Fildes and Sir William Llewellyn respectively in 1911. [These paintings are now in the Lahore Museum.]

F 14. THE INTERIOR OF THE COUNCIL CHAMBER

F 15. THE PIPALS RESIDENCE

F 14. THE INTERIOR OF THE COUNCIL CHAMBER

Photo, 1922.

At the southern end of the Council Chamber, the Speaker's chair stood elevated beneath a portrait of Queen Victoria. A copy of the coronation portrait of her son King Edward VII done in 1901 by Sir Luke Fildes hangs on the left.

The Council Chamber, lavishly refurbished in the 1990s, is now used as a Committee Room by the Punjab Government.

F 15. THE PIPALS RESIDENCE

Photograph, 28 August 1926

Described when this photograph was taken in August 1926 as 'The Residential Club for Members of the Legislative Council, Punjab', this building has retained both its name 'The Pipals' and its use as a hostel. It is located across the Secretariat on Sanda Road and is now designated Block A of the MPA Hostel for Members of the Punjab Provincial Assembly.

Goulding has left a detailed account of the antecedents of The Pipals: 'Further on [after Jhind House] we come to The Pipals, known among the Indian population as "Pincher-sahib-ki-kothi," being for many years the residence of the late H.C. Fanshawe, while that distinguished Punjab civilian was Secretary to Government [.] Other well-known officials occupied the house from time to time, among them being Mr. H. Maude and Sir Alfred Kensington (both Judges of the Chief Court), His Excellency Sir Edward Maclagan when he was Chief Secretary to Government, Mr. G.R. Elmslie ("Lachhmi sahib") and his son-in-law Sir Michael Fenton, both in turn Financial Commissioners. After it was vacated by Sir Michael, the house was taken by Government, as a residence for the officers of the Education Department. It is doubtful, however, whether there are any of the older residents of Lahore who remember that before The Pipals became a fashionable private residence, it was occupied by Messrs. Richardson and Co., Chemists, the predecessors of Messrs. Plomer and Co. But alas, the glory is fast departing from this part of the station, and European firms and distinguished officials are retreating eastwards before the advance of education, in the shape of schools, colleges and students' hostels.' [Goulding (1924), pp. 40-41.]

F 16. THE TOWN HALL

Photo postcard by B.N. Kapur, Lahore, c. 1920. (RS/40)

Opened on 3 February 1890, the Town Hall has remained the hub continuously of the Lahore Municipality, functioning over the past century under different labels but with essentially the same responsibilities for Lahore's civic administration.

Municipal House, Lahore

F 17. CHARBURJI GATEWAY

F 17. CHARBURJI GATEWAY

Watercolour by Major R. Mitford, c. 1880.

Originally the entrance to a garden, this gateway bears an inscription that confirms that the garden was laid out in 1646 by a lady, a Mughal grandee identified only as 'Sahib-e-Zebinda, Begam-e-Dauran (One endowed with elegance, The Lady of the Age'. [Waliullah Khan (1961), p. 62.]

Eastwick recorded that 'the N.W. turret has fallen down, perhaps from an earthquake, and has taken with it the wall on that side. This beautiful building is faced with blue and green encaustic tiles. [...] The S. side measures 58′ 5″. There has been a dome, but the greater part of it has fallen'. [Eastwick (1883), p.199.]

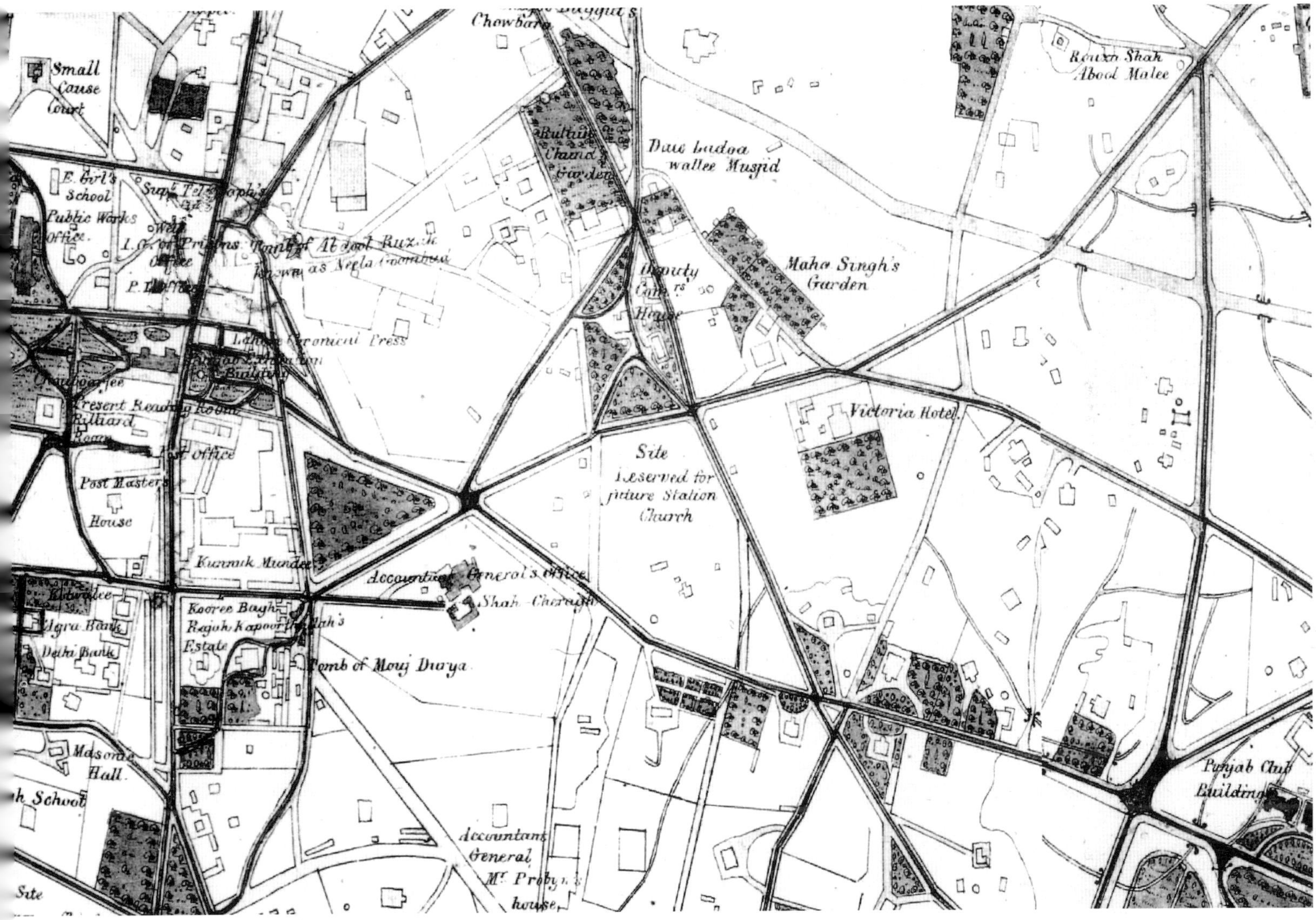

Detail from 1867 map.

THE MALL
(TOWARDS CHARING CROSS)

Detail from 1927 map.

THE MALL
[Towards Charing Cross]

The Mall, now Shahrah-i-Quaid-e-Azam, begins from Nasser Bagh, once known despite its irregular shape as Gol or Round Bagh. Goulding recalled: 'The social life of Old Lahore centred round the now deserted Lower Mall in days not too far distant, when the Police Band played regularly twice a week in the Gol Bagh, then known as the Bandstand gardens, and the beauty and fashion of the station gathered there to exchange gossip and listen to the music.' [Goulding (1924), p.31.]

'From Anarkulli eastwards the station now stretches for a distance of nearly three miles, the Lawrence Gardens and Government House marking its eastern limit,' the Gazetteer noted. 'This eastern portion of the station is known as Donald Town, taking its name from the Lieutenant-Governor in whose time it was first occupied the late Sir Donald McLeod. It is connected with Anarkulli by the road now called the Mall, which runs down the station centrally from east to west. The old Mall is a splendid road, which runs from the city southwards through the Anarkulli portion of the station.' [Lahore Gazetteer (1883-84), p.164.]

In 1914, the buildings and shops ranged on either side of the Mall starting from Gol Bagh were:

LEFT	RIGHT
Chemical Examiner's Office	Mayo School of Arts
Chief Malaria Medical Officer	Museum
Punjab University Hall	General Market
Dalhousie Dairy Farm	Makhan Lal and Brothers
Messrs. Alfred & Co., Chemists	Alliance Bank of Simla
The Punjab Ice Co.	General Post Office
L.M. Datta, Bar-at-Law	Chief Court
K.R. Kalloo Mal &Co., Drapers	Statue of Lord Lawrence
Young Men's Christian Association	G Craddock & Co., Photographers
Rev. J.C.R. Ewing	Cook and Kelvey, Jewellers
Forman Christian College	E. Clarke & Co., Drapers
Bank of Bengal	Gyan Manzil
Govt. Telegraph Office	Bombay Cycle and Motor Agency
H.A. Levy & Co.	West End House
Lahore Boot House	Frank Bliss & Co., Chemists and Druggists
Oliver Commercial College	
W. Thorns & Co., Oliver Typewriter Agency	
Luke and Stonebridge, Elec. Engrs.	
E. Plomer & Co.	
Pioneer Commercial College	
The Exchange Trading Co.	
L.C. Smith Bros., Typewriters	
The Engineering Stores (Electrical)	
Jas. Davison & Co.	
English Warehouse	

G 1. PUNJAB UNIVERSITY HALL

G 1. PUNJAB UNIVERSITY HALL

Photo postcard, c.1920. (RS/47)

The proposal to establish a university at Lahore was first made in 1868. Initially, a Punjab University College was established in January 1870, with the objectives 'to promote the diffusion of European science as far as possible through the medium of the vernacular languages of the Punjab, and the improvement and extension of vernacular literature generally; to afford encouragement to the enlightened study of Eastern classical languages and literature; and to associate the learned and influential classes with Government in the promotion and supervision of popular education.'

The University College first established an Oriental School and College, and subsequently after the charter had been granted to the university in October 1882, the Punjab University came formally into being.

In 1903, the Lieutenant Governor Sir Charles Rivaz granted to the university the land hitherto used by the Roberts' Institute, upon which the new University Hall was constructed in 1905. The building was designed by Bhai Ram Singh, who later in 1911 also designed the University Library.

G 2 (a & b). THE ZAMZAMA CANNON

Cast at Lahore in 1757 on the orders of Shah Wali Khan, the senior minister of Ahmad Shah Abdali, the Zamzama cannon was one of a pair, cast from a mixture of copper and brass and paid for out of the *jazia* or tax levied by Muslim governors on Hindu citizens. Used by Ahmad Shah at the famous battle of Panipat in 1761, it was left behind at Lahore when Ahmad Shah returned to Kabul. He took with him the companion piece which sank during the crossing across the river Chenab.

Captured by the Sikh Bhangi sardars in 1762, it passed through many inconsiderate hands until it fell into the hands of the young Sikh chieftain Ranjit Singh. He used it in a number of campaigns until 1818 when it was damaged during his attack on Multan. Put out of commission, it remained on display outside Delhi gate until the visit of Alfred Duke of Edinburgh (the second son of Queen Victoria) to Lahore in 1870, when it was shifted to a site in front of the old Tollinton Market, facing the Anarkali bazaar. It was relocated to its present site on a traffic island opposite the National College of Arts during the early 20th century.

G 2 (a). THE ZAMZAMA CANNON

G 2 (a). THE ZAMZAMA CANNON

Stereoscopic photograph by James Ricalton, 1888. (RS/K)

Captioned 'Ancient Cannon and Street Idlers, Lahore' by the photographer Ricalton in his travelogue. Ignoring the idlers in the foreground, Ricalton waxed lyrical about the cannon itself: 'That grim old muzzle has dealt forth so much of death, has roared so often and so loudly in many wars, that it became a proverb "Who holds Zamzamah (The roaring lion) controls the Punjab." The Sikhs call it the Bhangianwali Top[e], which signifies the cannon of the Bhangi confederacy. After the battle of Multan [in 1818], it was placed at the Delhi Gate of Lahore, where it remained for over forty years, when it was removed to its present place of honor [in 1870].' [Lucas (1990), pl.16 and p.69.]

G 2 (b). THE ZAMZAMA CANNON

G 2 (b). THE ZAMZAMA CANNON

Photo postcard, c.1920. (RS/20A)

In the background is the Punjab University. The signboard above the arch on the right reads: 'Educational Office'.

G 3 (a & b). THE LAHORE MUSEUM

G 3(a). THE FAÇADE OF THE LAHORE MUSEUM

Photo postcard, c.1920. (RS/44)

The foundation stone of the new Lahore Museum had been laid on 3 February 1890 by HRH Prince Albert Victor of Wales, the eldest son of Prince Albert Edward Prince of Wales and grandson of Queen Victoria. He had arrived in Lahore by a few days earlier on 25 January. The Museum had been designed as part of the Victoria Jubilee Institute to commemorate the Jubilee of Queen Victoria in 1887. Financed out of the funds raised from the Province, the Institute included the Museum, a Lecture hall and an Art College (now the National College of Arts). The building was completed in 1893. [Lahore Gazetteer (1916), p. 247.]

The B & R Report for 1905-6 mentions that 'the entrance porch of the Lahore Museum was reconstructed in marble, and the old inferior window frames were removed and teak frames fixed in their place. These works were carried out under the supervision of the Curator, and have vastly improved the lighting of the rooms.' The total expenditure for these improvements was Rs 18,825.

G 3(a) THE FAÇADE OF THE LAHORE MUSEUM

A detailed description of its structure and contents was given in the Gazetteer 1916: 'The general plan of the building resembles a letter E with the entrance porch in the centre of the back face. The centre gallery is devoted first to a few fine specimens of carved Mughal doorways and woodwork and secondly to a fairly representative collection of Indian paintings dating from the Indo-Persian, Mughal, Sikh and Kangra schools up to a few examples of Modern Indian paintings of the new Calcutta School; the cataloguing and arranging of this collection is now complete.' Lionel Heath, as Curator, had written in his report on the museum for 1913-14 that 'Mr S.N. Gupta has classified and arranged the collection of pictures in the Museum. He has written descriptive notes and labels which are now affixed to each picture. When his catalogue of this section is complete, it will be of great artistic interest and add much to the educational value of the exhibition.' [Gupta's catalogue was published in 1922.] 'In order to accommodate the increasing number of Indian paintings and facilitate their exhibition, all the cases in the central gallery have been remade. All the paintings have now a good light on them.' [The paintings managed to oust the photogravures of the Lieutenant Governors.]

The Gazetteer continued: 'The south wall of the gallery has been decorated in Persian style by the students and teachers of the Mayo School of Art from designs by the present Vice-Principal, M. Sher Muhammad, who also designed the whole of the wood and plaster work seen in the building. Two galleries run east and west of the central gallery, that on the west being devoted to models, raw products, etc., and that on the east to art industries of all kinds amongst which may be noted fine collections of musical instruments, *huqas*, jewellery, textiles, pottery, and a small collection of armour. At the end of the east gallery is the gallery containing the famous collection of Graeco-Bactrian Gandhara sculptures [.]

Parallel to the Sculpture Gallery is a smaller gallery in which are shown some interesting small collections of Tibetan painted banners, statuettes, carved curios, Nepalese brass work, and a case of manuscripts. In this room too is a case containing the recent finds of gold and silver ornaments and objets d'art from Taxila and loaned to the Museum [.] The museum has been extended this year by the addition of one large gallery, a library, office, and record room, opening out of the central gallery at the back. This gallery will be shortly filled by Sir Aurel Stein's latest finds in Central Asia.'

The entire area of the Museum in 1916 covered 35,582 square feet. It remained a popular tourist spot, attracting 400,000 visitors each year. By comparison, the attendance in 2001-2 has been 265,610 visitors.

G 3(b). THE LAHORE MUSEUM, SEEN FROM THE PUNJAB UNIVERSITY

G 3(b). THE LAHORE MUSEUM, SEEN FROM THE PUNJAB UNIVERSITY

Photo postcard, c. 1938. (RS/7A)

Photographed from the upper floor of the Punjab University opposite, the Museum entrance with its multi-tiered domes and the projecting eastern gallery are visible.

The statue in the foreground is of Dr Alfred C. Woolner, Vice-Chancellor of Punjab University(1928-1936). Its sculptor was Gilbert Ledward, R.A. The inscription below it reads:

Alfred Woolner
1878-1936
A Great and Beloved Leader.

It is the only statue of a human figure to be left in situ in Lahore. The others of British royalty and notable personages such as Lala Lajpat Rai (which stood near the Lahore Museum) have been removed. Their whereabouts are not always known.

G (a - d). TOLLINTON MARKET

G 4 (a). UNDER CONSTRUCTION

G 4 (a). UNDER CONSTRUCTION

Photograph, 1863.

The annual report of the Buildings and Roads department for 1863-64 gives this prosaic mention of the construction of Lahore's first major exhibition hall: 'A building was erected at Anarkullee, Lahore, from Local, Provincial and Imperial Funds, for the Punjab Exhibition of natural products, arts and manufactures, which was opened on 20th January 1864, and closed in the first week of April. The building is now to be used, one wing for the Lahore Museum, and the other for public meetings and general purposes.'

A livelier eye-witness account has been left by a British administrator G. R. Elsmslie who served in the Punjab between 1858 and 1893, and was present at the formal opening: 'The chief event at Lahore in the early part of 1864 was the opening of an Industrial Exhibition, in a building specially built for the purpose in Anarkali. This Exhibition imposed much extra work on the local Civil Officers, who were placed in charge of the different departments. I am afraid I did not feel very much enthusiasm in the matter, having inherited a prejudice against 'Exhibitions' as savouring of humbug to a considerable extent. An indirect advantage was that the opening ceremony brought the principal Punjab officers to Lahore, and helped to no small extent to promote better acquaintance among them.'

From his dairy notes, Elmslie recalled: 'January 17... The State opening of the Exhibition takes place on Wednesday next, the 20th. This week is to be the regular week of tamashas. A large number of Commissioners and Deputy Commissioners are collected in Lahore, with Rajas and Nawabs *ad lib*. The European visitors are principally located in a large camp in Anarkuli. The native grandees are on the plain on the north of the city. Tomorrow is fixed for the grand durbar or levee for the reception of the Native Princes, etc. The Civilians have to appear in evening dress at twelve noon! A terrible go, is it not, for those whose dress suits have had much wear and tear? However, there is no help for it. Sir Robert [Montgomery] will no doubt be resplendent in diplomatic uniform, cocked hat, gold lace, orders, etc. On Tuesday H.H. the Lieutenant-Governor gives a grand fete at Shalamar to all residents and visitors. On Wednesday the Exhibition is to be opened with all possible pomp. On Thursday come a grand review and ball. Friday, State visit to the city. Saturday, Amritsar will be illuminated... Of course, cutcherry is entirely suspended, but I would rather spend the holidays shooting in the jungles than at the monster fetes and revelries...'

The actual occasion proved to be a denouement: 'January 20 The Exhibition excitement is at its height. This is the opening day. The Lieutenant-Governor proceeds in grand procession from Government House at twelve o'clock, receive our address, and replies to the same from a magnificent velvet dais, marches around the building, and finally declares the Exhibition open... As for the Exhibition, it is a very mild affair.' [Elmslie (1908), pp.101-2.]

Within a year, 'the Exhibition building was repaired and partially fitted up as a central museum. Furniture [was] purchased for the museum at Multan.' (B & R Report, 1864-65, p.6.)

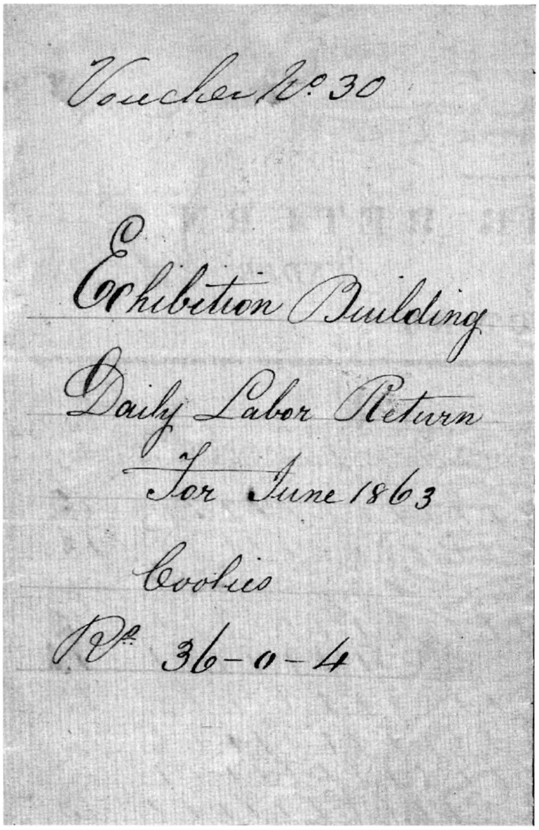
Voucher No. 30

Exhibition Building

Daily Labor Return

for June 1863

Coolies

Rs. 36-0-4

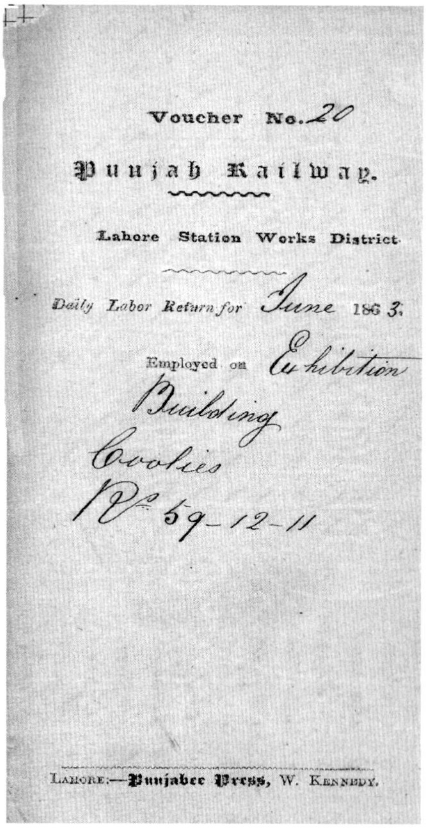
Voucher No. 20

Punjab Railway.

Lahore Station Works District.

Daily Labor Return for June 1863.

Employed on Exhibition Building

Coolies

Rs. 59-12-11

Lahore:—Punjabee Press, W. Kennedy.

G 4 (b). DAILY LABOUR RETURNS FOR JUNE 1863.

G 4 (b). DAILY LABOUR RETURNS FOR JUNE 1863.

These two sheets of Daily Labour returns for the payments to labour employed during the construction of the Industrial Exhibition building were retrieved by the author from a rubbish pile where they had been discarded during the renovation of the Lahore Museum in 1966.

One of the returns for Rs 59-12-11 (i.e. rupees, annas and pice) lists the attendance and the wages of 24 coolies. While the lowest daily rates were 2 annas, most of them received either three and a half annas or four annas, with the supervising mate getting 6 annas per day. It is interesting to compare the rates paid some years later, in 1851-52, to similar categories of workmen employed during the renovation of Government House: 'in those early days a European overseer could be obtained for Rs 40 per mensem; a Munshi for Rs. 12; head masons and carpenters for Rs. 16, while ordinary masons were paid from 4 to 6 annas a day.' [Goulding (1926) pp.29-30.]

G 4 (c). TOLLINTON MUNICIPAL MARKET

G 4 (c). TOLLINTON MUNICIPAL MARKET

Photo postcard, c.1920, by B. N. Kapur, Photographic Dealer, Lahore, No.15. (RS/50)

G 4 (d). POULTRY FOR SALE AT REAR OF TOLLINTON MARKET

G 4 (d). POULTRY FOR SALE AT REAR OF TOLLINTON MARKET

Photo postcard, c.1920. (RS/45)

The main building of the market was occupied by general merchants, grocers and a few confectioners. At the rear of the building, poultry was sold from makeshift stalls.

G 5 (a & b). WAZIR KHAN'S BARADARI

G 5 (a). WAZIR KHAN'S BARADARI

G 5 (a). Stereoscopic photograph by James Ricalton, 1888. (RS/L)

One of the few ancient buildings of Lahore to have remained in continuous use since its construction, this baradari built by Hakim Ilmuddin Khan (Wazir Khan) in the late 1630s was originally designed as a grand pavilion set in a large garden, called according to Latif 'the *Nakhlia* garden of Wazir Khan, from its containing a large number of date trees.'

G 5 (b). WAZIR KHAN'S BARADARI

G 5 (b). Photo postcard, c.1920. (RS/43)

Goulding's recollection of the transformations this stately building underwent reads: 'After the annexation of the Punjab, it was used first for military purposes, than as a Settlement office, next as a Telegraph office, and temporarily as a museum. The writer's first recollection of it is as the Anarkali Book Club for the European residents. It contained a fairly good collection of books and magazines which used to be circulated to the members. [in 1883-84, the monthly membership of the Book Club was four rupees per month.] When this library was transferred to the Lawrence Hall and became part of the Lahore and Mian Mir Institute, now known as the Gymkhana, the *baradari* was made available for the present public Library.'

By the time of this photograph it had been adapted to become the Punjab Public Library.

G 6. THE PUNJAB PUBLIC LIBRARY

G 6. THE PUNJAB PUBLIC LIBRARY

Photograph, 1938.

The modern red-brick adjunct to the baradari of Wazir Khan was completed in 1939-40. One of the finest public libraries in Lahore during its day, the Punjab Public Library has recently fallen into sad neglect, its collection of books depleted and its regular membership a fraction of what it once enjoyed.

G 7. PWD BUILDING

G 7. PWD BUILDING

Photo postcard, c. 1920. (RS/53)

The PWD or Public Works Department building. located on the road now known as Library Road between the Lahore Museum and Tollinton market, has been absorbed into the corpus of large complex of official buildings that could easily be mistaken as a block of civilian barracks housing various departments of the Punjab Government.

The area in and around old Anarkali was originally populated by military barracks. Goulding recalled 'Many of the old barracks were, however, reserved for use as public buildings. Some of these stood in parallel lines on the area between the Anarkali bazaar and the Municipal Gardens (Gol Bagh). Two were utilised for the accommodation of the Boys' and Girls' High Schools. They occupied the ground on which the Senate Hall, the gift of His Highness the Nawab of Bahawalpur, now stands. Another was used until recently for the offices of the two branches of the Public Works Department, Buildings and Roads, and Irrigation. This has been demolished to make room for the handsome building, still under construction, in which the Chemical Laboratory of the Punjab University will be fitted up. It was here that the midday gun was fired for many years previous to its removal, first to the Telegraph Office and later to its present position on the crest of the old brick-kiln in the Lawrence Gardens. The only one of this group of old barracks which still exists in a recognizable form is that occupied by the Educational offices. The northern end was, however, transformed beyond recognition when converted into the Punjab University Library. The offices of the Inspector-General of prison and of the Sanitary Commissioner were also accommodated for many years in this barrack.' [Goulding (1924), p.21.]

G 8. OLD ANARKALI

G 8. OLD ANARKALI

Photo postcard, c. 1920. (RS/48)

Although this suburb of Lahore was built after the 1850s, the architecture of decorated overhanging wooden balconies echoes those seen within the old walled city.

G 9. YOUNG MEN'S CHRISTIAN ASSOCIATION (YMCA)

G 9. YOUNG MEN'S CHRISTIAN ASSOCIATION (YMCA)

Photo postcard, c. 1920. (RS/C)

The Lahore branch of the YMCA was founded by a Major Edward Newbury, a British Engineer, as a result of an evangelistic meeting with the Revd. J. Somerville in the previous year. According to the records of the YMCA, the first broadcasting station in the subcontinent was established in 1928 in this building.

The roads flanking the corner YMCA building are the Mall on the left leading westwards to the Lahore Museum, and on the right the road leading to Nila Gumbad.

G 10. THE NILA GUMBAD AREA

G 10. THE NILA GUMBAD AREA

Photo postcard, c. 1920. (RS/54)

The area shown in this photograph is the triangular garden in front of the Nila Gumbad shrine of Abdul Razzak Makai (hidden by trees on the left). Makai was a divine from Ghazni who settled in Lahore during the reign of Humayun. On the right, also hidden from view, would have been King Edward Medical College, and in the far distance are some of the shops on the road that led to New Anarkali. One of these S.R. Khosla's Hair Dressing Saloon - advertised himself ambitiously in the Lahore Directory of 1914 as the 'Cheapest Hair Dresser in the Punjab' and in case any potential customer misconstrued the word cheap, added ' Cleanliness guaranteed in every respect.'

The statue in the foreground is of King Edward VII (1901-1910), in naval uniform. This statue is now in the Lahore Fort.

G 11. KING EDWARD MEDICAL COLLEGE

G 11. KING EDWARD MEDICAL COLLEGE

Photo postcard, c.1920.

Identified on this postcard as Mayo Hospital, the building is in fact the King Edward Medical College. The College had been established in 1860 as a medical college to impart training to local Punjabis, as it was found that Bengali doctors imported into the Punjab found less favour with the local population and in any case tended to feel homesick. [Latif (1892), p.301]

The first site of the nascent medical college, according to Latif, was 'on the site of the present Government College, and the Hospital was formed in Raja Suchet Singh's stable, in the Tibbi Bazar near the Taxali Gate of the city.'

The domed block was known as the Patiala Block, completed in 1915. The building on the right became Ewing Hall.

G 12. FORMAN CHRISTIAN COLLEGE

G 12. FORMAN CHRISTIAN COLLEGE

Photo postcard, c. 1920. Photo by Fred Bremner, Lahore and Quetta.

A valuable image of the Forman Christian College building that once stood opposite the General Post Office on the Mall. Latif, writing in 1891, could still describe it as 'the new building of the Lahore Mission College' that faces 'the plains, not far from the Telegraph Office.' He described its establishment: 'In November 1849, or forty-two years ago, the Revd. Messrs. Newton and Forman, members of the Board of Foreign Missions of the Presbyterian Church in the United States of America, arrived in Lahore, and opened the first English School, the building known as "Rang Mahal", in the newly acquired city. At first there was a great aversion to the study of English, partly owing to religious considerations, and partly because the people were not sure how long the English occupation would last.' [Latif (1892), p.283.]

Khosla's Lahore Guide of 1932 provides the additional information that the Forman Christian College was established first in 1866, and for the first four years prepared its students for the F.A. and B.A. examinations of Calcutta University. The College went into a hiatus following the death of its Principal Mr. Henry, but was revived in 1886, after which the candidates prepared for the examinations set by the Punjab University.

Three years after the college was opened in Rang Mahal, it shifted to its new premises in 1889. The new building was completed at a cost of Rs 56,000 on 14 acres of land provided by the Government of the Punjab. The building was finally demolished after the Forman Christian College moved to its present premises in the 1940s. The Annual Lahore City Guide for 1942 reported that 'the College has recently shifted to its new premises near the Canal.'

G 13. GOVERNMENT TELEGRAPH OFFICE

G 13. GOVERNMENT TELEGRAPH OFFICE

Photo postcard, c. 1920. Photo by B. N. Kapur, Photogoods Dealer, Lahore. (RS/73)

The main building of the Government Telegraph Office, located opposite the General Post Office, was completed in 1882 and expanded a decade later. In 1916, the main office was connected to 16 telegraph offices seven within the city in Anarkali, Charing Cross, Civil Secretariat, Dabbi Bazar, Sadar Bazar, Naulakha and Mughalpura. The other nine were in rural areas Balloke, Changa Manga, Chunian, Kasur Mandi, Kot Radha Kishan railway station, Patti, Pattoki Railway station, Raiwind and Shahdara Mills. [Lahore Gazetteer (1916), pp.169-170.]

G 14. THE BANK OF BENGAL BUILDING

G 14. THE BANK OF BENGAL BUILDING

Photo postcard, c. 1920. (RS/52)

One of the early banks to establish its offices at Lahore, the Bank of Bengal building stood adjacent to the Telegraph Office on the Mall, opposite the General Post Office. The first Bank of Bengal branch had been near the Magistrates Court, the site being vacated to accommodate the Veterinary College. [Goulding (1924), p.13.]

In 1876, according to Thornton, Lahore had three banks, all located in Anarkali: Agra Bank, Punjab Bank, and Bengal Bank. By 1914, two new names were added Alliance Bank of Simla and the National Bank of India. The Bank of Bengal building has since been demolished.

G 15. THE GENERAL POST OFFICE

G 15. THE GENERAL POST OFFICE

Photo postcard, c.1920. Photo by B. N. Kapur, Photogoods Dealer, Lahore. No.16. (RS/72)

The General Post Office building stood at the junction of the Mall and Nabha Road. Described in the Lahore Gazetteer of 1916 as ' a handsome structure surmounted by a Clock Tower and four minarets and is of the Indo-Saracenic order of architecture. It was completed in 1904 and occupied by the Post Office in the same year.'

The Gazetteer of 1916 mentions that Lahore 'is well-equipped with street letter boxes [One of these, bearing the monogram of Queen Victoria (who died in 1901), is still in use in Anarkali.] of which there are 132, the distant boxes being cleared by bicycle peons. Bicycle peons are also utilized to exchange mails between the General Post Office, Charing Cross, the Lahore cantonment and Mughalpura Post Offices. Mails are conveyed to and from the Railway Station in mail carts drawn by horses and several of the postmen serving distant beats are conveyed to their beats in these horse-drawn mail carts. Two flags are flown weekly at the General Post Office, a red one to indicate that the foreign mail has been signaled at Bombay and is expected at Lahore, and the Royal Mail Standard (a white one) to indicate the day of dispatch of the foreign mail from Lahore.' [Lahore Gazetteer (1916), p.169.]

G 16. THE GENERAL POST OFFICE

G 16. THE GENERAL POST OFFICE

Photo postcard, c. 1940.

This later photograph, taken perhaps in the 1940s, shows the traffic roundabout that has since been removed, and a cat's-cradle of telephone wires that should have been.

G 17.

G 17. THE PUNJAB HIGH COURT (FROM THE EAST)

Photograph, c. 1920.

The elegance of the Punjab High Court building is seen to best advantage in this photograph. The building was designed by Mr Brossington and completed at a cost of Rs 3,21,837 in March 1889 under the supervision of Mr. J.E. Hilton, Executive Engineer.

'The whole structure,' Latif wrote admiringly, 'which is in the form of a quadrangle is built of solid bricks, in lime mortar, with all mouldings, cornices and projections of specially moulded bricks and the arch fillings of terra cotta trellis work. One great peculiarity of the work was that no chipping of bricks was allowed.

The front arches of the Judge's verandah and the porch outside, and portions of the main towers, are built of Nowshera marble, with marble trellis work [.] On all four sides, both inside the quadrangle and round the outside of the entire building, are spacious verandahs, bringing the whole of the courts and offices in direct communication with one another.

The two towers, which form the central feature, are carried up square for half the height, above which, they are fluted and have bold cones thrown out, somewhat after the model of those of the Kutab Minar at Delhi. The total height of the central towers to the vane is 95 feet, and that of the two at the end 72 feet.' [Latif (1892), pp.284-5.]

In the foreground, located in the small park, is the statue of Lord John Lawrence.

G 18. THE PUNJAB HIGH COURT (FROM THE WEST)

G 18. THE PUNJAB HIGH COURT (FROM THE WEST)

Photograph, c. 1925.

Seen from the approach road opposite the General Post Office, the west side of the Punjab high Court building housed rooms for 'the Jury, the Bar, Bar Library, Deputy Registrar, the Translating Department, Reader's Room, and the Superintendent of the Vernacular Office.' [Latif (1892), p.284.]

THE HIGH COURT, LAHORE.
Bar Association Library.

G 19.

G 19. THE HIGH COURT BAR ASSOCIATION LIBRARY

Photograph, 1933.

The extension of the Punjab High Court building was made in 1933 for the use of the Bar Association to replace 'the somewhat restricted and inconvenient accommodation now occupied in the main building of the High Court.' [B & R Report (1933-34), p.9.] The cost of these extensions, begun in 1932 was Rs 925,000.

G 20. THE LAHORE CATHEDRAL

Photo postcard, c. 1925. (RS/108)

Until 1867, the Anglican community in and around Lahore came under the jurisdiction of the Calcutta diocese. In December that year, Lahore was constituted as a separate see, under its first Bishop the Right Revd. T.V. French. His new diocese included the province of Sindh.

In 1883, the Lahore Gazetteer reported: 'Several years ago the small size and inconvenient situation of the old tomb near the Civil Secretariat, used as the station Church induced the congregation to build a more convenient church, and site was obtained on the high ground to the right of the road to the Railway Station, opposite the new Government Telegraph Office, and foundations sunk. But in December 1867 the Punjab was constituted a separate diocese; and as the church was not completed and the design was poor, it was resolved to enlarge the building into a larger church fitted as a Cathedral, with library, chapter-house, etc. The design was furnished by Mr Oldrid Scott, son and successor to the late well-known Sir Gilbert Scott, and is being carried out in fine red brickwork and grey stone from the Taraki quarries beyond Jhelum. The work is being vigorously carried on by Messrs Burn and Co. of Calcutta, who have agreed to construct the fabric of the Cathedral, without the western towers and without any ornamentation or furniture, for Rs 2,76,535. The Church, dedicated to "All Saints" is expected to be sufficiently complete for use in 1885.' [Lahore Gazetteer (1883-84), p.125.]

The foundation stone was laid in 1874 and largely due to the efforts of the first Bishop T. Valpy French, the building was completed and duly consecrated on 25 January1887. The two western towers were added in 1913, 'one being a memorial of the Lahore episcopate of Dr Lefroy [third Bishop of Lahore, 1899-1913] and the other in memory of the late Archdeacon Spence Gay.' [Archdeacon 1905-6]

G 20. THE LAHORE CATHEDRAL

G 21. THE LAHORE CATHEDRAL

G 21. THE LAHORE CATHEDRAL

Photo postcard, c. 1930.

The Lahore Cathedral Church of the Resurrection as it appears today, without the two spires on its Norman towers. The North tower houses the clock manufactured in 1862, and the South tower six of the bells received from England and cast in 1903 by John Taylor and Co. of Loughborough. 'The largest bell is about one ton in weight and when in use, the foundations used to vibrate.' [*The Centenary Volume, The Cathedral Church of the Resurrection, Lahore 1887-1987.*]

The building on the right is known as St Hilda's and is used as a guest house for visiting clergy.

G 22. THE STATUE OF LORD JOHN LAWRENCE

Photo postcard, c. 1920.

The statue of Lord John Lawrence, Viceroy and Governor-General of India (1864-69) had been erected to commemorate his tenure as a member of the Board of Administration and after its dissolution, as the first Lieutenant-Governor of the Punjab in 1859. The statue stood in a small garden on the same side of the Mall as the Punjab High Court, separated from it by Fane Road. The statue was cast by Sir Joseph E Boehm (1834-1890), sculptor-in-ordinary to Queen Victoria, and presented by him to the Lahore Municipality to commemorate Queen Victoria's Jubilee. It was unveiled by Lawrence's successor as Lieutenant-Governor Sir Charles Aitchison on 30 March 1887.

The sculptor took the liberty of paraphrasing Lawrence's declaration in 1848 to the Trans-Sutlej states: "I have ruled this district three years by the sole agency of the pen, and if necessary, I will rule it by the sword", compressing it into the pithy warning: 'By which will ye be governed - the pen or the sword?'

In the 1920s, agitation was fomented objecting to the condescending inscription that many nationalists found offensive. In October 1921, the General Committee of the Municipal Committee passed a resolution to the effect that (1) the statue should be removed, (2) it should be stored temporarily in the Town Hall, and (3) that a sub-committee should deliberate on the final disposal of the statue. For a resume of the debate on whether the statue should be permitted to remain or not, see Goulding (1924), pp.36-8. Predictably, the formation of the sub-committee ensured that no action would be taken, and the statue remained in place until its final removal on 25 August 1951 to the Lahore Fort.

G 22. THE STATUE OF LORD JOHN LAWRENCE

G 23. THE STATUE OF LORD LAWRENCE

G 24. A VIEW OF THE MALL

G 25. A VIEW OF THE MALL

G 23. THE STATUE OF LORD LAWRENCE

Photo postcard, c. 1920. (RS/77)

In this photograph, the building in the background is the Holy Trinity Church and the one on the right is Forman Christian College.

G 24. A VIEW OF THE MALL

Photo postcard, c. 1930. (RS/58)

Looking eastwards towards Regal Chowk. The cupolas of the Punjab High Court are visible on the right.

G 25. A VIEW OF THE MALL

Photo postcard, c.1930. (RS/60)

Looking westwards towards Regal Chowk. The road on the right would be Hall Road.

G 26. HALL ROAD JUNCTION

G 26. HALL ROAD JUNCTION

Photograph, December 1941.

G 27. CATHEDRAL GIRLS' HIGH SCHOOL

G 27. CATHEDRAL GIRLS' HIGH SCHOOL

Photo postcard, c. 1900. Photo by Bremner. (RS 31/A)

The Cathedral High School was located on Hall Road, adjacent to the Cathedral of the Resurrection. This particular postcard bears a franking date of 1904 and was sent by the Deaconess Katherine Beynon to a Lady Young in St. Leonards-on-Sea, United Kingdom.

G 28. A VIEW DOWN THE MALL

G 28. A VIEW DOWN THE MALL

Photo postcard, c. 1930. (RS/59)

View down the Mall westwards from Charing Cross, with the statue of Queen Victoria on the right.

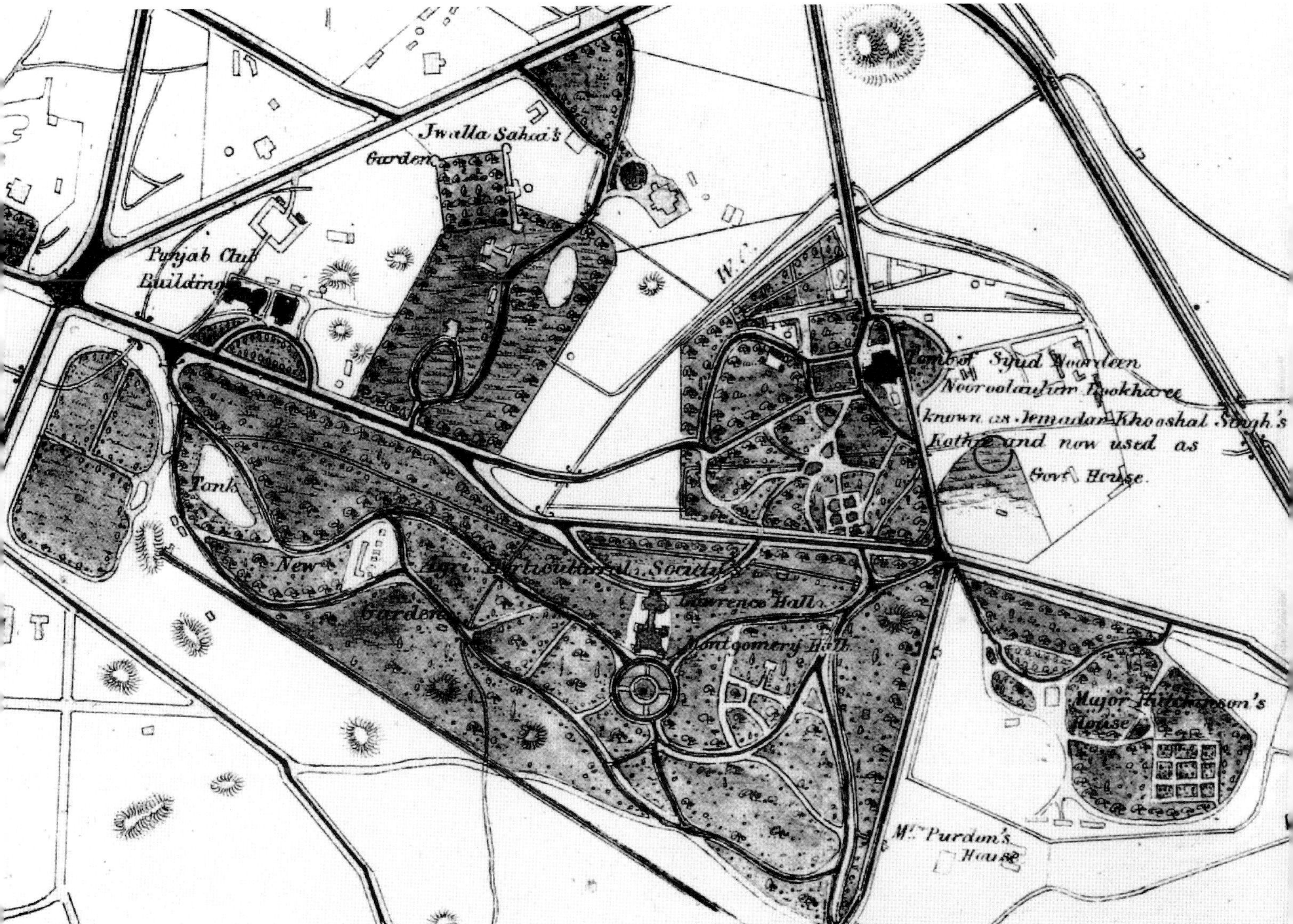

Detail for 1867 map.

THE MALL
(AT CHARING CROSS)

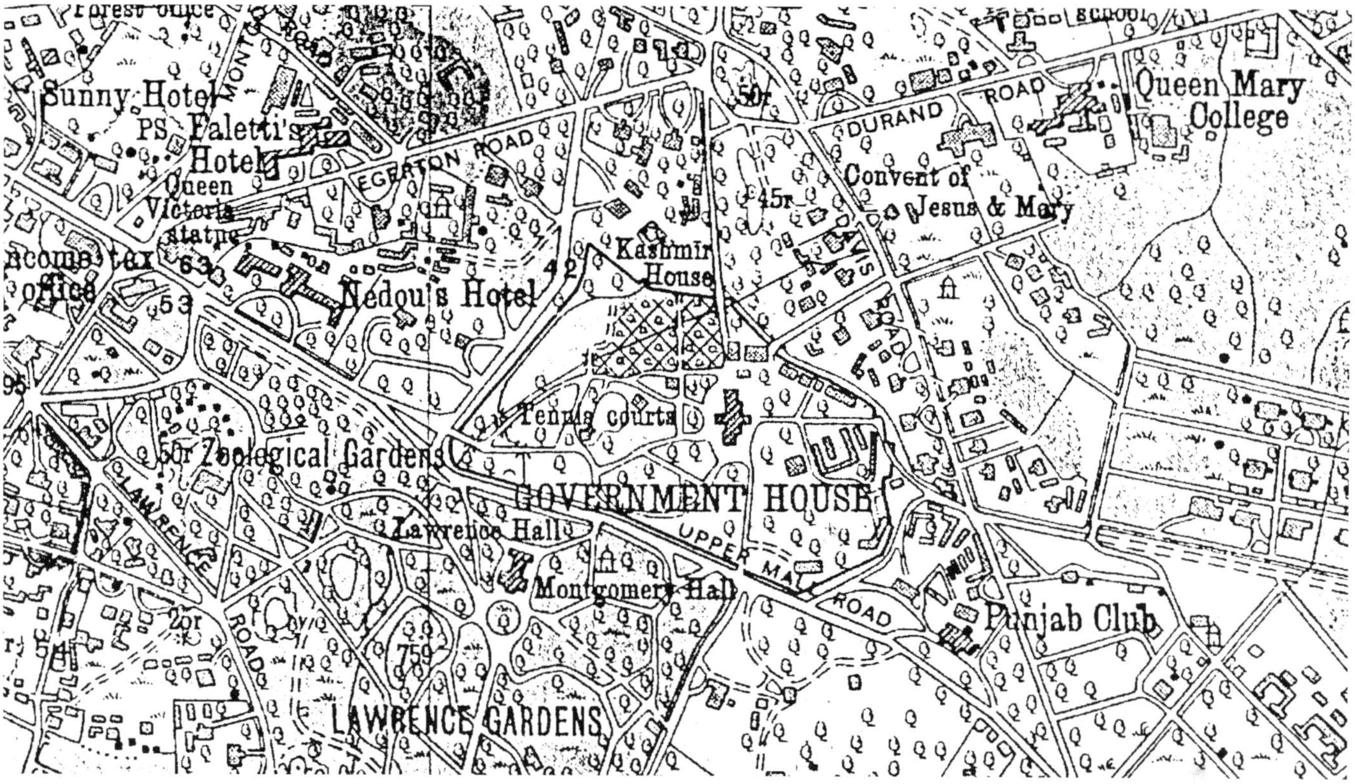

Detail from 1927 map.

Originally named Donaldtown after Mr. Donald McLeod, then President of the Lahore Improvement Committee and later Lieutenant-Governor of the Punjab (1865-70), the name Charing Cross would appear to have been given to the area by the First World War.[Elmslie (1908), p.78.]

The B & R report for 1918-19 mentions that the Charing Cross Scheme 'has now been finalized at its less important (southern) end by the completion of the Masonic Hall and by the laying out of roads, paths and grass. The remainder of the undertaking, consisting of a group of very large Secretariat buildings which was postponed during the War, is now to be pushed forward. The most difficult part of the site has been dealt with, however, and when the new buildings are erected, standing as they will among harmonious surroundings, they should form a fitting and durable monument of the civil administration of the Punjab.' [B & R report (1918-19), p.10.]

Eventually, the scheme had to be shelved as funds were not available in the post - war economy.

The new Masonic Hall replaced the old Masonic Hall on Lodge Road. The former building is still standing within the compound of what is now the Lady Maclagan Government High School.

H 1. AERIAL VIEW OF CHARING CROSS AND THE CENTRAL MALL

H 1. AERIAL VIEW OF CHARING CROSS AND THE CENTRAL MALL

Photograph, c. 1920.

In the centre of the photograph is the white cupola of the statue of Queen Victoria. The Mall flows diagonally west to east, passing Charing Cross. On the left are the Masonic Lodge and Shah Din Manzil buildings flanking the commencement of Queen's Road, and on the right, a row of shops located in Mela Ram and Jodha Mal buildings. They were pulled down, to make way for WAPDA House. To the right is Nedou's Hotel (now the Avari Lahore Hotel). Work on the Punjab Assembly building had not been started when this photograph was taken.

Following the Mall in an eastward direction the shops and monuments one would have passed in 1914 would have been:

LEFT	RIGHT
Ranken and Co., Civil and Military Tailors	Haye's Stores
Civil & Military Gazette Press	M/s Varcados & Co., Cigarette Manufacturers
M/s Cutler Palmer & Co., Wine Merchants	Depot of Muir Mills Co. Ltd.
Sunny View Hotel	M/s Hakman & Co., Court Hairdressers
M/s Peer & Sons, Motor Car Dealers	M/s Phelps & Co., Tailors and Outfitters
M/s Smith & Campbell, Chemists	Mr. Imrie, Court Milliner
M/s L. Richards & Co., Drapers and Outfitters	Price Edwards & Co., Opticians
Queen Victoria's statue	M/s Hayat & Bros.
M/s Walter Locke & Co., Gun makers	Mr. Fred Bremner, Photographer
Mr J. D. Bevan, Pianoforte dealers	
M/s Watts & Co., Bootmakers/Saddlers	Savoy Hotel
M/s Whiteway Laidlaw & Co.	Motor and Cycle Agency
M/s Ball, Moody & Co., Civil & Military Tailors	Ghulam Husain, Milliners
M/s J. Morris & Co., Wine and General Merchants	M/s Setna & Sons
Mr G.T. Fillingham, Tailor	Paplos & Co., Cigarette Manufacturers
M/s R. Dill & Co.,	Mr. E. L. Stiffle, Confectioner
Charing Cross Post Office	M/s C. Steirt & Co., Music Saloon
	M/s Max Minck & Co. Jewellers and Watchmakers

Advertisement for Ranken & Co., Outfitters, Lahore. Probably c. 1925.

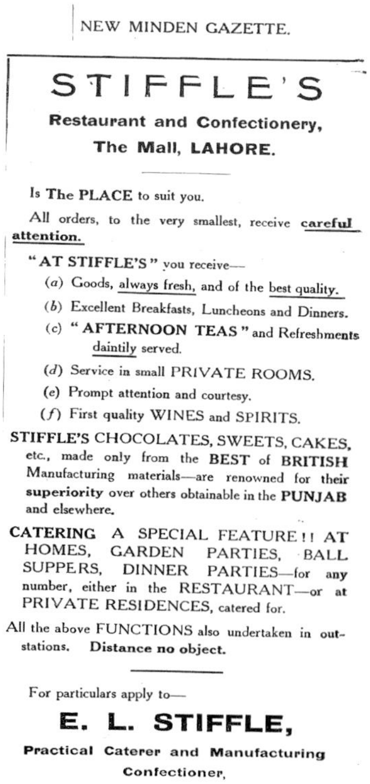

Advertisement for Stiffle's Restaurant, Lahore. Probably c. 1925.

H 2. THE STATUE OF QUEEN VICTORIA

Photograph, c. 1930.

The most prominent monument to the British presence was for many years the bronze statue of Queen Victoria, wearing her small Imperial crown on a veil of her favourite Honiton lace, cradling the sceptre and holding the orb. The statue had been cast in London by B. Mackennal in 1900, the year before Queen Victoria' death in January 1901. The marble pavilion protecting the statue had been designed by Bhai Ram Singh Mistri, Deputy Principal of the then Mayo School of Arts. Although the statue was taken to the Lahore Museum in 1951, the marble pavilion remains covering now a bronze model of the Holy Quran.

H 3 (a-o). THE PUNJAB ASSEMBLY BUILDING

The plan to shift the Punjab Legislature from its temporary accommodation (see F 10-14) in what is now the Civil Secretariat near Anarkali had been initiated in 1918-19, with the acquisition of ten acres of land at Charing Cross. [B & R Report (1918-19), p.4.] The original scheme anticipated a large complex of administrative buildings. In November 1932, the Government of India decided to build on Charing Cross site. The cost was estimated at approximately Rs 900,000. The Working Drawings and Estimates were expected to be ready by December 1933, and the structure by December 1935. It was planned to be 'one of very considerable architectural beauty, [and] will form the first stage in a scheme, to include on this site, a completely new Civil Secretariat with subsidiary local government offices. This scheme, however, is unlikely to materialize for many years to come.' Meanwhile additions/alterations to the Temporary Legislative Council cost Rs 39,000, and were completed in October 1933.

The B & R Report for the following year (1933-34) advised that 'two detailed estimates with drawings for a part of the new roads were prepared and sanctioned [.] The detailed drawings and estimates for the Council Chamber itself were proceeded with.' [B & R Report (1933-34), p.8] During the following year 1934-35, filling, realignment and remaking of existing roads and the new circular road around the site were completed. Estimates and drawings were prepared upon the basis of which tenders were called in November 1935.

H 3(a). Layout in front of site.

During 1935-36, work on the foundations and basement up to the plinth level was undertaken under a separate contract pending the receipt of tenders for the whole building. The large area in front of the Council Chamber itself was laid out and grassed and two avenues of trees planted. The foundation stone of the Council Chamber was laid on 17 December 1935 by Sir Jogendra Singh, the Punjab Minister for Agriculture. [B & R Report (1935-36), p.10.] Work on the superstructure started on 8 March 1936, and by March 1937 was 'in full swing', with an estimated completion target of summer 1938.

In 1936-37, 'work on the substructure having been completed, tenders for the superstructure were invited and the work was started on 8 March 1936'. A Committee, convened by the Hon'ble the President of the Legislative Council, considered the plans and specifications of the building and recommended additional items and better materials in various parts of it. The cost of these were worked out. After lengthy discussions, a number of these were sanctioned by Government on 26 February 1937. There was a delay while decisions were being reached and the revised estimates were being prepared. The work was consequently not in full swing until March 1937. The portion of the building being constructed is expected to be completed by the summer of 1938.'

By 1937-38, work had slowed because 'better materials than those in sanctioned estimate' needed to be used. Plaster, for example, being replaced by stone because of the difficulty of procuring stone following of the quarries in 1937. Secondhand girders were taken from the Railways. The building was planned to be in use from October 1938. The buildings were finished in October 1938, and opened by the Governor on 10 November 1938. [B & R Report (1936-37), p.10.]

The B & R report for 1938-9 mentions that an accurate plan of the whole complex is still awaited. The buildings proposed are: 'New Secretariat, PWD Block, Record Rooms, His Excellency's Office, quarters for Member of the Assembly, quarters of a Caretaker, garages for the Speaker, Ministers and Secretaries, service room for caterers, parking ground for cars, public taxi stand, and post office.' [B & R Report (1938-39), p.11.] Two years after its occupation, the Punjab Legislative Assembly building was found to be inadequate. Additional space was required. 'The need for additional accommodation was felt and the Secretary, Provincial Legislative Assembly has asked for additional accommodation.' Also additional lavatories were demanded for the Public and the Press.

H 3(b). Foundation Raft under construction. The buildings in the background are the Freemason's Hall (first occupied in 1917) on the left, and the Shah Din building (completed in 1914) on the right. The statue of Queen Victoria is seen against the latter building.

H 3(c). Laying the foundation stone by Punjab Minister for Agriculture Sir Jogendra Singh, on 17 November 1935.

H 3 (d). Centering for the Reinforced Concrete floor above basement.

H 3 (e). Foundation raft approaching completion.

H 3 (f). Girders being placed below Council Chamber.

H 3 (g). Concreting the floor above the basement.

H 3(h). Front elevation in progress.

H 3(i). Masons at work on capitals of the columns in the main entrance.

H 3 (j). View of completed Assembly building, from the Mall.

H 3(k). North View of the Council Chamber.

H 3(l). Grand staircase with vestibule in the hall.

H 3(m). The first floor vestibule.

H 3 (n). Council Chamber

H 3 (o). Tea Room

H 4. THE PUNJAB LEGISLATIVE ASSEMBLY BUILDING

H 4. THE PUNJAB LEGISLATIVE ASSEMBLY BUILDING

Photo postcard, c.1940. (RS/62)

A view of the newly constructed Punjab Assembly building, photographed from the roof of the Shah Din building. The area marked by the signboard as the Charing Cross taxi stand is now occupied by the Al-Falah Building, the foundation stone of which was laid by President Ayub Khan on 30 November 1962.

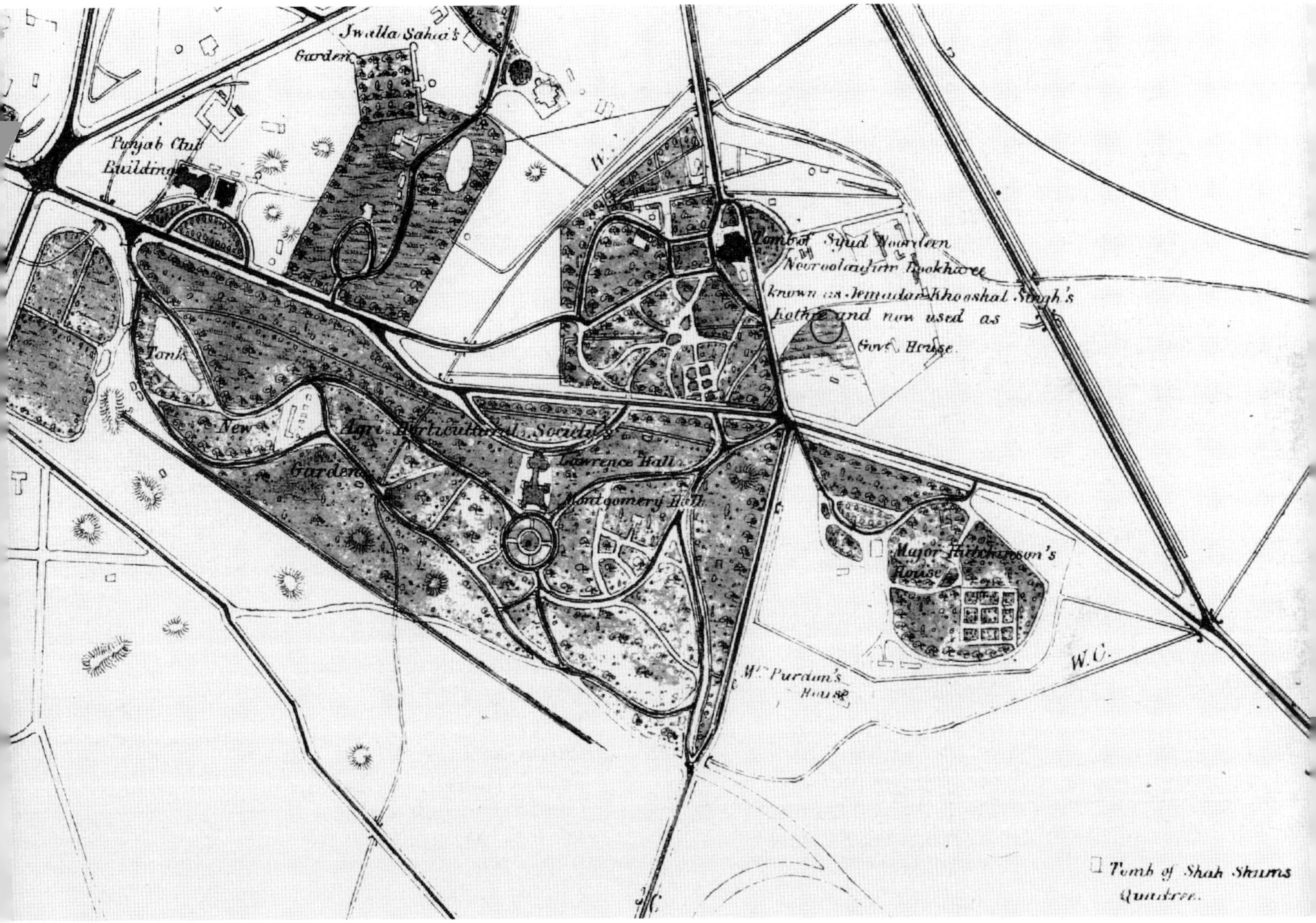

Detail from 1867 map.

THE MALL
EASTWARDS FROM CHARING CROSS

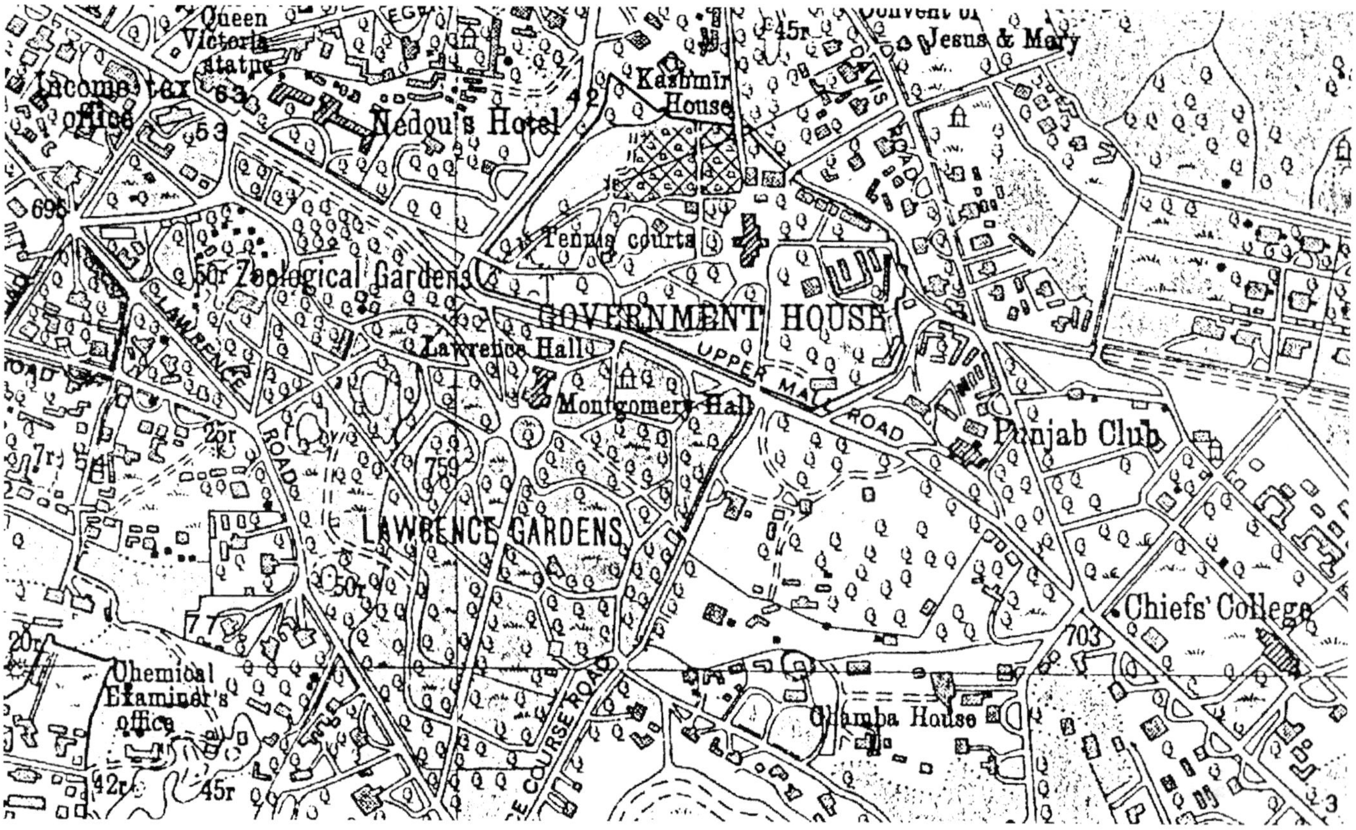

Detail from 1927 map.

Travelling along the Mall in an easterly direction towards the Cantonment, the following buildings would have been encountered in 1914:

LEFT	RIGHT
Nedou's Hotel	Agri-Horticulture Gardens
Mr Morton	Lawrence Hall
Punjab Club	Police Post
Mr. A.R. Ross-Redding	Government Agri-Horti Garden
Mr Rup Narain	Patiala House
Mr. F. A. Leslie-Jones [Principal, Aitchison College]	Garden of Chote Lal
Chief's College [Aitchison College]	Mr R.A. Mant, ICS
	Police Post
	Chief's College
	Mr A. C. Edger
	Octroi post
	Mr D. Macfarlane
	Chamba House
	H. H. the Chief of Kalsia [A village in Kasur District.]
	Mr A.H. Joscelyne

I 1. NEDOU'S HOTEL

I 1. NEDOU'S HOTEL

Photo postcard, c.1940. (RS/61)

In 1876, Thornton cautioned visitors to Lahore with the warning that 'the hotels in Lahore are poor, though there is little doubt that a really good hotel would pay, owing to the large influx of travelers at certain seasons of the year. The Punjab hotel, Mrs. Clark's Hotel, the Victoria and Montgomery, are those most frequented by European visitors.'

For those who preferred something more traditional, there was always the dak bungalow: 'The Dak Bungalow in Anarkali, opposite to the Katchery and adjoining the union Church, affords good accommodation on the usual terms.' The Dak Bunglaow stood on a ridge and was absorbed within the grounds of Government College. It was demolished in the 1960s.

In 1914, fifteen hotels are given mention in the Lahore Directory:

Bombay Hindu Hotel, Anarkali
Braganza Hotel, McLeod Road
Cambridge Hotel, Empress Road
Cecil Hotel, Cooper Road
Central Hotel, Empress Road
Faletti's Hotel, Egerton Road
Imperial Hotel, Railway Road
Lahore Hotel, Nicholson Road
Nedou's Hotel, The Mall
Savoy Hotel, The Mall
Shelbourne Hotel, Empress Road
Sunny View Hotel, The Mall
Schneider & Co., McLeod Road
St John's Hotel, Museum Road
Puri's Hindu Hotel, Circular Road

Any traveller using the agency of Thos. Cook and Son could buy Indian Hotel Coupons which would be surrendered at its selected hotel - Nedou's for a full day's board. In 1910, a coupon for Rs 7 per day covered:

Bedroom, lights and service, with bath
Chota hazri, or early tea with toast
Burra hazri, or meat breakfast
Tiffin or lunch
Dinner

By 1930, the Automobile Association advised its members of the following hotels in Lahore:
- Faletti's on Egerton Road, with 76 bedrooms at a tariff of Rs 11 per day for a Single and Rs 20 per day for a Double; Nedou's on The Mall, with 84 bedrooms at a tariff Rs 10-11 per day with special terms for commercial travellers; Sunny View Hotel, Kashmir House, with 41 bedrooms at a tariff of Rs 9 per day, Rs 240 per month/Double Rs. 18 per day, Rs 500 per month; Braganza and Sons Hotel, opposite Railway Station, with 40 bedrooms at a tariff of Rs 6 to Rs 9 per day.

This photograph of Nedou's' Hotel shows the façade of Dane Block, completed in 1908 and named after Sir Louis Dane, Secretary to the Punjab Government (1898) and later Foreign Secretary to the Government of India (1903).

Nedou's Hotel was demolished to make way for the present Avari Lahore Hotel, the foundation stone of which was laid on 23 September 1973. It opened in 1977.

I 2. GOVERNOR'S HOUSE

Wood engraving, *Illustrated London News*, 27 November 1869.

Muhammad Qasim Khan, a blood relation of the emperor Akbar, lived long enough to see a third generation of Mughals on the throne at Delhi. He died during the reign of Shah Jahan and was buried in a large garden that would have been at that time an uninhabited wilderness. Subsequent occupation by Sikh sirdars who made random additions to its structure during Ranjit Singh's reign in the early nineteenth century did little to improve its isolation. Even by the end of the century, when the American painter Edwin Lord Weeks visited Lahore in the late 1880s, he wrote about the jackals that frequented the area. In his memoirs, he recalled:'Government House, the seat of the Lieutenant Governor of the Punjaub, stands in attractive grounds near the fine park known as Lawrence Gardens, on the outskirts of the civil station. The flower-beds and the parterres which adorn the public and private grounds in this neighbourhood are more luxuriant and varied than the winter gardens of the Riviera. In the early morning, as well as at night, they are much frequented by jackals, which show their appreciation of them by trotting about in couples through the shrubbery. An open-air fete has been held in one of these gardens in the afternoon, and when the last guests had departed, many of them in furs and ulsters, and while we were standing before the chimney fire within, the conversation was interrupted by the howls of a band of these nocturnal ramblers just outside the doors.' [Weeks, E.L., *From the Black Sea through Persia and India* (New York, 1895), p.173.]

In 1905, Government House was substantially renovated on the occasion of the visit of the Prince and Princess of Wales (later King George V and Queen Mary) in early 1906. 'Extensive alterations and additions had to be made to Government House, Lahore,' the B & R Report records, '...[and] camps on a large scale were laid out for the accommodation of Their Royal Highnesses' suite and escort. [...] Certain rooms on the north side were enlarged, and the floors relaid with teak, and ceilings and cornices decorated with canvas plaster mouldings. The painted designs on the walls of the dining room were renewed in oil paint by the School of Art, and an ornamental plaster ceiling was provided for a portion of the dining room.' In addition, a new boundary wall was constructed round the estate, for which the estimate was Rs. 63,572 and actual expenditure during the year 1905-6 was Rs 55,250.

I 2. GOVERNOR'S HOUSE.

I 3(a). THE NORTHERN EXTENSION TO GOVERNMENT HOUSE

I 3(a). THE NORTHERN EXTENSION TO GOVERNMENT HOUSE

Photograph, 1915.

Ten years later, a report described the state of Government House in 1914-15: 'Rooms of various shapes and sizes (most of them badly lighted and ventilated) were from time to time built round the tomb, and afforded scanty and inconvenient accommodation for receptions. Architecturally, too, the building was bad as owing to the unsightly additions which had been made the front bristled with excrescences, sweepers' staircases, etc. By the new proposals most of the objectionable features of the old residence had been obviated. Two separate wings are substituted for the mass of shapeless rooms on the north part of the house; each of them is double storied and will provide well-lighted and well-ventilated bedrooms, and office of the Lieutenant-Governor and his staff and large cloak rooms. A ballroom 50 ft x 76 ft is also to be added as the use of the drawing room is not only inconvenient, but the room itself is too small for the purpose. During the course of the year Rs 41,000 have been spent on collection of materials for the work, which will be carried our during the summer of 1915.' The architect for the northern wing extension that contained the ballroom (now the Durbar Hall) and private apartments above the Governor's office suite was designed by an architect, Mr Basil M. Sullivan.

The report made a disparaging reference to the quality of the plaster-work: 'the quality of the plaster and woodwork are not of a very high standard, excepting that prepared in the Mayo School of Arts'.

In 1918-19, it was reported: 'Two pairs of entrance gates have been fixed at Government House. The Bhaganwala stone piers and the wrought iron gates have been carried out entirely by local smiths and masons. This is a better method than indenting on Bombay or Calcutta which has been the custom in the past, as it is more economical and encourages local handicrafts. A design from additions to the garden staircase from the ballroom has been prepared and the work has been executed.'

In subsequent years, the Council Chamber was converted in 1919-20 into a suite of rooms for visitors, and in 1934-35, the prominent fireplace in the Drawing room was redesigned by the Mayo School of Arts.

Since Independence the main building has remained intact except for periodic refurbishment. Any additions that have been made have been of a lakeside pavilion and to the gardens.

I 3 (b). CARVED BRACKETS IN GOVERNMENT HOUSE

Photograph, 1915.

The carved brackets in Government House were designed by Basil Sullivan and modeled by Lionel Heath, then Principal of the Mayo School of Arts, Lahore.

Front View.

Designed by Basil M. Sullivan, A. R. I. B. A.
Modelled by Lionel Heath Esq.

Photo-engraved & printed at the Offices of the Survey of India, Calcutta, 1916.

Side View.

Model of Carved Bracket.

I 4. THE LIEUTENANT-GOVERNOR'S CAMEL-CARRIAGE

I 4. THE LIEUTENANT-GOVERNOR'S CAMEL-CARRIAGE

Photograph, c.1930.

I 5. ENTRANCE GATE TO LAWRENCE GARDENS

I 5. ENTRANCE GATE TO LAWRENCE GARDENS

Photograph, c. 1920.

This photograph shows the Victoria Gate entrance to Lawrence Gardens (now Jinnah Bagh). The Victoria Gate, designed by the architect Mr Barry M. Sullivan, ARIBA, led into Lawrence Gardens from the Mall. The other gates on the south side of the gardens and accessible from Lawrence Road were the Rivaz Gate and the Montgomery Gate.

Thornton in his guide book of 1876 recorded that 'the Lawrence Gardens - the Kensington Gardens of Lahore - cover 112 acres on the right hand side of the Mall between Anarkali and the Lawrence and Montgomery Halls. In 1860 the land now occupied by them was a desolate wilderness. In that year a portion of the ground was laid out as a garden, and in 1868 the portion on the far side of the mounds was added, having been purchased from the proceeds of the sale of the old Government garden near the fort known as Badami Bagh. [The site of the Old AHC Society's Garden or Bedamee Bagh is clearly visible, north of the Fort and adjacent to the samadhis of Jamadar Khushal Singh and Teja Singh on the 1867 map.] Part of the garden is in the occupation of the Agri-Horticultural Society of the Punjab and laid out as a botanical garden under the superintendence of a gardener from Kew [Gardens London] ; part is occupied by a menagerie [the forerunner to the present Lahore Zoo.]; the rest is held by the Municipality and used as a public pleasure ground sacred to badminton, archery and cricket; and on Saturday evening the Lahore Police Band perhaps one of the best native bands in India plays in the space fronting the Montgomery Hall.' [Thornton (1876), pp.80-81.] According to Khosla, the Police Band and sometimes the Military band played there every Tuesday and Friday evenings. [Khosla (1876), p.17.]..

The first tree was planted in this extensive garden in January 1862. G. R. Elmslie, who had arrived in Lahore to take up duties as Assistant Commissioner Lahore, recalled the occasion: 'One morning I accompanied Mr. Forsyth [then Commissioner Lahore] to the newly laid out Lawrence Gardens, then little better than a wilderness, where Miss Forsyth, now Mrs. George Parker, planted the first tree of what was destined to become one of the most beautiful pleasure grounds of Upper India.' [Elmslie (1908), p.77.]

By 1876, that single tree planted by Miss Forsyth had been augmented by thousands more. Thornton reports: 'The garden is watered by a cutting from the Lahore branch of the Bari Doab Canal and contains nearly 80,000 trees and shrubs of 600 different species including, in addition to the trees usually met with in the plains of India, the *chil (Pinus longifolia),* the Australian gum tree (Eucalyptus globulus), and the carob tree of Syria and the South of Europe. The cost of the garden is defrayed partly by the Municiaplity, partly by subscription, and partly by grants in aid from the Provincial Revenues.' [Thornton (1876), p.81.]

Lawrence Gardens had two mounds, assembled from bricks collected from surrounding areas. Khosla wrote that 'one has been turned into a terraced garden with a huge plain on top, where scores of people sit down in the evening to rest a while.'

I 6. LAWRENCE HALL

I 6. LAWRENCE HALL

Woodcut engraving, published in *Illustrated London News, 31 December 1864.*

Designed by Mr G. Stone, then Chief Engineer, Lawrence Hall had been built in 1861-2 in honour of Sir John Lawrence (Chief Commissioner of the Punjab 1853-57, and then Viceroy of India 1863-69).

In 1883-84, the Gazetteer reported that 'Lawrence Hall is frequently used as an assembly room for public meetings and theatrical entertainments.' After an extended period of use as the Lahore and Meean Meer Institute (later the Lahore Gymkhana), the building is now part of the Jinnah Library complex.

I 7. MONTGOMERY HALL

I 7. MONTGOMERY HALL

Photograph, c. 1910.

Montgomery Hall, the southern adjunct to Lawrence Hall and connected to it by a corridor was designed by Mr Gordon, Chief Engineer, and constructed out of contributions by local chiefs in 1866. Soon after it was completed, the roof was repaired and the floor relaid with 'a splendid teak floor for rinking and dancing'.

I 8. THE PUNJAB CLUB

I 8. THE PUNJAB CLUB

Photo postcard, c. 1920. (RS/65)

One of the premier and most exclusive clubs of Lahore, the Punjab Club stood on the Mall, a neighbour of Government House. It appeared first on the list of nine clubs against only four hotels listed in the Automobile Association Handbook for Northern India (c.1929):

Punjab Club	Lahore Gymkhana
Lahore Race Club	Commercial Gymkhana
Cosmopolitan Club	Northern India Flying Club
Punjab Assoc. Club	Murray Club (Cantt.)
Roberts Volunteer Club	

The gracious building has now become the Pakistan Administrative Staff College, and the Punjab Club has been relegated to much smaller premises in Danepur Road, GOR I.

I 9. AITCHISON COLLEGE

I 9. AITCHISON COLLEGE

Photo postcard, c. 1920. (RS/64)

The foundation stone of Aitchison College was laid on 3 November 1886. G.R. Elmslie wrote in his diary after witnessing the event: 'November 3 Afternoon, the ceremony of the laying of the foundation-stone of the Punjab Chiefs' College by the Viceroy came off... The arrivals of the various Chiefs were imposing.' [Elmslie (1908), p.330.] The Viceroy - the Marquess of Dufferin and Ava - gave it the name of Aitchison College.

The area selected as the site for Aitchison College lay on the north side of the Mall. It covered a little over 176 acres. The architecture of the Main Building was a merger of two designs, the exterior being derived from the design submitted by J. Lockwood Kipling and Bhai Ram Singh (Principal and Vice Principal respectively of the Mayo School of Arts) while the interior was planned by Col. Swinton Jacob (1841-1917), a relation of John Jacob after whom Jacobabad in Sindh was named. Swinton Jacob designed a number of such buildings in the Indo-Saracenic style throughout India, including St Stephen's College, Delhi, and the Secretariat at Simla.

This particular building, the nucleus of the college that over the past century has expanded across its extensive campus, contains the Hall of Remembrance on the left, classrooms flanking the Main Assembly Hall in the centre, and more classrooms on the right. At the time, the building cost about Rs 2,18,000. One principal subsequently lamented the extravagance of investing so much money in 'decorative but unsuitable bricks and mortar' instead of in an Endowment Fund, while another complained that interior had sacrificed 'practical utility to artistic effect.' In the foreground are the college tennis courts.

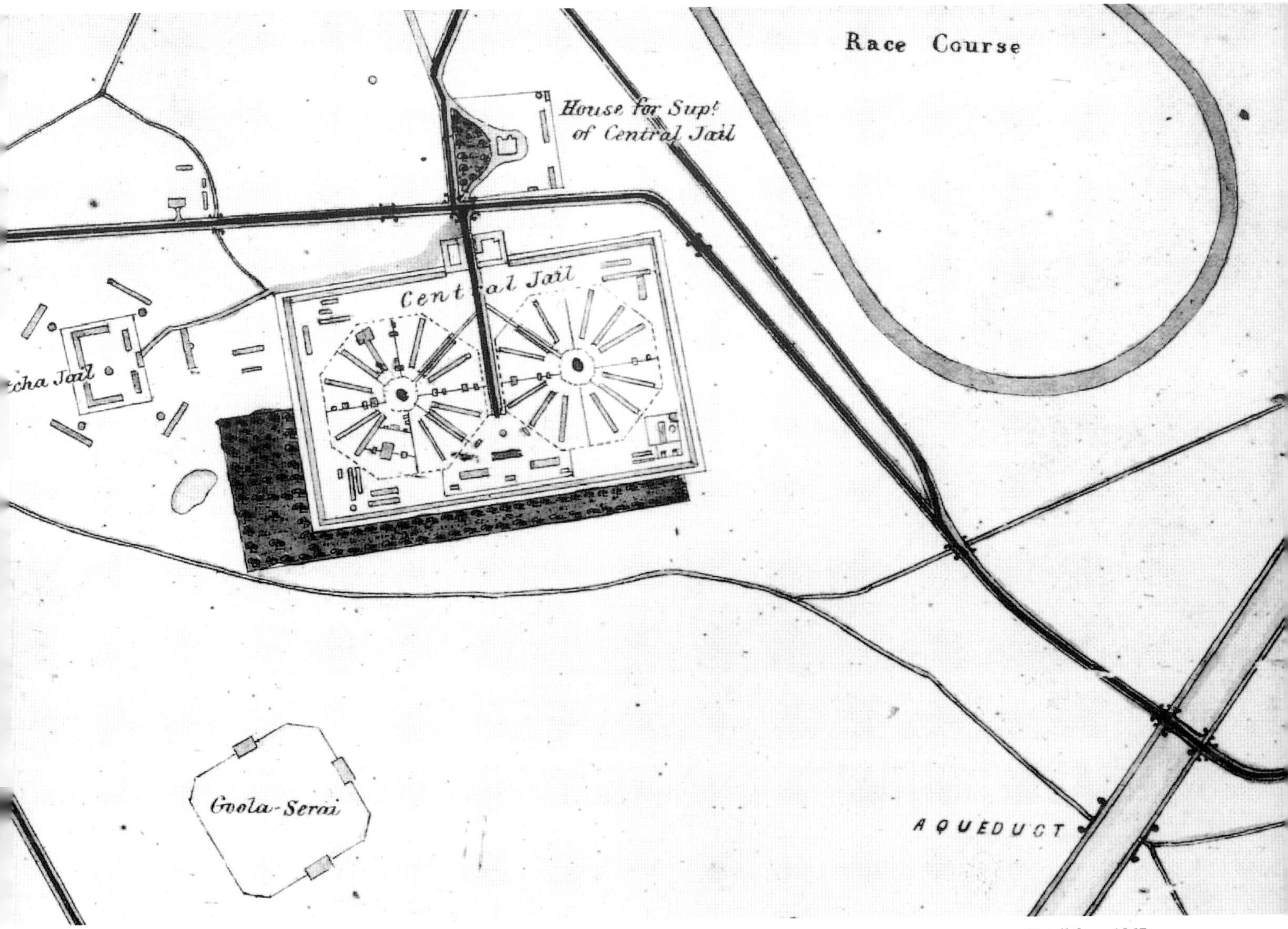

Detail from 1867 map.

GAZETTED OFFICERS' RESIDENCES (G . O. R. I)

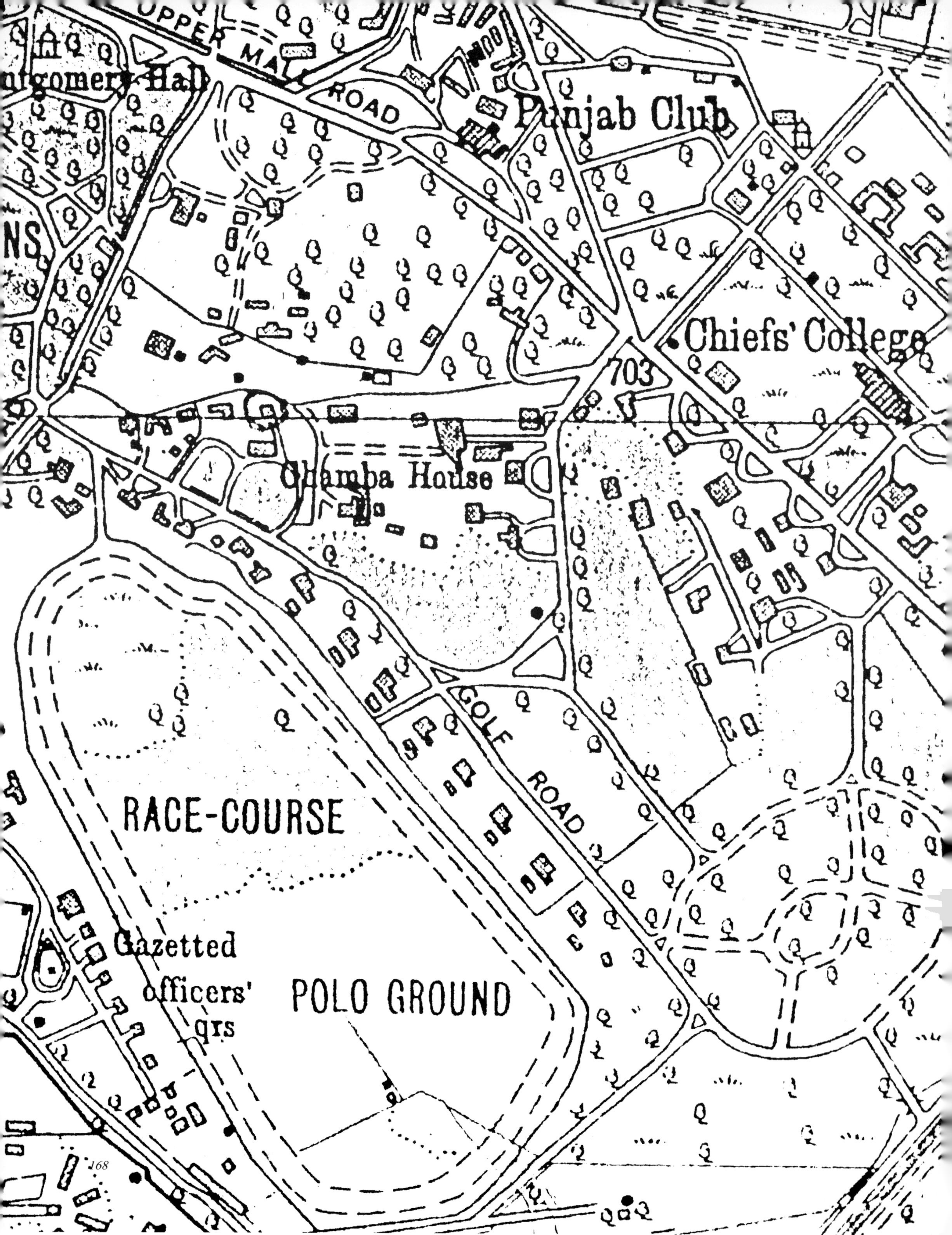

Detail from 1927 map.

GAZETTED OFFICERS' RESIDENCES (G . O. R. I)

In 1914-15, the Government of the Punjab was informed that 'owing to the difficulty found by officers in obtaining suitable houses at Lahore, a scheme has been prepared for the construction of official residences and awaits the sanction of the Secretary of State.

As a preliminary measure, however, permission has been accorded to the purchase of a site, and the old golf links (between the main road to Lahore Cantonment and the Race Course) an area of 192 acres has been acquired at a cost of Rs 3,24,369. Roads on the portion of this land on which it is proposed to construct the first houses, have been laid out in accordance with a plan prepared by the consulting architect and avenues planted.' [B & R Report (1914-15), p.4.]

Four years later, in the post-First World War situation of 1918-19, the Buildings and Roads Department reported on their progress: 'Six houses have now been built and three more have been designed and are under construction, all of which will probably be occupied next cold weather. A considerable demand for these houses is anticipated, although, owing to a great rise in the cost of materials, it has been found necessary to cut out of the designs everything which could possibly be considered a luxury. When it is considered that the cost of rolled steel beams rose from about Rs 6 per cwt. in 1913 to Rs 55 per cwt. before the armistice, while the rates for bricks, timber, coal, freight and wages also rose, it will be realized how difficult if not impossible it is, at the present time, to design a house with reasonable accommodation at a rental which, while not exceeding 10 per cent of the occupant's salary, will show a return to the Government on the capital cost. The general question of housing is to be considered by a Committee which will probably make representation on the subject to the Government of India.

An interesting experiment has been made in the construction of two of the houses, where small Indian bricks from demolished structures were used, which is poor in colour and shape, and to economise in cost. The former object was effected but the cost of the extra number of mortar joints largely neutralized the saving in the cost of the bricks. Designs have also been prepared for a post and telegraph office for the estate and a small bazaar for the use of the servants employed by the residents. During the year the vacant sites have been ploughed up and crops sown upon them with the object of reducing the *reh* which is abundant over large areas of the ground. The sale of crops should provide a set-off against the cost of this treatment. More trees have been planted and roads consolidated. While the plantations along the canal bank have been cleared and greatly improved. Though the progress of this scheme, like many others, has been impeded by the War a distinct advance has been made; while nature, untroubled by strife, has not slackened her efforts, with the result that many of the roads already have avenues of trees of considerable size.' [B & R Report (1918-19), p.11.]

The following year, in 1919-20 nine houses had been constructed; and after a gap of a number of years, in 1927-28, the Buildings and Roads Department estimated the costs of Type II-A Houses at a total of Rs 88,800, another three of a lower category at Rs 73,524, and one Special Type House at Rs 36,670. In 1929-30, six houses were completed and handed over for occupation in October 1929.

The Commissioner's House was estimated in 1934-35 to cost initially Rs 48,900, but that estimate was revised upwards to Rs 50,100 because of 'various additions requested by Government.' The building was completed on 28 Sept 1936.

The Deputy Commissioner's House constructed during the same period cost Rs 44,700. Other buildings completed in subsequent years were a residence for the Chief Secretary, started in June 1939 and completed before the end of 1940, and two residences for the Financial Commissioners and thirteen other residences for lower grades of gazetted officers constructed in 1946-47.

Although most of the GOR estate had been acquired and developed by the Government, certain pockets of privately-owned property remained. A layout plan of these privately-owned buildings was delineated in 1939-40.

Other prominent buildings constructed during this time were:

J 1. THE RESIDENCE FOR THE CHIEF JUSTICE

J 1. THE RESIDENCE FOR THE CHIEF JUSTICE

Photograph, 1935.

The original estimate prepared in 1935-36 for the residence of the Hon'ble Chief Justice of the Punjab was revised to Rs 67,100 due to 'a considerable number of alterations made in the original designs and its services. The two storeyed building was completed in November 1936.

J 2. THE RESIDENCE FOR THE MINISTER OF FINANCE

J 2. THE RESIDENCE FOR THE MINISTER OF FINANCE

Photograph, 1938.

The residence of the Punjab Minister of Finance (now the Chief Minister's official residence) on Club Road was completed and occupied in October 1939. The building cost finally Rs 80,486, appreciably more than its first estimate of Rs 60,499.

J 3. THE RESIDENCE OF THE MINISTER OF EDUCATION.

J 3. THE RESIDENCE OF THE MINISTER OF EDUCATION.

Photograph, 1938.

This building was also completed in October 1939, at a final cost of Rs 59,270 against an estimate of Rs 48,970.

J 4. SPECIAL A-TYPE RESIDENCE.

J 4. SPECIAL A-TYPE RESIDENCE.

Photograph, 1927.

Completed in 1927-28, the building was estimated to cost Rs 36,670. The building is now the Pakistan Navy War College, and is located at the junction of Bromhead Road and Shahrah-i-Quaid-e-Azam, opposite the entrance to Aitchison College Junior School.

J 5. TYPE III-A RESIDENCE

J 5. TYPE III-A RESIDENCE

Photograph, 1927.

This building was also completed in 1927-28. It is now No. 14 Aikman Road, and reserved for occupancy by the Deputy Inspector General of Police, Punjab.

Detail from 1867 map.

QUEEN'S ROAD

(FORMERLY OLD FEROZEPUR ROAD, AND NOW FATIMA JINNAH ROAD)

Detail from 1927 map.

QUEEN'S ROAD
(Formerly Old Ferozepur Road, and now Fatima Jinnah Road)

Reverting back to Charing Cross, the road that the statue of Queen Victoria faced was not surprisingly called Queen's Road. Before that it was known as Ferozepur Road, and more recently it has undergone another change of name to Fatima Jinnah Road.

Walking down that road in 1914, one could have expected to see the following buildings, many of them residences. Prominent amongst them was the on the left side of the road an open area behind the zoo that became the site of the new Civil Station Police Lines (see K 1), the residence of the Hon'ble Khan Zulfiqar Ali Khan, CSI, of Malerkotla, and further down closer to what is now Jail Road, the Salvation Army Girls' Boarding School and the Salvation Army Headquarters & Boarding School. On the right would have been M/s Simon & King, Chartered Accountants, and the Office of the Punjab Light Horse (see K 3).

K 1 (a & b). THE CIVIL STATION, POLICE LINES

In the B & R report for 1933-34, the following scheme for the construction of a new police lines was disclosed:

Block A.	Police Station, barracks for 120 foot constables, 8 Head constables and 2 sub-Inspectors' quarters.
Block A-1.	Two cook houses and two dining rooms.
Block B.	Six flats for European Inspectors.
Block B-1.	Eighteen servants' quarters and six motorcycle rooms for European Inspectors.
Block C.	Four flats for European Sergeants.
Block C.1	Eight servants' quarters and four motor cycle rooms for European Sergeants.
Block D.	One married Sub-Inspector's quarters, two married Assistant Sub-Inspectors' quarters and two Head Constables' rooms.
Blocks E-L.	For married Head Constables, foot constables, menial's quarters, facilities and for stables.'
	[B & R Report (1933-34), p.8.]

In its Report for 1935-36, the B & R Department mentioned that 'the main block was nearly completed at the end of the year. The general progress on the subsidiary buildings was that work had been started on the married quarters for constables etc.' The following year, in 1936-37, 'the Main Block building was completed and occupied by the Police Department on 15 January 1937.'

The building today houses the offices of the City Police Chief, the SP (Administration), the Foreigners' Registration office, and the Police Complaint Cell.

K 1 (a). THE POLICE STATION ON FEROZEPUR ROAD UNDER CONSTRUCTION

Photograph, 1936.

K 1 (b). THE FAÇADE OF THE COMPLETED POLICE STATION

Photograph, 1937.

K 2. THE ROMAN CATHOLIC CATHEDRAL, LAHORE

Photo postcard, c. 1920. (RS/56)

Thornton's Guide of 1876 records one Roman Catholic church in use at Lahore - the Church of the Immaculate Conception in Anarkali [Thornton (1876), p.91.] The subsequent history of the presence of the Roman Catholic Church in the Punjab was summarized in the Lahore Gazetteer of 1916. It stated that: 'The Punjab was erected on the 18th September 1880 into a Vicarate Apostolic distinct from that of Hindustan. Dr P. Tosi was appointed Bishop and Vicar Apostolic of the Punjab. Under the Hierarchy proclaimed in 1886, the portion of the Punjab which extends northward from the river Sutlej to the river Jhelum was constituted into a separate See of Agra. The first Bishop of the new diocese of Lahore was Dr Symphorian Mourad, OC. When in 1910, the new Archdiocese of Simla was created, the Diocese of Lahore became on the 22nd of May 1913 a Suffragan See to the Metropolitan See of Simla. The present Bishop of Lahore, the fourth in succession, is Dr F.A. Oestermans, OC, consecrated on the 29th June 1905.' [Lahore Gazetteer (1916), p.76.]

In addition to the Cathedral of the Sacred Heart, the Gazetteer listed four churches under the jurisdiction of the Diocese of Lahore: The church of St Anthony (Railway Church), on Empress Road, the Church of the Immaculate Conception on Kutchery Road, St Joseph's Church on Thornton Road, and a second St Joseph's Church in Lahore Cantonment.

K 2. THE ROMAN CATHOLIC CATHEDRAL, LAHORE

K 3. THE PUNJAB LIGIIT HORSE HEADQUARTERS

K 3. THE PUNJAB LIGHT HORSE HEADQUARTERS

Photograph, 1921.

The Punjab Light Horse was a volunteer corps, raised in 1893 with Mr Arthur Grey as it first Commandant. Initially, this volunteer corps had only 50 members, all of them Europeans including the future explorer Aurel Stein and his companion Fred Andrews.

By 1916, this number had increased to 423 with a Northern Squadron covering Peshawar, Rawalpindi, Khewra, and Lyallpur (now Faisalabad), and a Southern Squadron covering Ambala, Montgomery (now Sahiwal) and Lahore where the force had its headquarters. [Lahore Gazetteer (1916), p.211.]

The building itself was located opposite the Salvation Army headquarters and cost Rs 111,500 to construct. [B & R report (1918-19), p.10.] It has since been demolished.

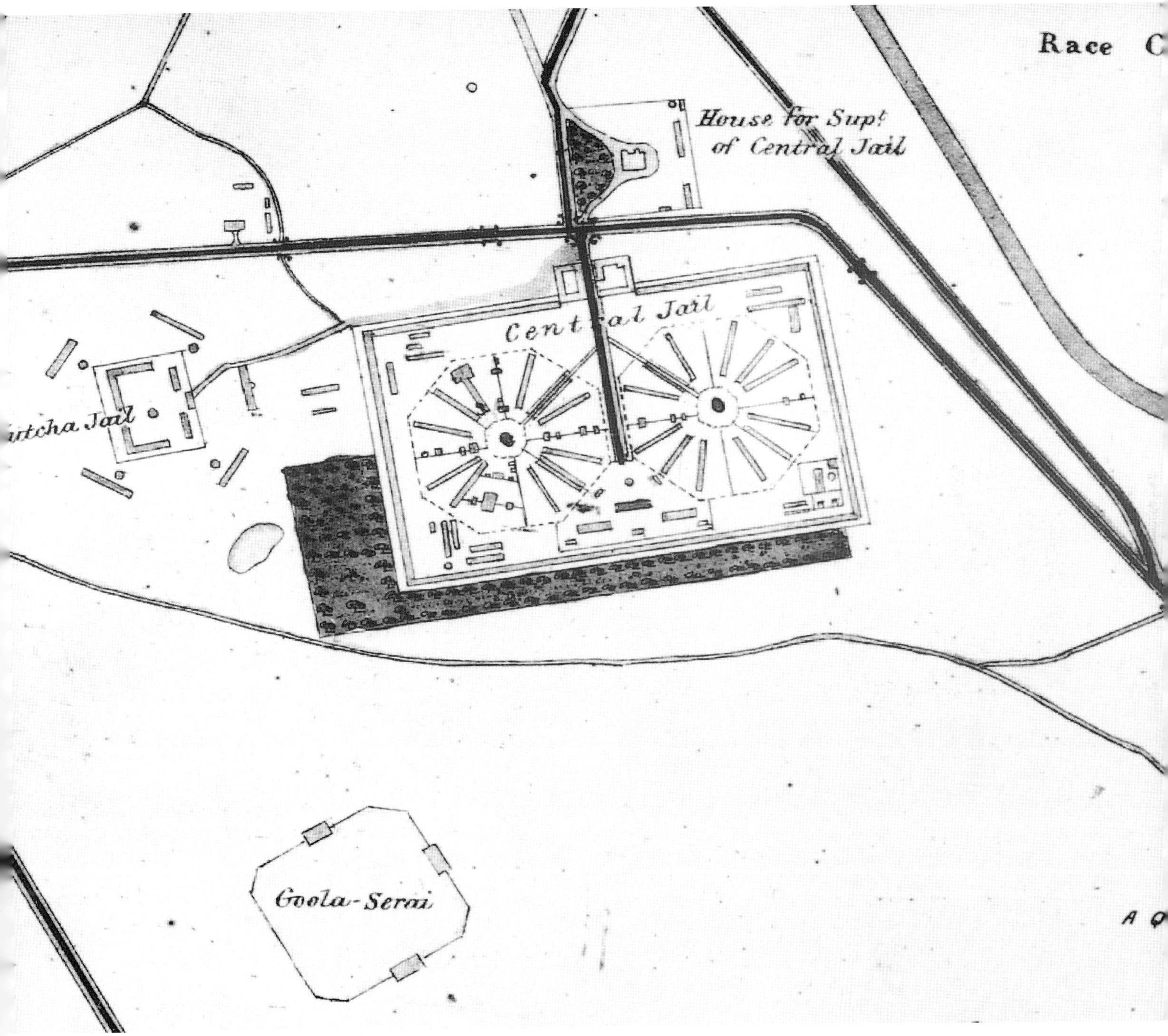

Detail from 1867 map.

JAIL ROAD

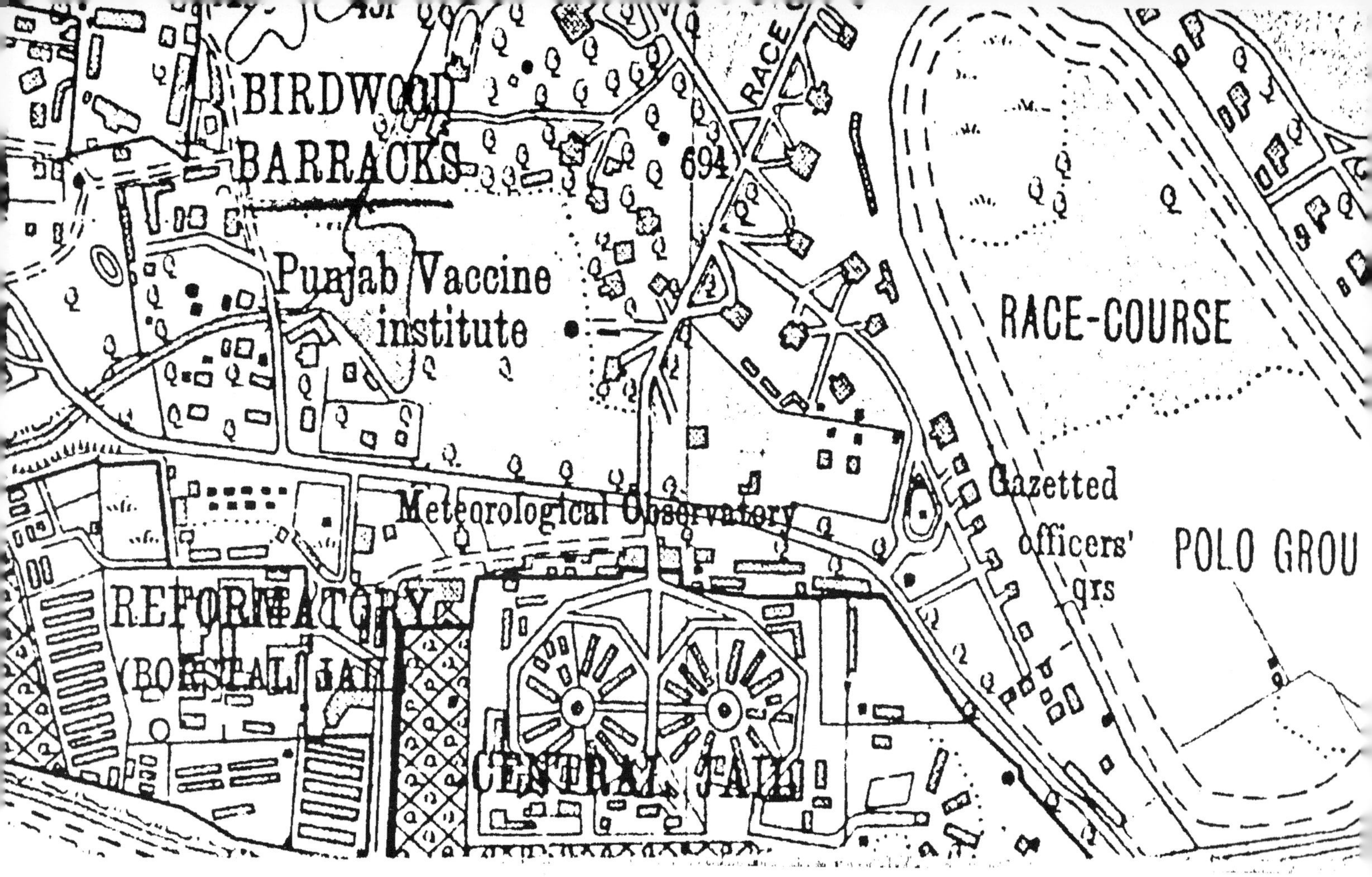

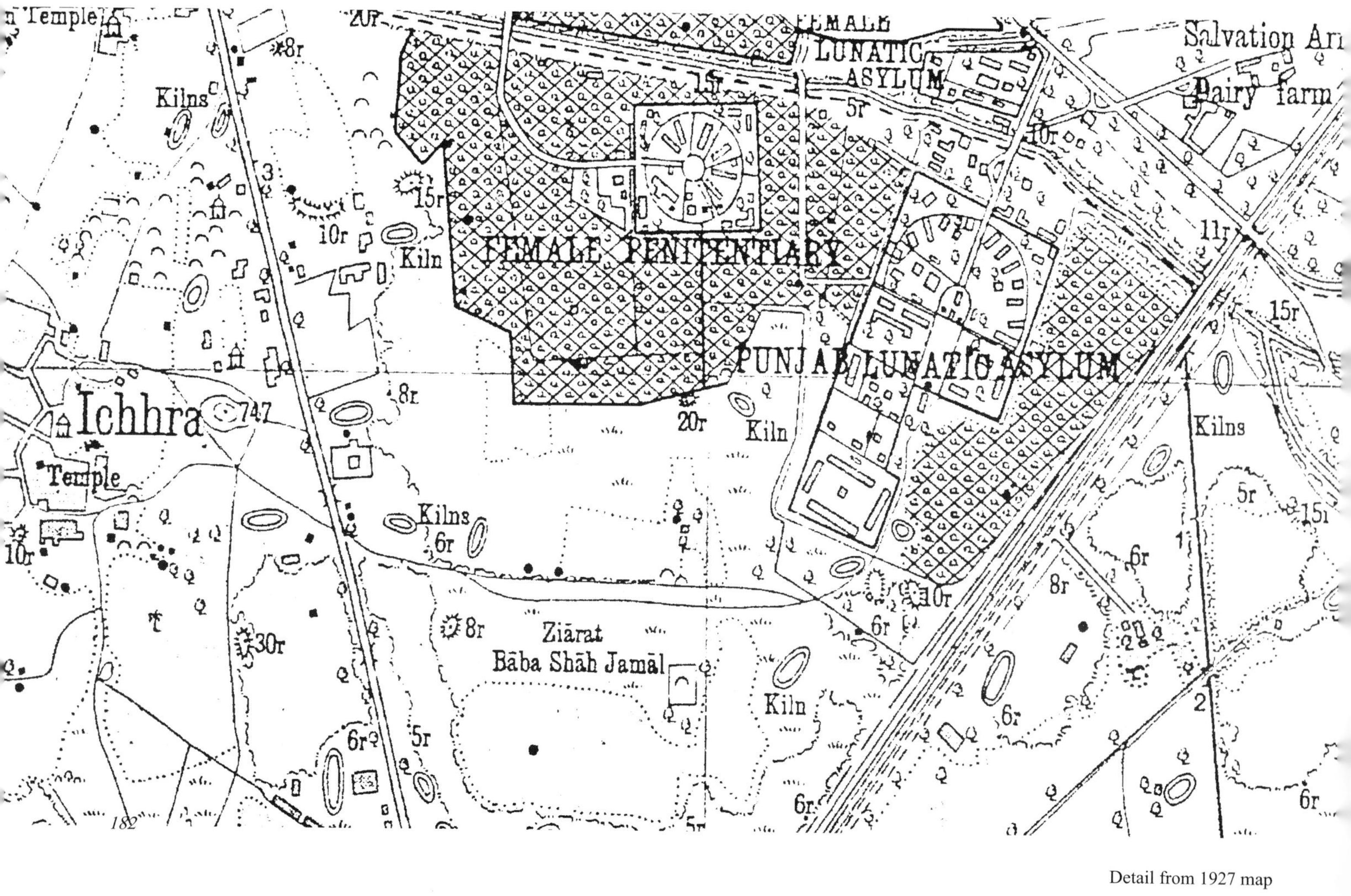

Detail from 1927 map

JAIL ROAD

If in 1914, one moved down Jail Road from the Canal, Khosla's Guide of 1932 (p.18) gives the canal its full name 'the Upper Bari Doab canal' and mentions that it irrigates the districts of Gurdaspur, Amritsar and Lahore. He describes a scene, unchanged over the past seventy years, of during the summer months 'a seething crowd...walking along the towpath to get relief from the heat of the steamy summer days.' Khosla foresees the inevitable: 'Bungalows are now fast springing up in the vicinity, and it would be before long that there would be a large number of people living about it.' One would have passed on the right the Criminal Settlement under the Salvation Army and the Salvation Army Farm (now the site of Kinnaird College for Women), the Race Course Office and Ground (now Race Course Park), a number of private residences, the Government Workhouse, the Central Jail garden, and then more private residences. On the left would have been a garden, the residence of a Mr Hemmy, the Lunatic Asylum, Central Jail, Central Jail Dairy, another residence, the Meteorological Observatory, Borstal Central jail, and the residence of a Mr Hodgkins.

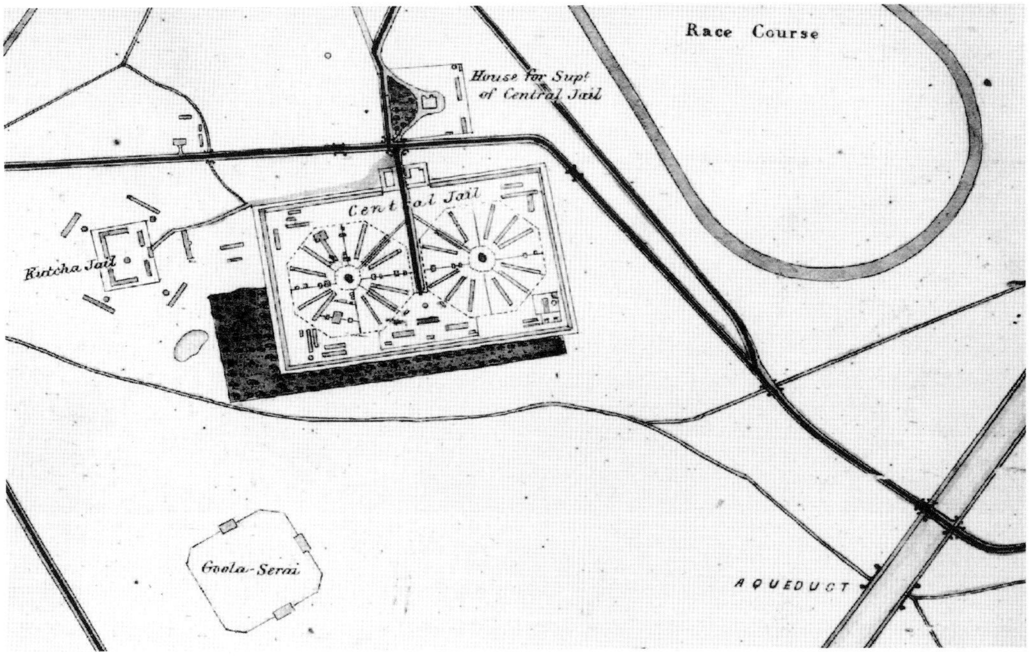

L 1. LAHORE CENTRAL JAIL

L 1. LAHORE CENTRAL JAIL

Detail of 1867 map.

In 1883, Lahore had three main jails - the Lahore District Goal built for 694 prisoners, the Lahore Penitentiary that could accommodate 1767, and the Female Penitentiary for 296 inmates.

The Lahore District Goal was located in the Gola Serai (see map) which had been converted in 1872-73 into a jail with a capacity for 585 prisoners. The District goal was completed in 1875-76 and included a hospital for 40 patients, arrangements for holding 96 in solitary confinement, 54 in quarantine, 20 under trial and 15 debtors. Female prisoners were kept separately in a jail for 268 women prisoners in 48 cells, with provision for 12 in quarantine and 8 juvenile prisoners. When in 1915 the Central Jail was redesignated the District Jail for the whole of Lahore District, the old District Goal became the Borstal Central Jail.

In 1876, Thornton described the situation of the Central Jail: 'This prison is on the radiating principle, with accommodation for 2,276 prisoners on the associated system. It consists of two octagons, each containing 8 compartments radiating from a centre in which is a watch-tower, from which a full view of the whole prison can be obtained. At the divergence of the 2 octagons is placed the hospital, 3 fine barracks en echelon in an enclosure of its own. The octagons and hospital enclosure are surrounded by iron railings so that the free circulation of air all over the prison is not interfered with.'

Thornton continued later: 'Each compartment of the octagon forms in itself a separate and complete prison, having its own workshop, so that dangerous characters need not be taken out to work. [...] One of the octagons of the prison was finished in 1853, and the other in 1862.' [Eastwick (1883), pp.195-96.]

The statistical analysis of the convicts for the five years from 1877-78 to 1881-82 make interesting reading. At the Central Jail, the number of prisoners rose from 1,995 in 1887 to 2,024 in 1881. Muslims outnumbered Hindus by about 3:1, and the bulk of the prisoners came from agricultural occupations. Most of the patients were serving sentences of two years or more. The cost of maintaining each prisoner in 1880 was Rs 60.By 1915, the cost had risen to Rs 81 per prisoner.

Eastwick, writing in 1883, mentions that 'the prisoners are allowed 36 superficial and 648 cubic feet of sleeping space,' and that 'the most notable manufactures in the prison are blankets (that cost Rs 2 ½ each; they threat them in water in order to make the stitches closer), and cloths, mats, and floorcloths (called *daris*), tents, rugs, carpets (that were sold at Rs 10 a yard, the prisoner doing a bit 2ft long and 4 inches broad per day), scarfs, shawls, lithographic printing, and country paper.' The carpets resemble those of Persia, and tradesmen in London purchase them annually to the value of about Pounds 2,000)'. [Eastwick (1883), pp.195-96.]

Eastwick advised his readers that 'as the central prison is one of the best managed in India, the traveller will perhaps like to visit it. Should he be desirous of purchasing tents or carpets for a journey to the hills, he will as a matter of course purchase them there.'

L 2. SALVATION ARMY FARM

The site of the present Kinnaird College for Women was originally the Salvation Army Criminal Settlement and Dairy Farm. The Gazetteer of 1916 gives the background: ' On Jail Road, there is a settlement known as "Danepur," where released prisoners from the Borstal Jail are received and cared for, and there are also some members of the Sansi tribe. The inmates are given employment in a Dairy and in cultivating the 25 acres of land attached to the Settlement as well as in the Government Gardens.' The report also mentions that there is a Settlement for Criminal tribes in Changa Manga forest.

Detail from 1927 map.

L 3 (a & b). THE MENTAL HOSPITAL

The origin of the Lahore Mental Asylum on Jail Road is traceable to the latter days of the Sikh Raj, when a European Dr Martin Honigberger was given responsibility for administering to lunatics at the hospital he established during his second tenure at the Sikh court between 1839 and 1849. On 1 May 1849, the twelve patients under the care of Dr Honigberger were transferred to a British Dr Hathaway, and in 1853, the rudimentary asylum was relocated to some barracks in Anarkali that had been formerly occupied by married artillerymen. [Thornton (1876), p.100.]

In 1876, Thornton mentions that the Lunatic Asylum was now in a building near the railway station known as Lehna Singh's Chauni. It had accommodation for 500 patients although on an average at a time, there were never more than 373 patients, of whom 100 were male. The ascertained causes for insanity, Thornton contended, were the addictive use of hemp and its preparations. 'There are also many cases of epileptic mania and congenital deficiency of intellect. Melancholia is not uncommon, but it may possibly be a characteristic of the Punjab temper in matters of faith that it more frequently arises from grief than from religion.' [Thornton (1876), p.101.]

The Lahore Gazetteer of 1916 gives an unusually lengthy account of the state of the Asylum. It mentions that after the transfer of the inmates from the old Naulakha asylum to the new one on Jail Road in 1900, 'its popularity is shown by the ever-increasing number of its inmates and the fact that patients from distant quarters of Northern India are brought here for treatment.' [Lahore Gazetteer (1916), pp.241-2.]

The buildings in the photograph were constructed in the 1930s.

L 3(a). GENERAL VIEW OF PUNJAB MENTAL HOSPITAL

Photograph, 1937.

L 3(a). GENERAL VIEW OF PUNJAB MENTAL HOSPITAL

L 3(b). BARRACK FOR FEMALE PATIENTS

L 3(b). BARRACK FOR FEMALE PATIENTS

Photograph, 1939.

L 4. THE VILLAGE OF ICHHRA

Detail of 1867 map.

Elmslie, on tour in the environs of Lahore in January 1881, recollected: 'As I rode along the Ferozepore road, a few miles from Lahore, I asked the Tehsildar, who was accompanying me, the name of the large village on the right hand which seemed to contain a number of unusually high old brick buildings. The reply was, 'That is the ancient town of Ichra, in comparison to which, in olden times, Lahore was an unimportant village; the tradition of Ichra's greatness has survived to the present day. The Benares Shroffs (bankers) still send their hundis (bills of exchange) address to "Lahore, near Ichra."' [Elmslie (1908), p.280.]

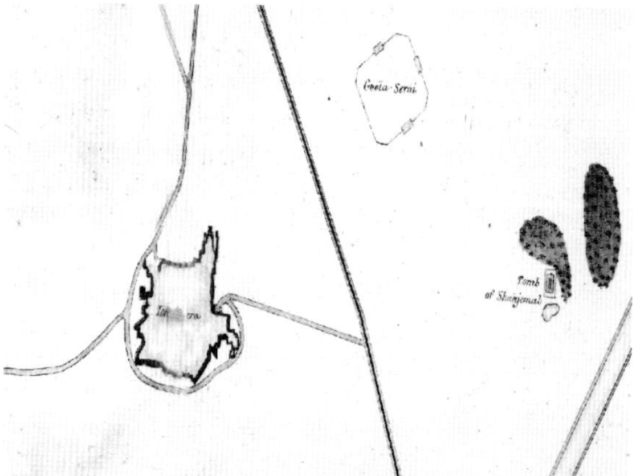

L 4. THE VILLAGE OF ICHHRA

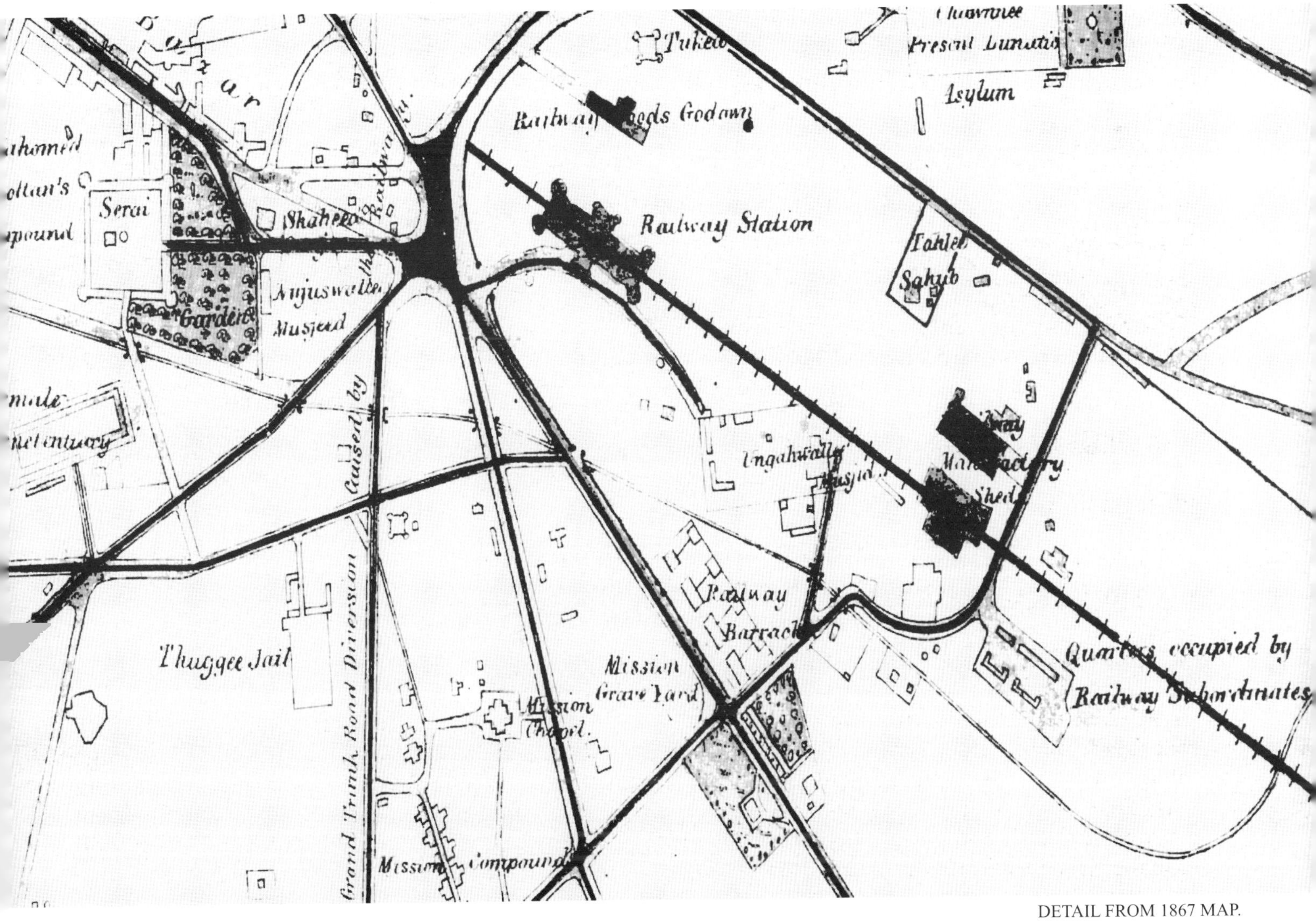

DETAIL FROM 1867 MAP.

EMPRESS ROAD & THE RAILWAYS

Detail from 1927 map

EMPRESS ROAD & THE RAILWAYS

The Gazetteer of 1883-84 mentions that 'some distance north of the Mall, and separated from it by an open and still desolate tract, lies the Railway station forming the centre of a colony of bungalows, principally those of Railway employees.' The Lahore Railway Station lay at the end of Empress Road. In 1914 journeying down Empress Road (now Abdullah bin Badees Road) one would have expected to see:

LEFT	RIGHT
Dr A. Jones, Dental Surgeon	Garden
Civil Police Lines	Waverley Board & Residence
Rev. Fr. Theodule, OC	Mr J. F. Rehill, Indian Police
Roman Catholic church [St Anthony's Church.]	
Roman Catholic Association Rooms	Mr Abdul Rahim, Distt. Engr.
Nawab Palace	Dr Francis and Mrs Anneley, Dentists
Mr P.O. Meakins, Punjab Police	Mr. P. J. Hammill
Mr. P.W. Meakins, Pleader	Mr W. Pitman
Cambridge Hotel	Office of the Manager, N.W.R.
M/s Nusserwanjee & Co., Contractors and Auctioneers	St Andrews' Church
Rev. H.D. Griswald	Central Hotel
Miss Greenfield	Mr. T. C. Bustard, piano/organs tuner
	Kinnaird Girls High School and Mission
	Rev. W. J. McKee

M 1. THE RAILWAY HEADQUARTERS

M 1. THE RAILWAY HEADQUARTERS

Photo postcard, c.1920. (RS/71)

With the identification of Karachi as a seaport in 1855, a proposal was prepared to establish a railway connection between Karachi and Lahore, and if possible beyond. The proposal envisaged a railway from Karachi to Kotri (in Sindh), steam navigation up to Multan, and from there, a further railway connection to Lahore. These four sections of the communication system were incorporatised as four separate companies Scinde Railway, Indus Flotilla Company, Punjab Railway and Delhi Railway. The Indus Flotilla Company was later wound up, and the remaining three were amalgamated in 1870 under the title 'Scinde, Punjab, and Delhi Railway Company'. In 1885, this company was purchased by the Government of India and integrated into the North Western Railway.

By 1916, the railway colony in the Naulakha area had taken on suburban proportions, commensurate with the extensive scale of the operations of the North-Western Railway. The Gazetteer of 1916 reports that 'a very large area, about a thousand acres of land was acquired in 1916 to the east between the Shalamar Road and the main railway line through Amritsar to Delhi. On this area entirely new Loco Shops and Carriage and Wagon Shops have already been built, the Railway having outgrown the old shops at the station.'

In 1916, the Railways employed about 1,200 Europeans and a large local population of junior support staff. For their recreation, a Railway institute was founded as early as June 1864, with reading rooms, a library, coffee rooms and swimming baths.

M 2. THE RAILWAY STATION

M 2. THE RAILWAY STATION

Photograph, c. 1920.

The Lahore railway station had been designed by Chief Engineer William Brunton and constructed at a cost of Rs 500,000 by Muhammad Sultan, a Kashmiri Muslim who had enjoyed a varied career as a wrestler during the reign of Ranjit Singh, a soap manufacturer and latterly as a major contractor patronized by the British administration. For a detailed description of the career of Contractor M. Sultan (c.1809-1875), see Kerr (1995), pp. 65-67. During his more affluent days, Sultan built a serai for the poor outside Delhi gate. His less laudable services to the Muslim community were the removal of bricks from old buildings, including the mosque of a Sitara Begum. The foundation stone of the station was laid by Lord John Lawrence in 1859, and although the fort-like building had not been completed by the time the first train commuted on the new line between Lahore and Amritsar (opened in April 1862), the station once operational became a symbol of a post-1857 assertion of colonial paranoia.

A recent history of the Pakistan Railways tells us that 'the Lahore station was built among the ruins of the ancient city, and great difficulty was experienced in laying the foundations of the various station buildings owing to the depth of the ruins overt he firm soil below.' [Malik (1962), p.10.] It mentions further that 'the first two platforms were 500 feet in length and 20 feet wide. The Grand Trunk Road which ran across the site had to be diverted. On the opening of the line to Multan [in 1865], offices of the Agent and the Chief Engineer, till then housed in Anarkali's tomb, were shifted to the station building.'

M 3. THE RAILWAY PLATFORM

M 3. THE RAILWAY PLATFORM

Photo postcard, c. 1920. (RS/67)

M 4. RAILWAY WORKSHOPS

M 4. RAILWAY WORKSHOPS

Photo postcard, c.1920. (RS/68)

According to the B & R Report for 1869-70, 'The construction of extensive workshops, fitted with all the machinery and appliances necessary for the constructional repairs of Rolling Stock, has been commenced at Lahore to meet the joint requirement of the Punjab and Delhi Railways. This building will probably be the last work of any magnitude carried out at the Punjab under the guaranteed system.' 'The first railway of Pakistan then known as the Eastern Bengal Railway and the Scinde Railway were constructed under this system. According to the contracts made with the railway companies, the Secretary of State for India agreed to provide land free of cost and to guarantee interest on the capital' invested by the railway companies. [(Malik (1962), p.4.)]

The Gazetteer of 1916 provides further information about the growth of these Workshops: 'The Carriage and Wagon Shops were built and first opened in 1910, and the new Loco Shops were started in 1910 and are now practically completed, the Locomotive Department having moved into them in 1914.' The workforce employed at the Workshops was almost 6,000.

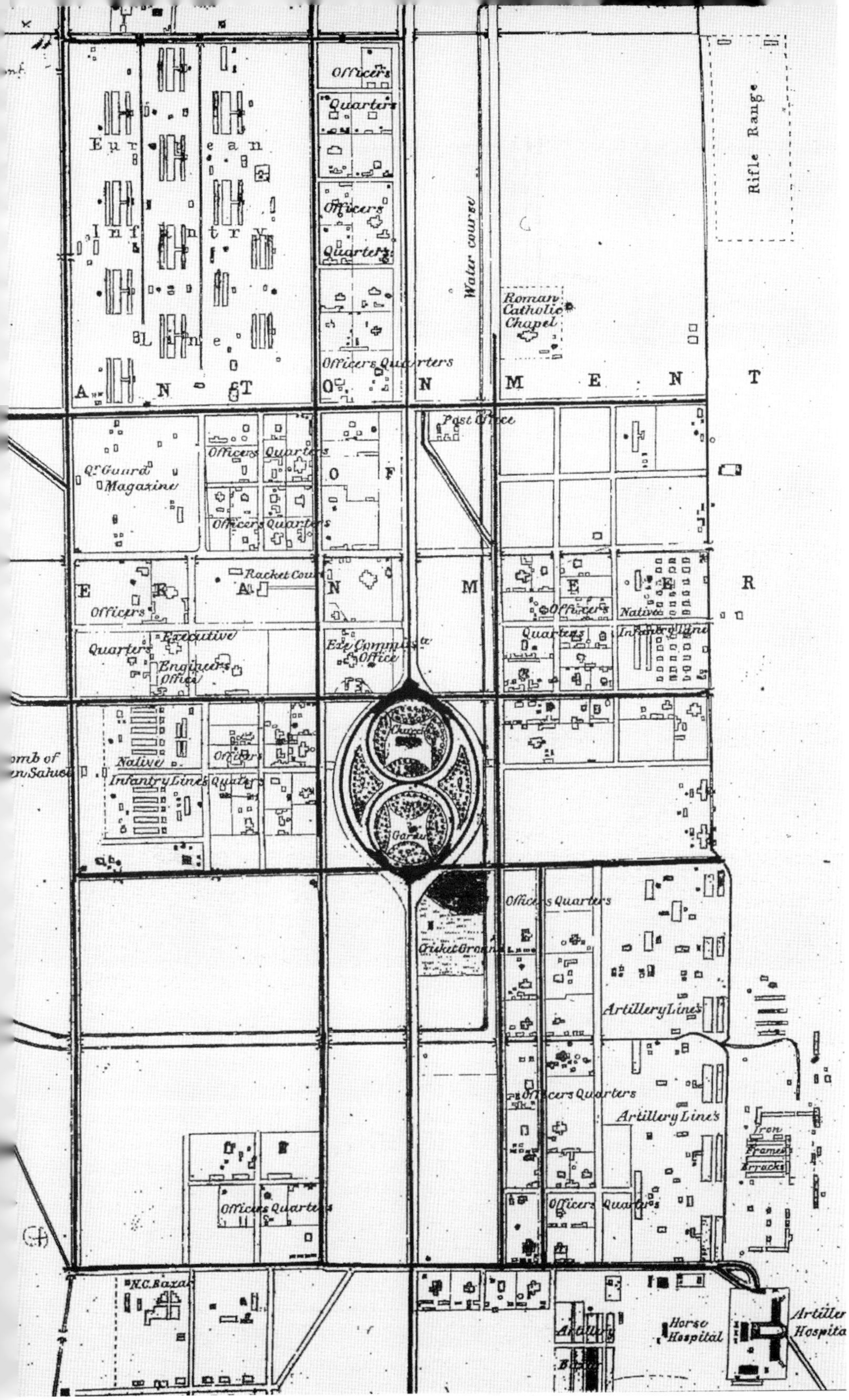
Officers Quarters
Officers Quarters
Rifle Range
European Infantry Lines
Water course
Roman Catholic Chapel
Officers Quarters
CANTONMENT OF MEERUT
Post Office
Officers Quarters
Qr. Guard Magazine
Officers Quarters
Racket Court
Officers
Quarters
Executive Engineers Office
Ex. Commissr. Office
Officers Quarters
Native Infantry Lines
Church
Garden
Native Infantry Lines
Officers Quarters
Officers Quarters
Cricket Ground
Artillery Lines
Officers Quarters
Artillery Lines
Iron Framed Barracks
Officers Quarters
Officers Quarters
N.C. Bazar
Artillery
Horse Hospital
Artiller Hospita

CANTONMENT

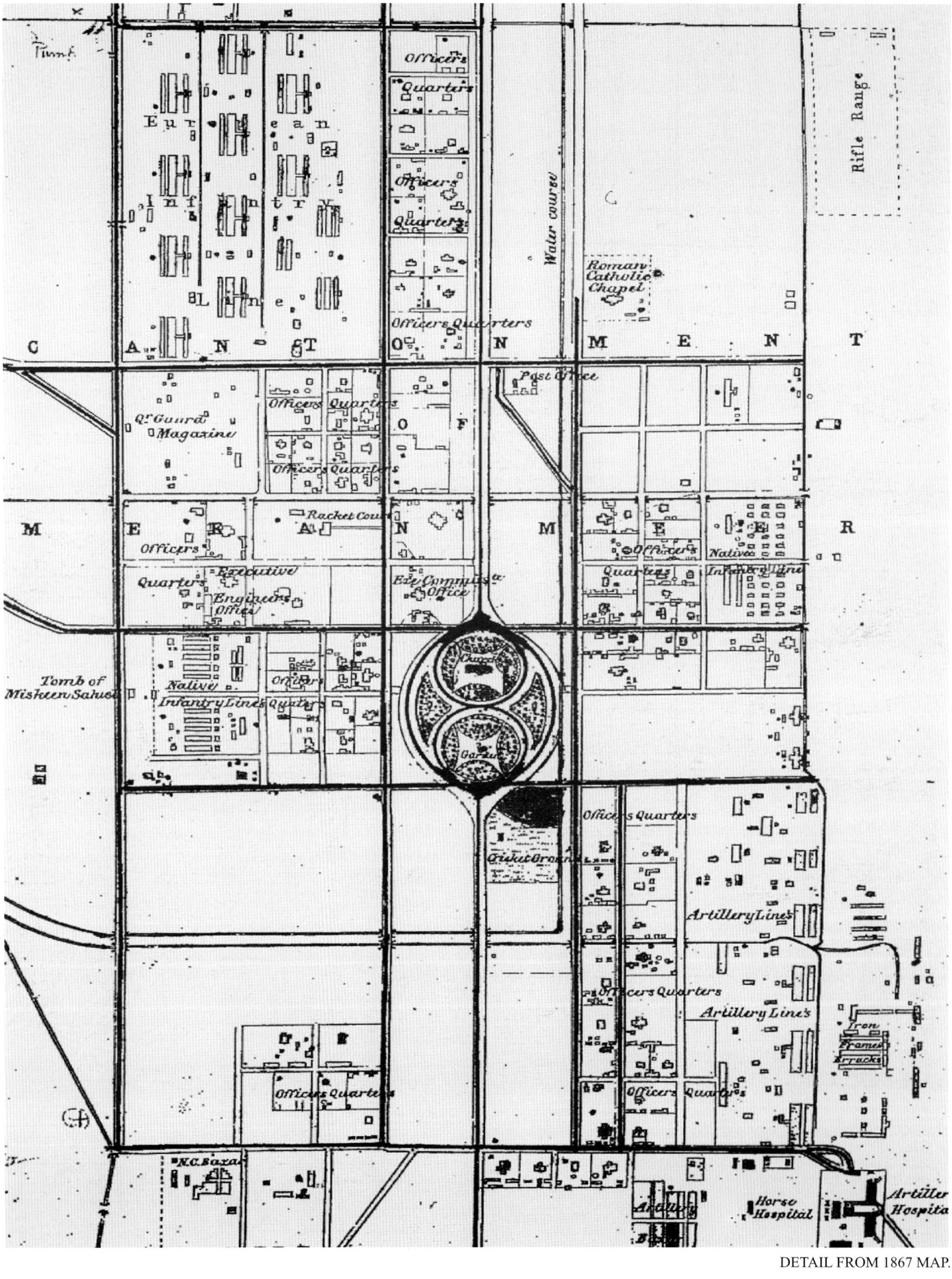

DETAIL FROM 1867 MAP.

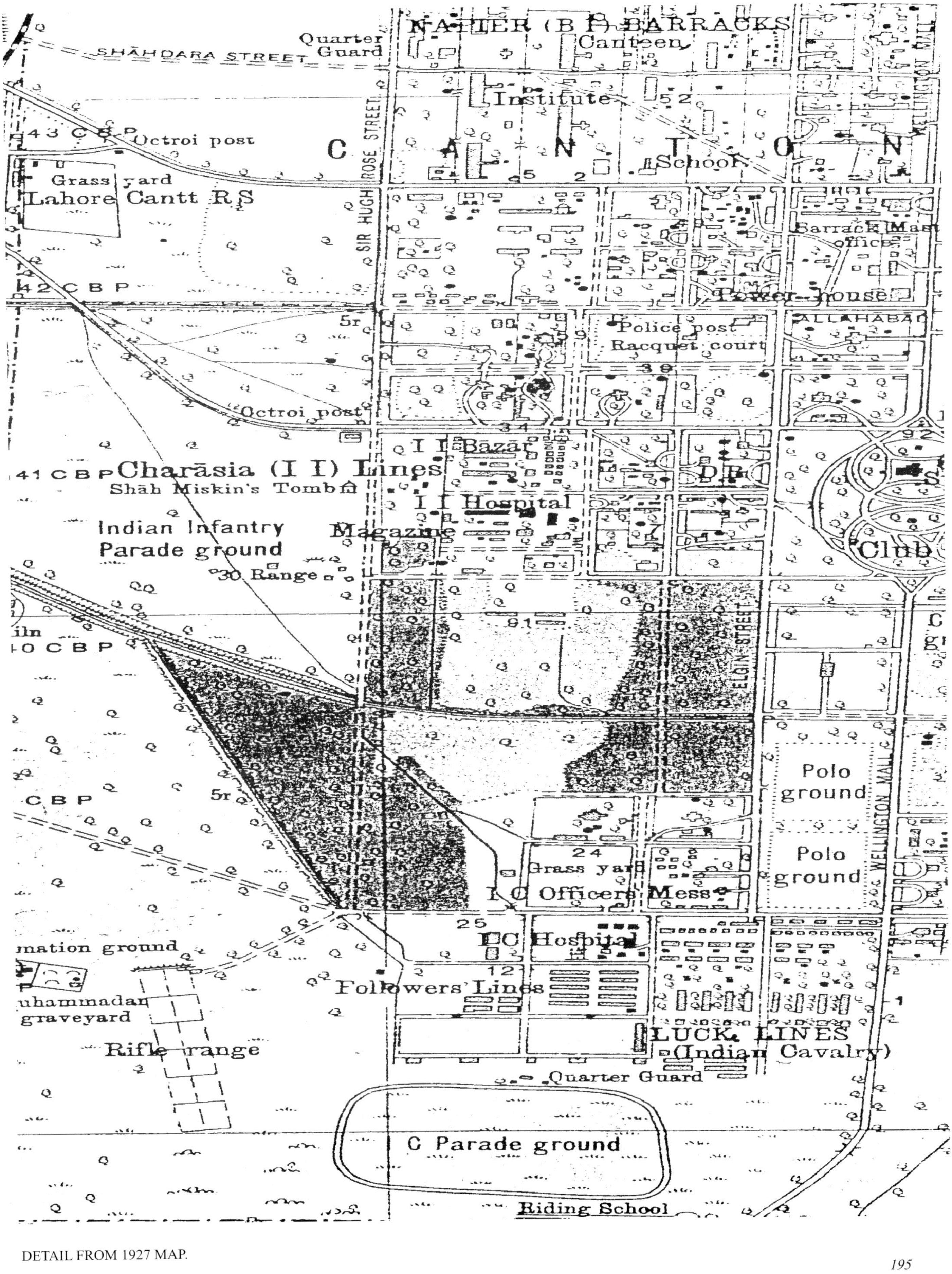

DETAIL FROM 1927 MAP.

LAHORE CANTONMENT

The story of the selection by Sir Charles Napier of the Cantonment of Lahore is now apocryphal. 'Napier decided that the Anarkali cantonment was to be moved. 'Why', Henry [Lawrence] remarked to Hardinge, 'I hardly know except that it is at Anarkali' and when pressed continually to choose the spot, finally took Henry and John on a mystery gallop to Meean Meer, where he announced that here was the spot. Anarkali was admittedly proving unhygienic, but Henry argued that improving, cleaning and draining the site would have been much less expensive than moving it.' [Lee (2002), p.280.]

Once the site had been identified, 'a large number of trees were planted in the cantonment, and all the trees were kept watered by an establishment maintained for that purpose'. [B & R report (1869-70), p.4.] However, even by 1883, the cantonments still had a deserted look about them. The Gazetteer of 1883 recorded: 'They stand in an open and exceedingly dreary plain, originally bare of trees but now gradually growing greener as canal irrigation extends and the trees planted by the roadside and assiduously fostered spring up.' [Lahore Gazetteer (1883-84), p.166.]

The later Gazetteer of 1916 mentions that the site of the Lahore Cantonment once a village called Haslimpur and known later as Mian Mir Cantonment - had been acquired by Prince Dara Shikoh (the ill-fated son of Shah Jahan), who gifted it to his religious preceptor Mian Mir.

N 1. THE CHURCH OF ST MARY MAGDALENE

N 1. THE CHURCH OF ST MARY MAGDALENE

Photo postcard, c.1920. (RS/24A)

The epicentre of the cantonment was the Garrison Church of St Mary of Magdalene, described by contemporaries as 'one of the most beautiful churches in Northern India.' It was consecrated in 1857. The church with its imposing steeple could almost have been transposed from a painting by Constable of a traditional English village.

N 2. INTERIOR OF THE CHURCH OF ST MARY MAGDALENE

N 2. INTERIOR OF THE CHURCH OF ST MARY MAGDALENE

Photo postcard, c.1920. (RS/6A)

The white marble flagstones used in this church were taken from the pathways of the small garden in front of the Diwan-i-Khas pavilion in the Lahore Fort. [Vogel (1911), p. 49.]

N 3. CHUMMERY

N 3. CHUMMERY

Photograph, 1890.

Chummeries were to solution to the chronic shortage of accommodation in the Cantonment: 'Quarters for officers in India were not provided, but instead they received a monthly rental allowance. Bachelors clubbed together to share a bungalow, or 'chummery'. [Lee (2002), p.20.]

N 4. CINEMA IN THE LAHORE CANTONMENT

Photo postcard, c, 1920. (RS/23A)

An interesting picture of a building in the Lahore Cantonment that bears the inscription 'Spencer Theatre 1920' and below it 'West End Cinema.'

N 4. CINEMA IN THE LAHORE CANTONMENT

N 5 . SADDAR BAZAAR IN LAHORE CANTONMENT

N 5. SADDAR BAZAAR IN LAHORE CANTONMENT

Photo postcard, c.1920. (RS/80)

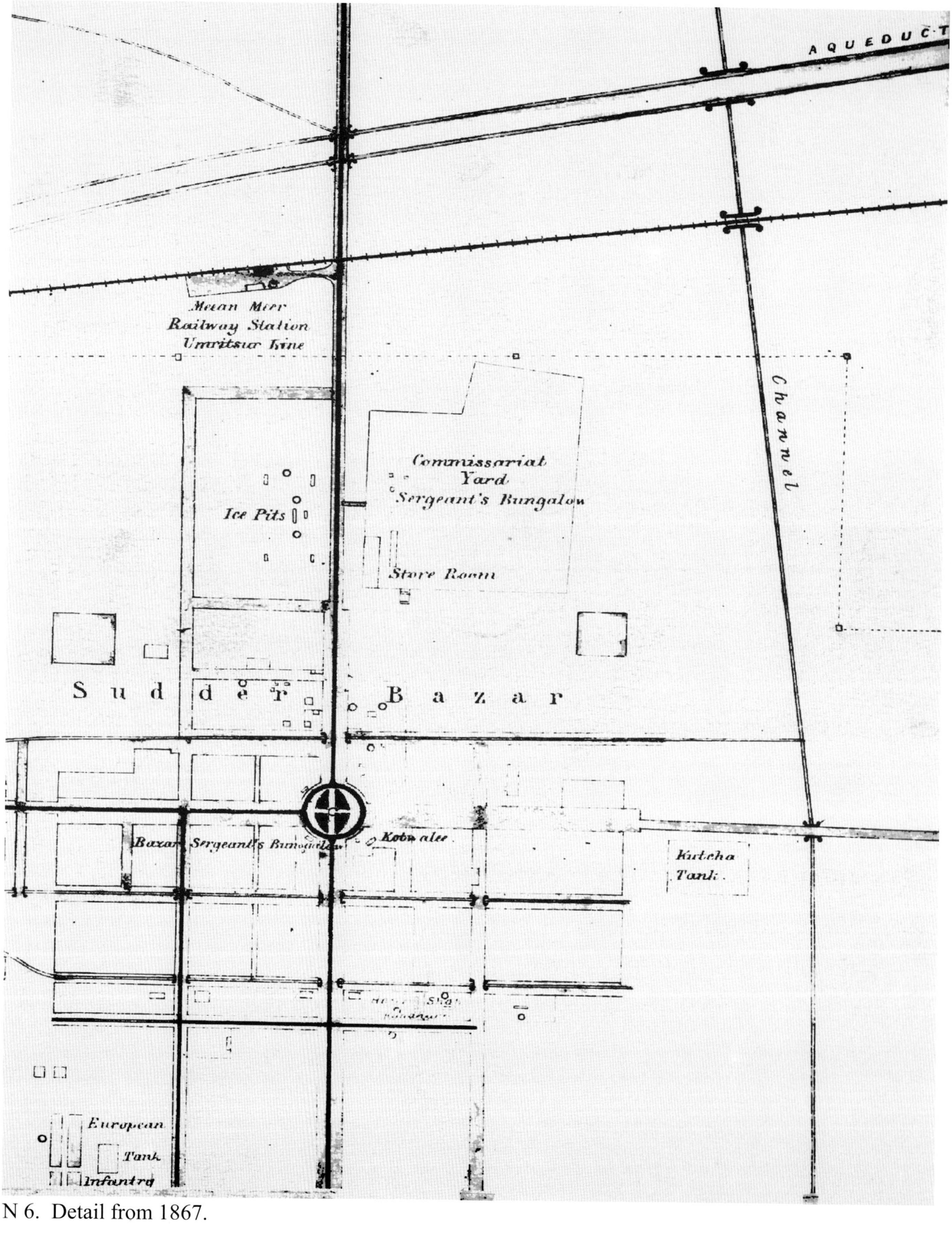

N 6. Detail from 1867.

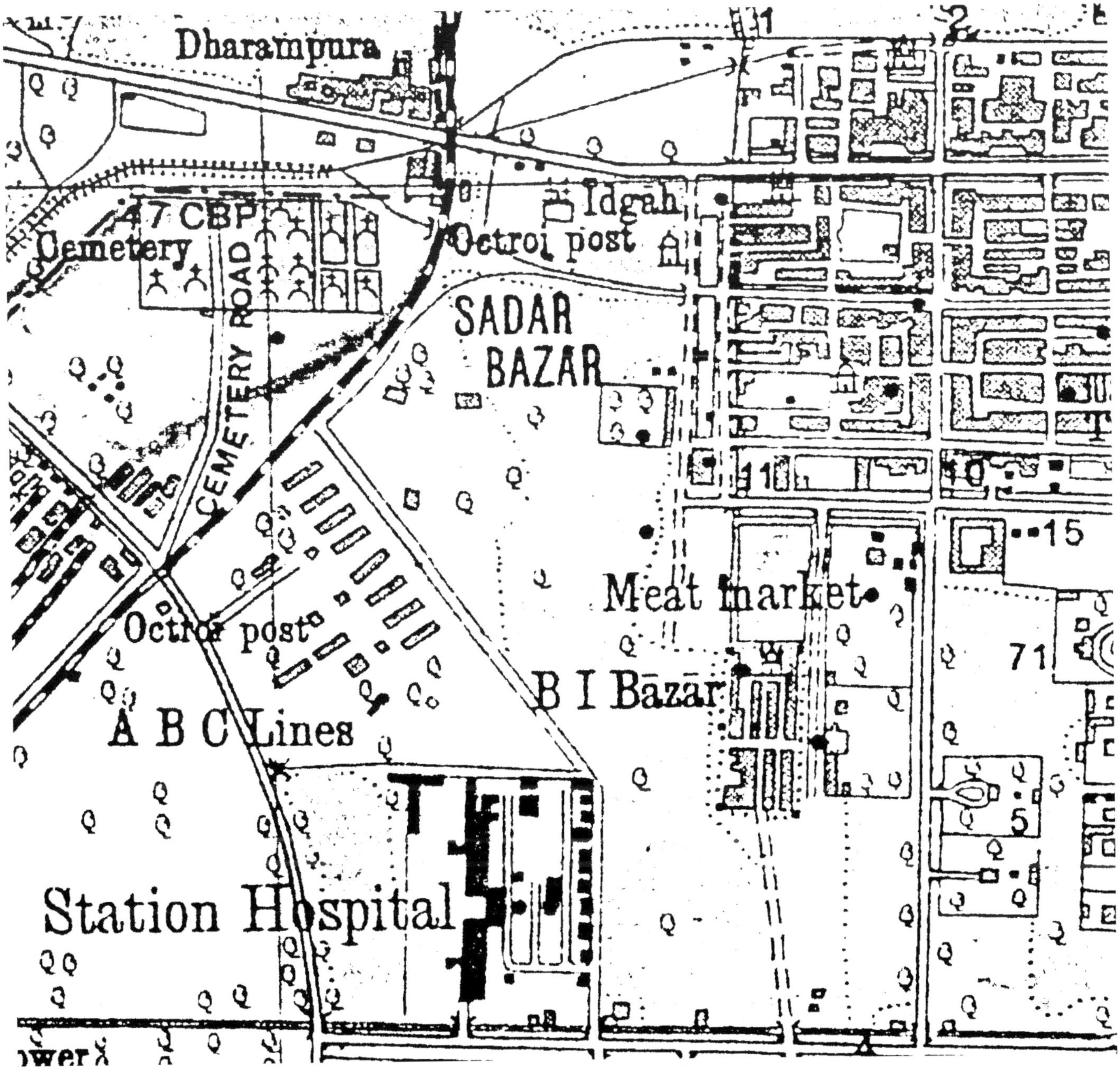

N 7. Detail from 1927.

AIRCRAFT PARK, LAHORE.

N 7. THE LAHORE AIRCRAFT PARK

Photograph, c. 1920.

An aerial view of what is now the Lahore International airport, recently renamed Allama Iqbal Airport.

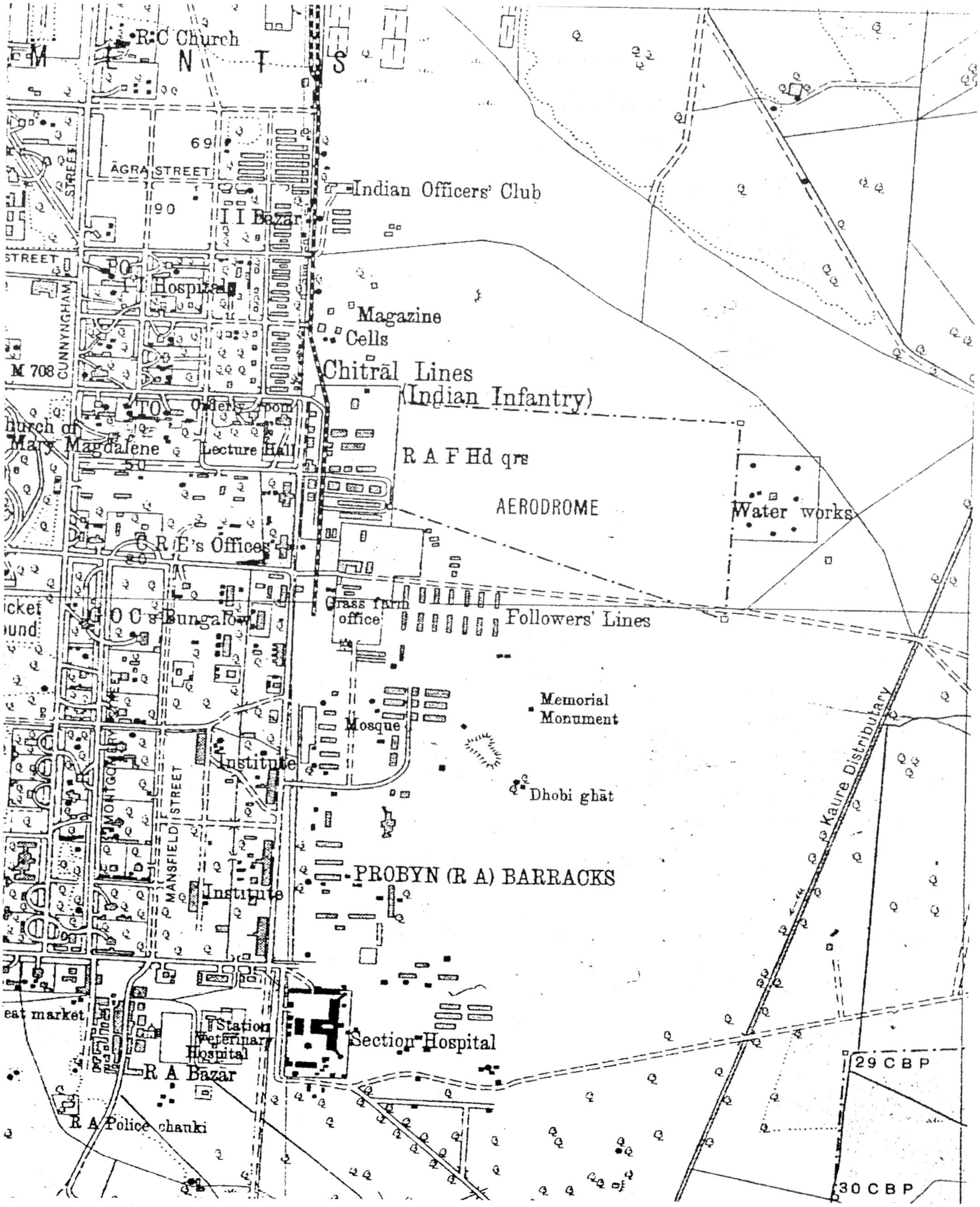

N 9. RAF HEADQUARTERS AT LAHORE AERODROME

Detail from 1927 map.

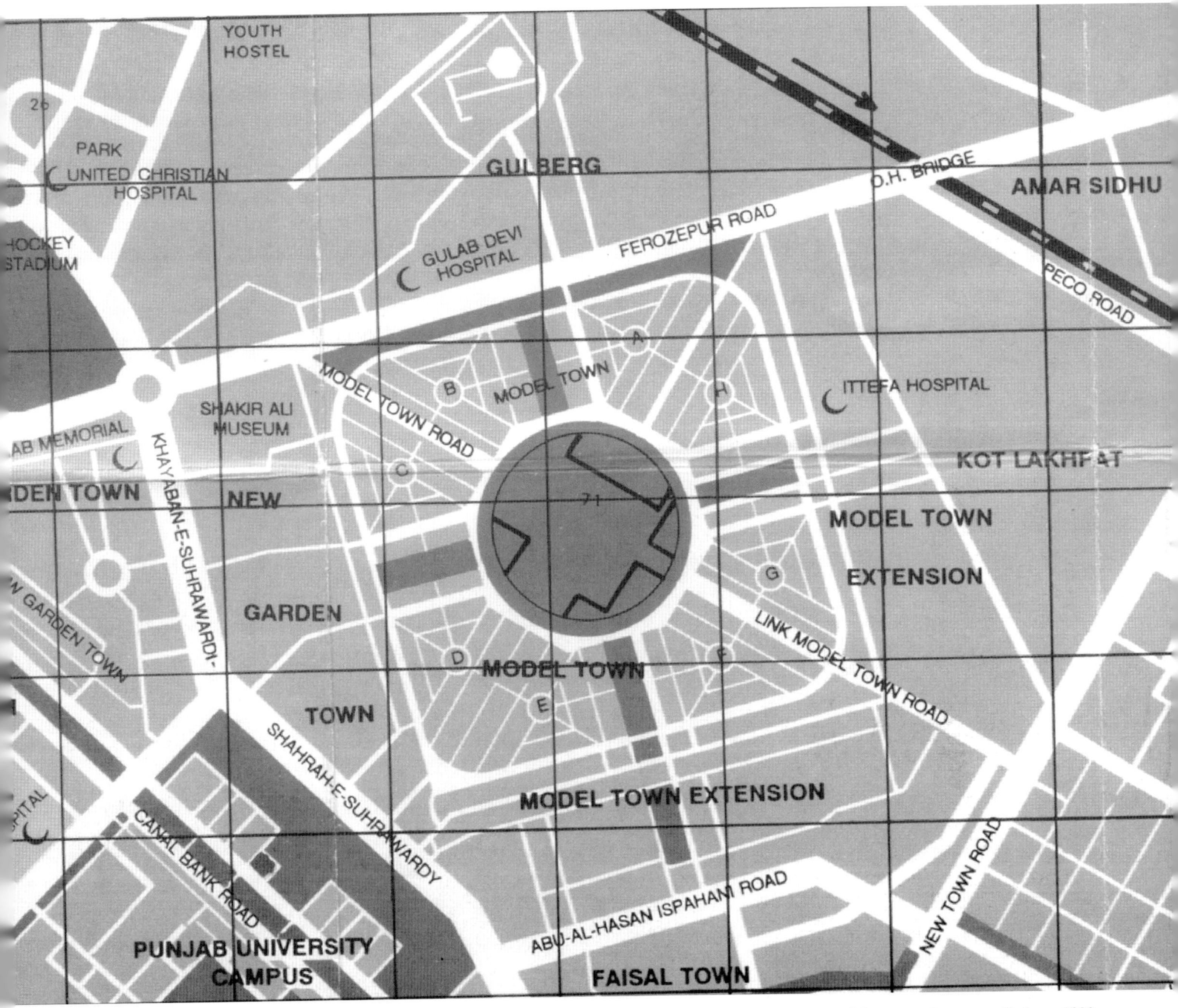

The Layout of Model Town. Detail from a modern map of Lahore, 1990.

MODEL TOWN

MODEL TOWN

The material for this section was derived from the report by Diwan Khem Chand: *The Scheme for Model Town and its Realization*, published in April 1930.]

If any suburb of Lahore could be regarded as the antithesis of its gradual, impulsive and often haphazard evolution, it must be the ordered geometrical symmetry of Model Town. Located five miles diagonally southeast of Anarkali, the scheme was the brain-child of Diwan Khem Chand, a lawyer of Lahore. The idea came to him 'in a faint form' when he was 14 years old and gestated in his mind during his studies in the United Kingdom until finally, at the riper age of 32, he published his ideas in January 1921. 'My scheme', he wrote, 'is that within easy reach of Lahore, say within 6 or 7 miles if it, about 1,000 acres of agricultural or waste land be purchased, and on it by built a town with all the conveniences of modern times.'

Khem Chand's original plan for his 'Ideal Town', congregating residents from 'different religions, different opinions, following different professions and coming from different parts of the country', had been to locate it on the Shahdara side of the river Ravi. Deterred by its low lying vulnerability to seasonal floods, he was taken by Sir Ganga Ram to see a wooded area at Rakh Kot Lakhpat to the south of Lahore. Khem Chand confessed that he 'fell in love with it immediately'.

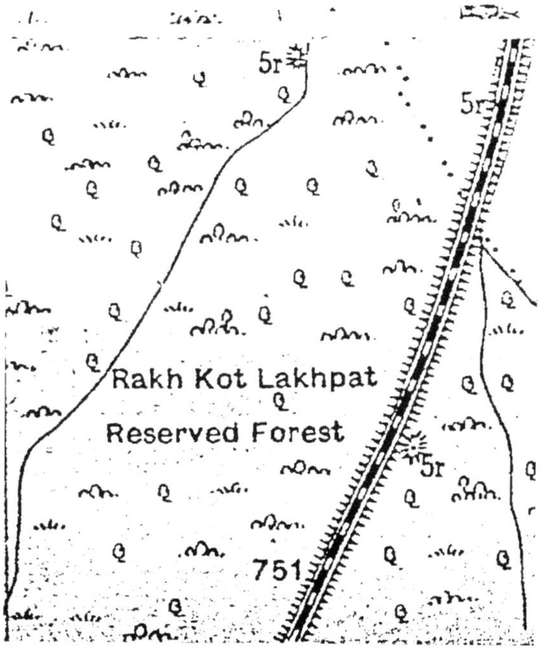

O 1. Rath Kot Lakhpat area. From a map of Lahore, 1927.

O 2. The forest on the site that later became Model Town, 1920.

The tract of land that won his heart lay 5 miles from Anarkali and 3 miles from the Lahore Municipal Boundary. 1963 acres of Forest land was purchased from Government at a cost of 9 lakhs of rupees, but due to the intransigence of the Forest Department, it took two years before possession was finally handed over on 5 January in 1923 to the new Society, which had been formed as a company and registered under the Cooperative Societies Act some years earlier.

At its first meeting, held in the Lahore Town Hall on 27 February 1921, the Founder members - each of whom was required to subscribe Rs 100 - elected Sir Ganga Ram as Chairman, Khem Chand as its secretary and appointed a Preliminary Committee of 21 persons to plan its implementation. Various options were considered and rejected for the name of the society. 'For want of a better name, "Model Town" was considered good enough to go on with, and it was then considered that a suitable name may be brought out later when the scheme had made some progress.' Over the past eighty years that name has remained.

The initial response to Khem Chand's novel scheme was lukewarm. 'Even Raja Narendra Nath [later the Society's first President, a post he was retain for the first 7 years of its existence] thinking the scheme to be merely a Utopian one, threw it into the waste paper basket, without reading it. It was only when Sir Shadi Lal, in a casual talk, informed him that the scheme was practicable, he sent for another copy and read it through. It was then that he became enthusiastic about it and took a prominent part on maturing the idea, as the first President of the Society,'

The first two years after the preliminary meeting in February 1921 were spent in laying out the plan of the Town. Progress was slower than Khem Chand would have wished, because 'only 400 copies of the brief outline of the Scheme were sent out. Response was great as, by September 1920, 184 individuals had filled out the forms and expressed a desire to build 200 houses'. A total of Rs 33,000 was collected from these subscriber members.

A prize of Rs 1220 was advertised for the best layout. 32 large scale plans were received and displayed on the Mall for a fortnight. A Selection Committee could not make up its mind among the final four and so the prize was divided between them. The second prize winner was invited to combine the best features of all the plans into one. He was paid an additional Rs 500 with expenses. His final plan 'won the admiration of members and others.'

The plan was a cat's-cradle of circles bisected by diagonals set within a square. In Khem Chand's words: 'The Town is square in shape. In the centre of the town is provided space for a Hill, Lake and Gardens. Encircling the garden is a Circular Road and on this Circular road are located the stores, market and Post Office, Boy's School, Girl's School, Nursery Club, Hospital, etc. All the public buildings are in the centre of the town. Between the Public Buildings and the outer road are located plots for residential purposes in a systematic order.' 'Near the centre of the Town there will be a circular lake about half a mile in circumference and 100 ft. in width. Work already started. Water deep enough for boating, and as the lake will be round it will look bigger than it actually is.'

The Society Byelaws stipulated that there could be only one house per plot with two-thirds remaining open for gardens and lawns. Khem Chand had envisaged an allotment pattern of four kanals of land for A type houses, two and a half for B type, and one and a half kanals for C-Type houses. He later wanted to double the entitlement but the Managing Committee of the Society decided otherwise and approved a six kanal plot for each A-type house, four kanals for a B-type house and two kanals for a C-type house. He anticipated the cost per house to be between Rs 9,000-12,000 for A type houses, Rs 6,000-8,000 for B type houses, and for C type Rs 4,000-Rs 5,000.

The first allotments were made in 1924. 'Each member was given marks according to a definite method, and members were invited to select their neighbours.' 95 % of the plots went to members, and the remaining 5 % to outsiders. By 1930, 834 plots taken up - 358 in A class, 169 in B, 307 in C. 'All members are literate and belong to the upper middle class,' Khem Chand wrote, with just a hint of snobbery.

Khem Chand's expectation that the cost of houses would range from Rs 4,000 to Rs 12,000 was overtaken

O 3. An 'A' Class house in Model Town, 1930.

O 4. An 'A' Class house in Model Town, 1930.

O 5. An 'A' Class house in Model Town, 1930.

O 6. A 'B' Class house in Model Town, 1930.

O 7. A 'C' Class house in Model Town, 1930.

O 8. A 'C' Class house in Model Town, 1930.

by inflation and the ambitions of some of the new members. The actual range began at Rs 4,000 but reached as high as Rs 40,000. The Society offered to act as agent to supervision of construction for a fee of 7 ½ % of the construction cost. The Members could choose from a menu of 100 plans of pre-designed houses, each combining 'the best features of Indian and European houses and designed to suit the Lahore climate.' Many were designed by the Society's own architect M.C. Khanna. By 1930, more than half the houses had been constructed through the Society. The speed and efficiency for such construction seems almost unbelievable. Khem Chand maintained in his report that the three built under his personal supervision, 'one of them was completed in 32 days, another in 6 weeks and the 3rd in 10 weeks. All the 3 houses have shown the greatest savings over estimated cost.' The Society charged a Municipal tax of 2 ½ % of cost of construction once.

The recommended material for construction was cement concrete with the roofs and lintels being made of reinforced bricks. An innovation was the introduction of flush systems. 'Many Members have installed flush system in the water closets, according to the Kentucky pattern, which are working satisfactorily (...) These sanitary closets can be installed at a cost of Rs 250 for a single and Rs 350 for 2 adjacent closets.'

For electricity, the Society relied upon its own generating plant. Power was supplied at the same rate as that applied to Lahore's citizens. 'If greater use of current is made,' Khem Chand argued, 'then it may be possible to reduce the charges to below Lahore rates. So far 100 connections have been given.'

Communications remained a luxury. 'As the Government charges for Telephones are exorbitant, greater

O 9. A 'C' Class house in Model Town, 1930. Built by Khem Chand in 32 days, at a cost of Rs 6,500.

use of telephones is not being made. At present there are only six telephones in the town connected with the Lahore exchange.' The Post and Telegraph office was located in an improvised building near the Club. The New building was proposed opposite Block A.'

The community services included a Dairy Farm (Khem Chand's scheme proposed a Cooperative Dairy farm, a five acre Poultry yard, 220 acres to be reserved for fruit growing, and six acres reserved for Children's Nursery. The first school was started on an experimental basis for two years. 'The experiment was a great success', and in October 1929, the School was raised to High School standard.

Social interaction between the 'different communities' was encouraged through clubs. A Ladies Club started in 1926 closed down for lack of interest. Two sites were earmarked, each of six acres, one for a Men's Club and the other for a Mixed Club. Only one was built, and that too served as an office for the Society and as a Dak bungalow for casual visitors. A Library was started in the club in 1927. A site was reserved for Hotel, attached to the hotel would have been a 'Barat Ghar' or Community Wedding Hall. A site was also demarcated for a cinema. Occasional Cinema shows, concert lectures and performances were held in the Club building.

O 10. Club Building at Model Town, 1930.

O 11. A View in Model Town, 1930.

Model Town's distance from main Lahore posed predictable problems regarding transport to and from the main city. From 1925 onwards, the Society maintained a regular Passenger Transport Service between Model Town and Lahore. Those who had to go daily to Lahore to attend their business could buy a monthly pass for Rs. 7.

By 1930, the total length of roads within Model Town measured 32 miles. 'The outer road 6 miles in length is 75 feet wide and has fruit garden on one side for its entire length. 4 Diagonal roads are 90 ft. wide, the Circular Road of 2 miles is 70 ft. wide and some roads are of 40 and 45 ft. width and a majority of roads are 50 ft. wide.' Khem Chand's proposal for the names of the roads was imaginative if not too practical: ' A new departure is to be made from the prevailing custom of calling them after names of persons, or the American system of giving them numbers. It is proposed to plant trees of the same kind on each road calling the road by the name of the tree plants along side of it.'

Perhaps the most sensitive aspect of this experiment in communal integration was the plan to accommodate the separate places of worship for the different religious communities. '8 sites have been reserved for Places of Worship. The Society has agreed to give land free, provided a Community wanting to build a decent place of worship collects at least Rs 10,000 for a good building suitable for that purpose. Attempts are being made by members interested in the matter to collect subscriptions for Mandir, a Musjid and a Gurdwara. Suitable sites have been set apart for cremation ground, burial ground as a cemetery.'

Cleanliness being next to godliness was assured with municipal services and keeping the streets clear of beggars: 'Street begging has been prohibited and all beggars and mendicants are turned out the area.'

The report Khem Chand authored and published a decade after his 'faint' idea had taken form included this paragraph that encapsulated his experience: 'In this country where the Garden City movement was non-existent and the Cooperative movement little understood, it was no easy matter to collect over 900 individuals belong to the most critical class and having different religions, different opinions, following different professions and coming from different parts of the country and to organize them into an Association not for making profits, but for spending money on a scheme which looked like a wild goose chase. It is remarkable that with a share capital of only Rs 90,000 we have laid the foundations of the Ideal Town on a firm base and managed to create assets of over 30 lakhs of rupees and, including the Share capital, have a liability of only 3½ lakhs. These results have been attained by tremendous hard work, considerable patience, a great deal of worry and after overcoming innumerable difficulties and obstacles.'

His Model Town has been the home of numerous generations of residents - among them Princess Bamba Sutherland (the granddaughter of the Sikh Maharaja Ranjit Singh) who resided in 104 A, and the plebeian Prime Minister Mian Nawaz Sharif whose family owned a row of houses in Block H. The 184 initial members who met in response to Khem Chand's solicitation in 1920 have grown over the years until by 2002, Model Town accommodates a population of 70,000 residents, most of them living in 6000 or so houses carved out of the expansive gardens he sought so assiduously to protect. Khem Chand's ambitious dream of achieving a population of 1000 homes has been more than surpassed, and his vision derided by many at the time more than vindicated.

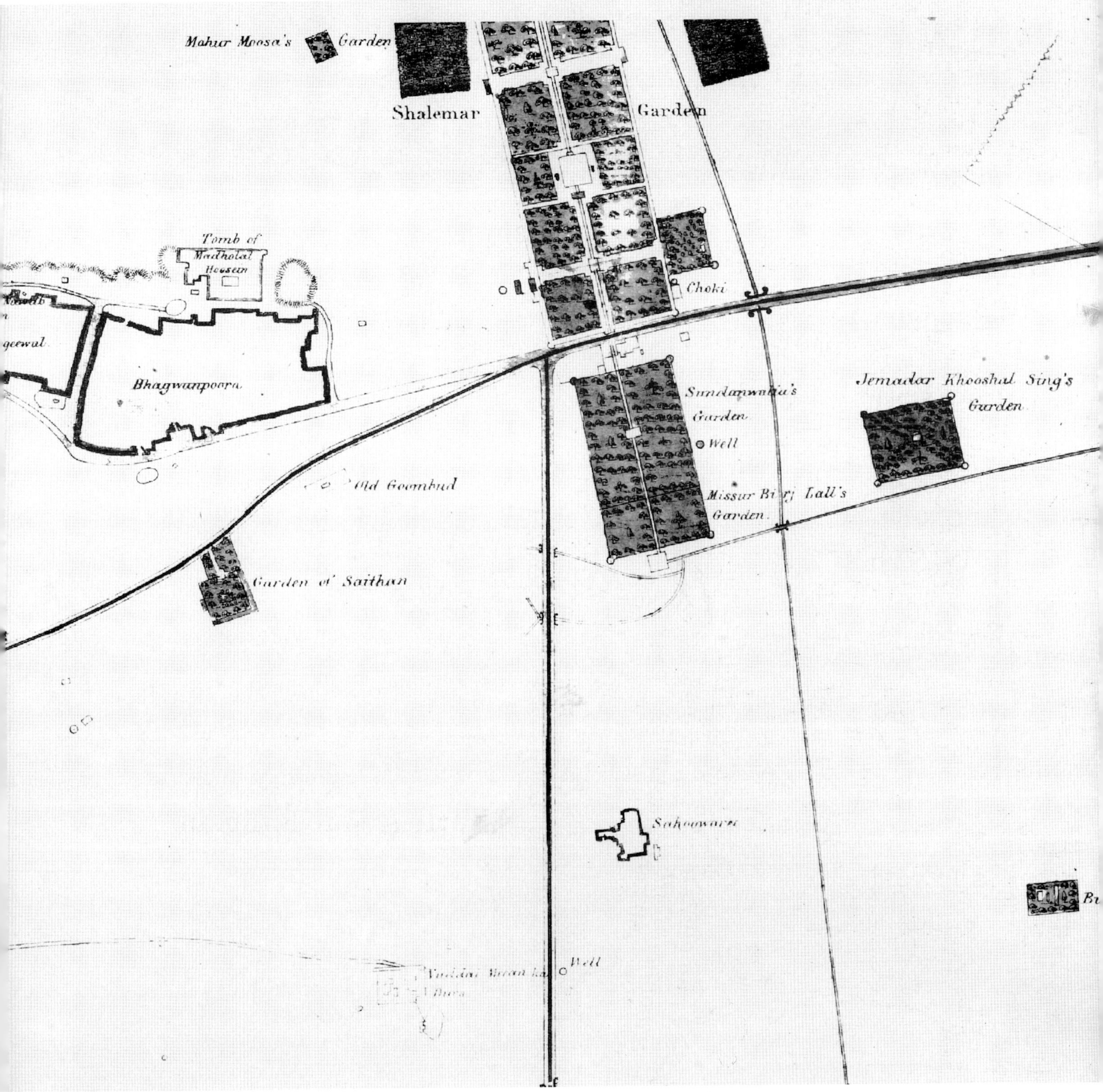

Detail from 1867 map.

SHALIMAR GARDENS

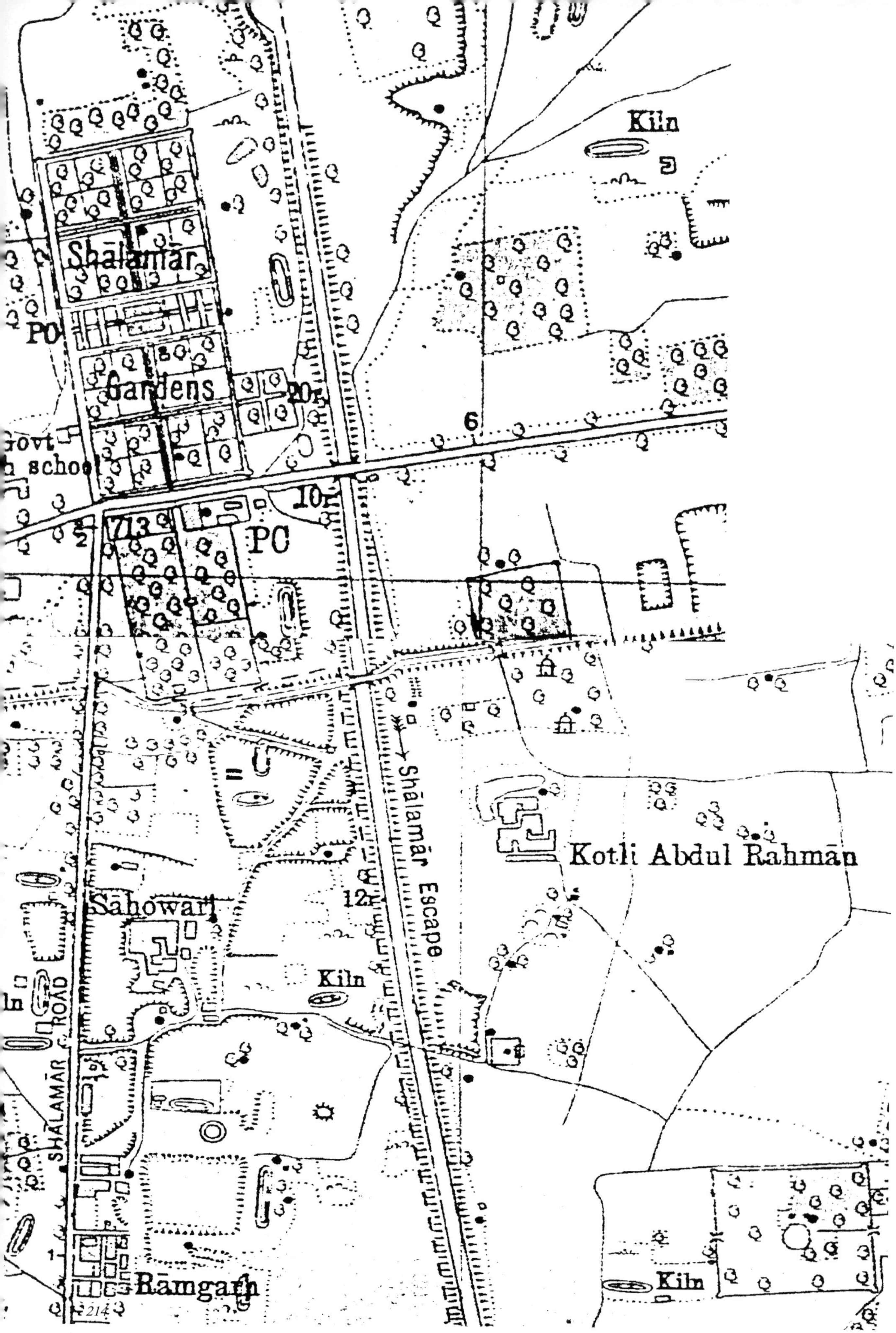

Detail from 1927 map

P 1. THE CHENTGHAR

P 1. THE CHENTGHAR

Published in W. Griggs, *The Journal of Indian Art* No. 19 (July 1887).

A gateway of Mughal times, this chromolithograph is the only record available of what must have been in its day a handsome monument, inferior to but not entirely overshadowed by the more sumptuous tiled Gulabi Bagh gateway near Shalimar Gardens on the Grand Trunk Road.

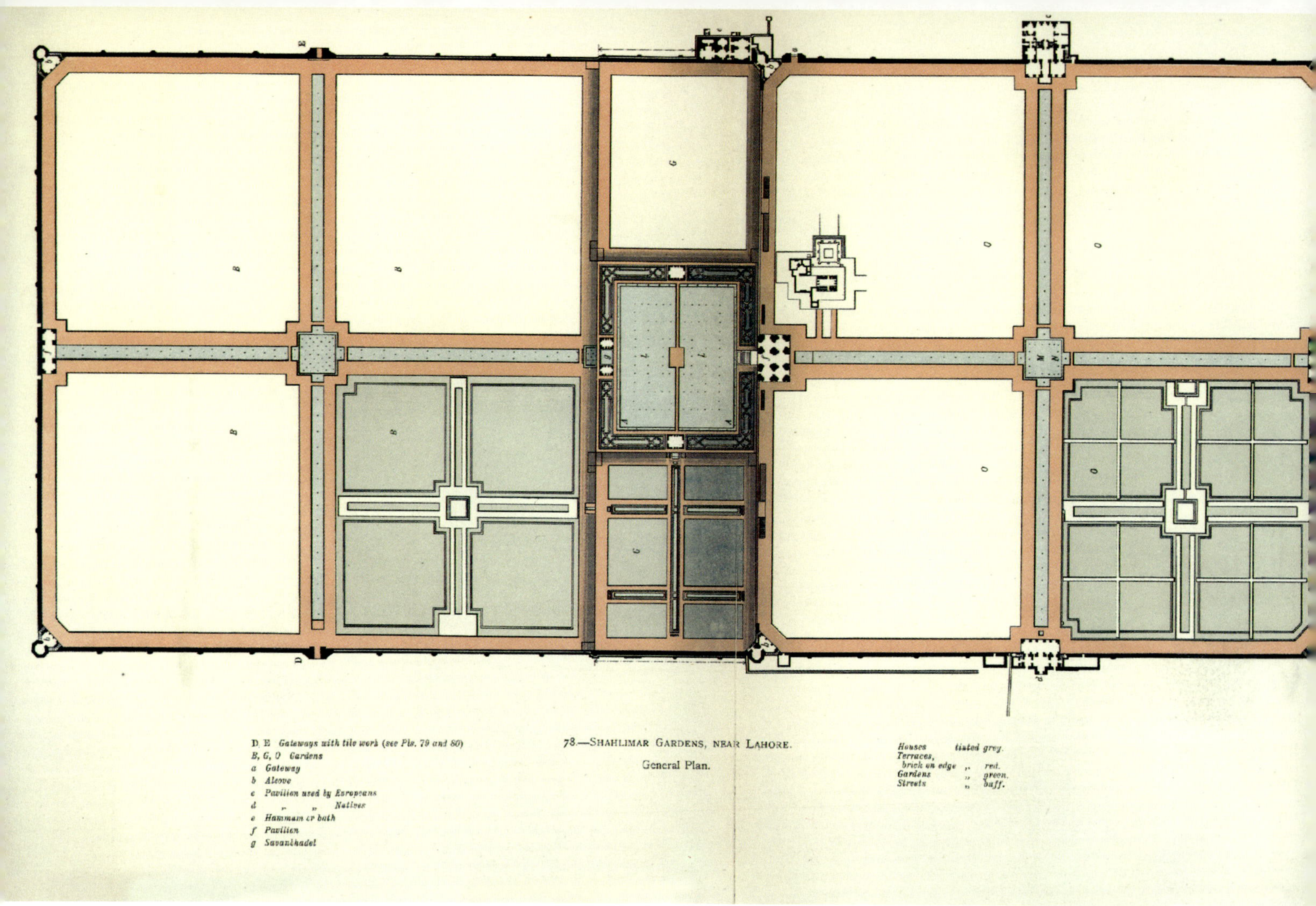

P 2. LAYOUT OF SHALIMAR GARDENS

P 2. LAYOUT OF SHALIMAR GARDENS

Liithograph published in W. Griggs, *India: Photographs and Drawings of Historical Buildings (London, 1896), no.78.*

This schematic layout shows to best advantage the ordered symmetry of the Shalimar gardens, one of the best surviving examples of the Mughals as horticulturalists.

Laid out under the orders of the emperor Shah Jahan over about 40 acres of land north east of the city of Lahore, it was completed in 1642 the collaboration of Ali Mardan Khan and Mulla Alaulmulk Tuni.

The enclosed gardens were a refuge for the emperor and his family, its enclosed walls providing a privacy court ritual dictated. Buildings afforded overnight accommodation, and the quartered gardens themselves, cooled by over 450 fountains, provided a pleasurable distraction from the heat of the apartments in the Lahore Fort, some three miles distant.

The original approach would have been from the lowest terrace, moving upwards and higher through the garden, from the lower Faiz Baksh (the Boon of Plenty) to the Farah Baksh (the Boon of Fragrance).

P 3. ARCHITECTURAL DETAILS OF SHALIMAR GARDENS

Three lithographs published in W. Griggs, *India: Photographs and Drawings of Historical Buildings (London, 1896), nos.79-81.*

i. Details of marble seat, borders and fountains (no.81).
ii. Gateway D (no.80).
Iii. Gateway E (no.79).

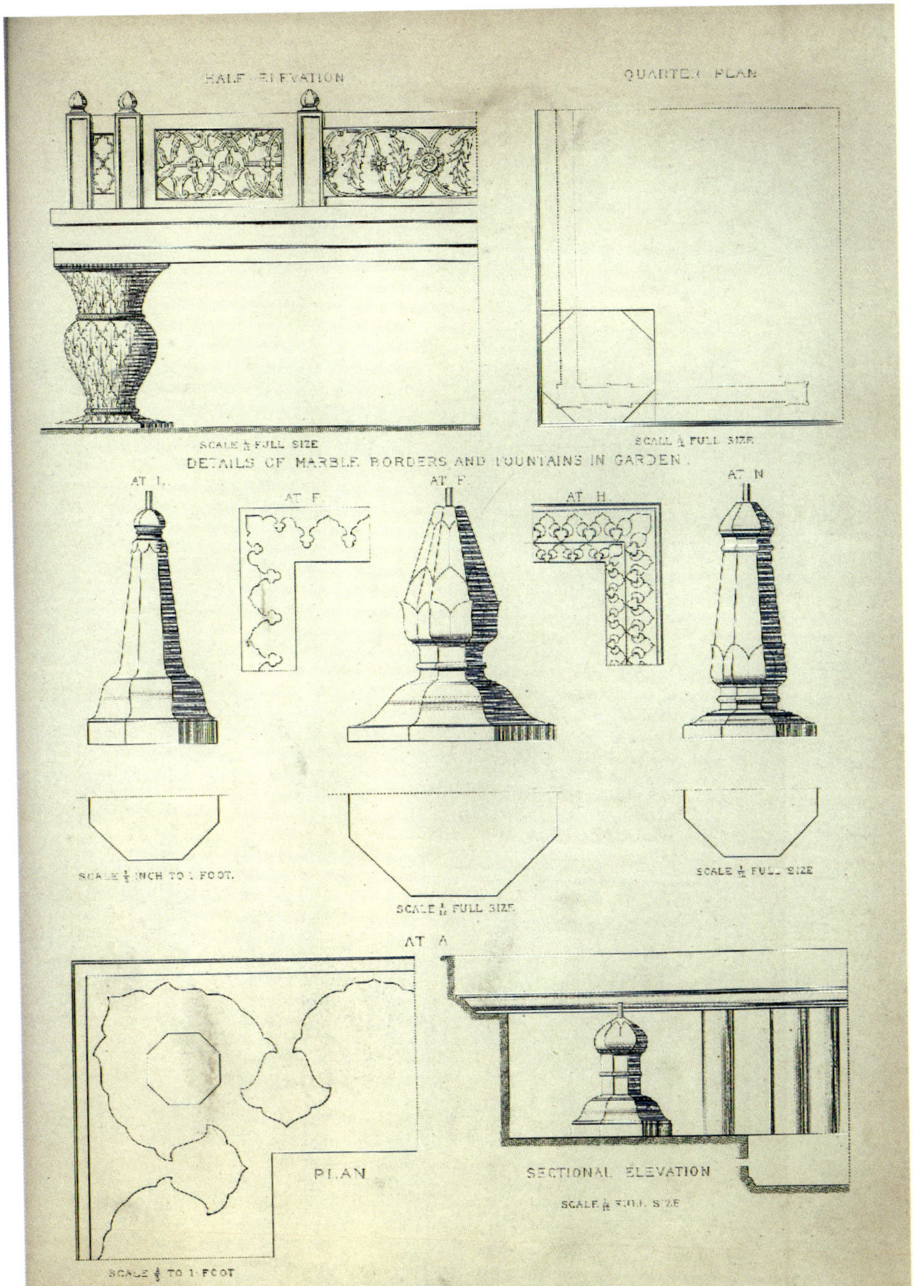

81.—SHAHLIMAR GARDENS, NEAR LAHORE.
Details of marble seat, borders, and fountains.

P 3 (i). Details of marble seat, borders and fountains (no.81).

79.—Shahlimar Gardens, near Lahore.

P 3 (ii). Gateway E (no.79).

P 3 (iii). Gateway D (no.80).

P 4. THE PAVILION AND MARBLE CASCADE

P 4. THE PAVILION AND MARBLE CASCADE

Photo postcard, c. 1930. Photo by B.N. Kapur, Photogoods dealer, Lahore. (RS/90)

The carved marble slab has been placed at an angle to allow water to ripple down, moistening the flowers carved in the white marble.

P 5. AN AERIAL VIEW OF THE GARDENS

P 5. AN AERIAL VIEW OF THE GARDENS

Photograph, c.1920.

This photograph, looking westwards in the direction of the city, shows the fountains in the second intermediate terrace of the gardens. On the left is the marble pavilion that overlooks the central reservoir, and on either side of the tank are two complementary structures, once made of marble but now of masonry. 'The marble pavilions, by the central reservoir,' Latif says, 'were used in adorning the Ram Bagh of Amritsar, and, in their stead, structures of brick and whitewash were substituted.' [Latif(1892), p.144.]

P 6. THE MIDDLE TERRACE

P 6. THE MIDDLE TERRACE

Photo postcard, c. 1920. (RS/92)

LIST OF ILLUSTRATIONS

B2(a). MAP OF THE WALLED CITY OF LAHORE. June 1846. Drawn by T. King, and printed at the Lithographic establishment of the Quarter Master General's Office, Horse Guards, London, 1847. (Courtesy: British Library.)

B 2 (b). A MODEL OF THE WALLED CITY. A wooden model of the walled city, c. 1925.

B 3. A SIKH PARTY ENTERING ONE OF THE CITY GATES
Lithograph based on a sketch by Prince Alexei Soltykoff, March 1842, titled: *Une Rue de Lahore* [A road of Lahore].

B 4. MASTI GATE . Photo postcard, c. 1920. (Rs/100)

B 5. DELHI GATE

B 5(a) Photograph, c. 1920.

B 5(b) Photo postcard, c. 1920. (RS/38)

B 6. MOCHI GATE. 1888.

B 7. SHAHALMI GATE.

B 7(a) Photo postcard, c.1920. (RS/37)

B 7(b) Photograph, c.1920.

B 8. RATAN CHAND'S TANK. Photo postcard, c.1910. Photo by Bremner. (RS/9A)

B 9. LAHORI GATE.

B 9(a). Sketch by B. Blascheck, n.d. (probably 1930).

B 9(b). LAHORI GATE. Photograph, c. 1920.

B 10. BHATI GATE. Photo postcard, c.1920. (RS/35)

B 11. TAXALI GATE. Watercolour by William Simpson, 1864.

C 1. MAP OF THE LAHORE FORT. Prepared from an original compiled from data provided by Fakir Qamruddin, 1883.

C 2. A PICNIC IN HAZURI BAGH. Photograph, c., 1870.

C 3. VIEWS OF THE LAHORE FORT.

C 3 (a). VIEW OF THE ALAMGIRI GATE AND THE LAHORE FORT. Photo postcard, c. 1930. (RS/9)

C 3(b). VIEW OF THE LAHORE FORT. Photo postcard, c. 1930.

C 4. THE MARBLE KACHERI . Photo postcard, c. 1930. (RS/21)

C 5. THE SHEESH MAHAL . Photo postcard, c. 1930. (RS/98)

C 6. THE INTERIOR OF THE SHEESH MAHAL. Photo postcard by Bliss & Tilden, c.1930. (RS/19)

C 7. THE VIEW FROM THE SHEESH MAHAL . Photo postcard, c. 1930. (RS/17)

C 8. THE NAULAKHA PAVILION. Photo postcard, c.1930.

C 9. THE ARMOURY. Photo postcard, c.1930. (RS/22)

C 10. SOME SIKH GUNS ON DISPLAY. Photo postcard, c.1930. (RS/23)

C 11. THE BARRACKS WITHIN THE LAHORE FORT. Photo postcard, c. 1920. Titled: '476. 6th Devon's Bungalow Fort Lahore'

C 12. THE VIEW FROM THE ROOF OF THE SHEESH MAHAL. Photograph by Samuel Bourne, c.1864 (no. 416).

C 13. ANOTHER VIEW FROM THE SHEESH MAHAL ROOF. Photo postcard by H.A. Mirza & Sons, Delhi, c. 1930. (RS/14)

C 14. THE HAZURI BAGH PAVILION . Photo postcard, c. 1930. (RS/24)

C 15. THE INTERIOR OF THE BADSHAHI MOSQUE. Photo postcard by Herman Dass & Sons, Umballa, c. 1930. (RS/26)

C 16. VIEW OF RANJIT SINGH'S SAMADHI AND BADAMI BAGH. Photo postcard, c. 1930. (RS/5)

C 17. A VIEW OF THE OLD CITY. Photo postcard, c. 1930.

C 18. A PANORAMIC VIEW OF THE OLD CITY. Photo postcard, c. 1930. (RS/4)

D 1. THE GOLDEN MOSQUE. Photo postcard, c. 1930. (RS/29)

D 2. A STEREOSCOPIC VIEW OF A LAHORE BAZAAR. Stereoscopic photograph by James Ricalton, 1888. (RS/L)

D 3. GATEWAY TO WAZIR KHAN'S MOSQUE., Chromolithograph, from a drawing by Amir Buksh, and published in W. Griggs *Journal of Indian Art* No. 19 (July 1887).

D 4. THE INNER SIDE OF THE ENTRANCE TO WAZIR KHAN'S MOSQUE. Chromolithograph by W.Griggs, from a drawing by Sher Muhammad. Published in *The Journal of Indian Art* No. 19, (July 1887).

D 5. THE INNER FACADE OF THE MOSQUE OF WAZIR KHAN, Watercolour by Muhammad Din, c.1880.

D 6. FRESCO DECORATION IN THE MOSQUE OF WAZIR KHAN. Chromolithograph by W. Griggs from a drawing by Mohamed Din, Allah-ud-din and Amir Baksh, c. 1880. Published in *The Journal of Indian Art* No. 19, (July 1887).

D 7. A CROSS-SECTION OF WAZIR KHAN'S MOSQUE. Drawing by Fred H. Andrews. Published in *The Journal of Indian Art* No. 19, (July 1887).

D 8. THE SHRINE OF MIRAN BADSHAH. Photograph, c. 1930.

E 1. VIEW OF THE INNER CITY . Photo postcard, c.1930. (RS/33)

E 2 STREET SCENE. Photo postcard, published by the Punjab Religious Book Society, Lahore, c.1930. (RS/34)

E 3. A HOUSE IN THE INNER CITY. Photo postcard, c.1930.

E 4. AN OIL PRESS WITHIN THE OLD CITY. Photograph, c. 1930.

E 5. HONORARY MAGISTRATES COURT . Photograph, c. 1880.

F 1. RAI MELA RAM'S BUILDING, Photo postcard, c. 1930. (RS/28)

F 2. LADY WILLINGDON HOSPITAL, NEAR TAXALI GATE . Photograph by Bali and Sons, 1933.

F 3. THE NEW DENTAL HOSPITAL. Photo, 1930.

F 4. CENTRAL MODEL SCHOOL. Photo postcard, c. 1930. (RS/41)

F 5. GOVERNMENT COLLEGE. Photo postcard, c. 1930.

F 6. GOVERNMENT COLLEGE HOSTEL.Photograph, 1921.

F 7. THE NEW VETERINARY COLLEGE. Photograph, 1916.

F 8. THE STAIRCASE OF THE NEW VETERINARY COLLEGE. Photo, 1916.

F 9. THE TOMB OF ANARKALI. Print from a sketch by an anonymous artist, c. 1900.

F 10-14. THE TEMPORARY LEGISLATIVE COUNCIL CHAMBER AND OFFICES.

F 10. THE TEMPORARY COUNCIL CHAMBER. UNDER CONSTRUCTION Photo, 1922.

F 11. THE COMPLETED LEGISLATIVE COUNCIL CHAMBER. Photo, 1922.

F 12. THE CHAMBER BUILDING SEEN FROM THE SOUTHWEST. Photo, 1922.

F 13. THE INTERIOR OF THE COUNCIL CHAMBER. Photo, 1922.

F 14. THE INTERIOR OF THE COUNCIL CHAMBER. Photo, 1922.

F 15. THE PIPALS RESIDENCE. Photograph, 28 August 1926

F 16. THE TOWN HALL. Photo postcard by B.N. Kapur, Lahore, c. 1920. (RS/40)

F 17. CHARBURJI GATEWAY. Watercolour by Major R. Mitford, c. 1880.

G 1. PUNJAB UNIVERSITY HALL. Photo postcard, c.1920. (RS/47)

G 2. THE ZAMZAMA CANNON.

G 2 (a). THE ZAMZAMA CANNON. Stereoscopic photograph by James Ricalton, 1888. (RS/K)

G 2 (b). THE ZAMZAMA CANNON. Photo postcard, c.1920. (RS/20A)

G 3. THE LAHORE MUSEUM.

G 3(a) THE FAÇADE OF THE LAHORE MUSEUM. Photo postcard, c.1920. (RS/44)

G 3(b). THE LAHORE MUSEUM, SEEN FROM THE PUNJAB UNIVERSITY. Photo postcard, c. 1938. (RS/7A)

G 4. TOLLINTON MARKET.

G 4 (a). UNDER CONSTRUCTION. Photograph, 1863.

G 4 (b). DAILY LABOUR RETURNS FOR JUNE 1863.

G 4 (c). TOLLINTON MUNICIPAL MARKET. Photo postcard, c.1920, by B. N. Kapur, Photographic Dealer, Lahore, No.15. (RS/50)

G 4 (d). POULTRY FOR SALE AT REAR OF TOLLINTON MARKET. Photo postcard, c.1920. (RS/45)

G 5(a). WAZIR KHAN'S BARADARI. Stereoscopic photograph by James Ricalton, 1888. (RS/L)

G 5(b). WAZIR KHAN'S BARADARI. Photo postcard, c.1920. (RS/43)

G 6. THE PUNJAB PUBLIC LIBRARY. Photograph, 1938.

G 7. PWD BUILDING, Photo postcard. c. 1920. (RS/53)

G 8. OLD ANARKALI, Photo postcard. c. 1920. (RS/48)

G 9. YOUNG MEN'S CHRISTIAN ASSOCIATION (YMCA). Photo postcard, c. 1920. (RS/C)

G 10. THE NILA GUMBAD AREA. Photo postcard, c. 1920. (RS/54)

G 11. KING EDWARD MEDICAL COLLEGE. Photo postcard, c.1920.

G 12. FORMAN CHRISTIAN COLLEGE. Photo postcard, c. 1920. Photo by Fred Bremner, Lahore and Quetta.

G 13. GOVERNMENT TELEGRAPH OFFICE. Photo postcard, c. 1920. Photo by B. N. Kapur, Photogoods Dealer, Lahore. (RS/73)

G 14. THE BANK OF BENGAL BUILDING. Photo postcard, c. 1920. (RS/52)

G 15. THE GENERAL POST OFFICE. Photo postcard, c.1920. Photo by B. N. Kapur, Photogoods Dealer, Lahore. No.16. (RS/72)

G 16. THE GENERAL POST OFFICE. Photo postcard, c. 1940.

G 17. THE PUNJAB HIGH COURT (FROM THE EAST). Photograph, c. 1920.

G 18. THE PUNJAB HIGH COURT (FROM THE WEST). Photograph, c. 1925.

G 19. THE HIGH COURT BAR ASSOCIATION LIBRARY. Photograph, 1933.

G 20. THE LAHORE CATHEDRAL. Photo postcard, c. 1925. (RS/108)

G 21. THE LAHORE CATEHDRAL. Photo postcard, c. 1930.

G 22. THE STATUE OF LORD JOHN LAWRENCE . Photo postcard, c. 1920.

G 23. THE STATUE OF LORD LAWRENCE. Photo postcard, c. 1920. (RS/77)

G 24. A VIEW OF THE MALL. Photo postcard, c. 1930. (RS/58)

G 25. A VIEW OF THE MALL. Photo postcard, c.1930. (RS/60)

G 26. HALL ROAD JUNCTION. Photograph, December 1941.

G 27. CATHEDRAL GIRLS' HIGH SCHOOL. Photo postcard, c. 1900. Photo by Bremner. (RS 31/A)

G 28. A VIEW DOWN THE MALL. Photo postcard, c. 1930. (RS/59)

H 1. AERIAL VIEW OF CHARING CROSS AND THE CENTRAL MALL. Photograph, c. 1920.

H 2. THE STATUE OF QUEEN VICTORIA. Photograph, c. 1930.

H 3(a -o). THE PUNJAB ASSEMBLY BUILDING.

H 3(a). Layout in front of site.

H 3(b). Foundation Raft under construction.

H 3(c). Laying the foundation stone by Punjab Minister for Agriculture Sir Jogendra Singh, on 17 November 1935.

H 3(d). Centering for the Reinforced Concrete floor above basement.

H 3(e). Foundation raft approaching completion.

H 3(f). Girders being placed below Council Chamber.

H 3(g). Concreting the floor above the basement.

H 3(h). Front elevation in progress.

H 3(i). Masons at work on capitals of the columns in the main entrance.

H 3(j). View of completed Assembly building, from the Mall.

H 3(k). North View of the Council Chamber.

H 3(l). Grand staircase with vestibule in the hall.

H 3(m). The first floor vestibule.

H 3(n). Council Chamber

H 3(o). Tea Room

H 4. THE PUNJAB LEGISLATIVE ASSEMBLY BUILDING, Photo postcard, c.1940. (RS/62)

I 1. NEDOU'S HOTEL, Photo postcard, c.1940. (RS/61)

I 2. GOVERNOR'S HOUSE , Wood engraving, *Illustrated London News*, 27 November 1869.

I 3 (a). THE NORTHERN EXTENSION TO GOVERNMENT HOUSE, Photograph, 1915.

I 3 (b). CARVED BRACKETS IN GOVERNMENT HOUSE, Photograph, 1915.

I 4. THE LIEUTENANT-GOVERNOR'S CAMEL-CARRIAGE, Photograph by Bourne and Shepherd, 1864.

I 5. ENTRANCE GATE TO LAWRENCE GARDENS, Photograph, c. 1920.

I 6. LAWRENCE HALL, Woodcut engraving, published in *Illustrated London News*, 31 December 1864.

I 7. MONTGOMERY HALL, Photograph, c. 1910.

I 8. THE PUNJAB CLUB, Photo postcard, c. 1920. (RS/65)

I 9. AITCHISON COLLEGE, Photo postcard, c. 1920. (RS/64)

J 1. THE RESIDENCE FOR THE CHIEF JUSTICE, Photograph, 1935.

J 2. THE RESIDENCE FOR THE MINISTER OF FINANCE, Photograph, 1938.

J 3. THE RESIDENCE OF THE MINISTER OF EDUCATION., Photograph, 1938.

J 4. SPECIAL A-TYPE RESIDENCE., Photograph, 1927.

J 5. TYPE III A RESIDENCE, Photograph, 1927.

K 1(a). THE POLICE STATION ON FEROZEPUR ROAD UNDER CONSTRUCTION, Photograph, 1936.

K 1 (b). THE FAÇADE OF THE COMPLETED POLICE STATION, Photograph, 1937.

K 2. THE ROMAN CATHOLIC CATHEDRAL, LAHORE, Photo postcard, c. 1920. (RS/56)

K. 3. THE PUNJAB LIGHT HORSE HEADQUARTERS, Photograph, 1921.

L 1. LAHORE CENTRAL JAIL, Detail of 1867 map.

P 2. LAYOUT OF SHALIMAR GARDENS.

P 3(i). ARCHITECTURAL DETAILS OF SHALIMAR GARDENS: Details of marble seat, borders and fountains (no. 81)

P 3(ii). ARCHITECTURAL DETAILS OF SHALIMAR GARDENS: Gateway D (no.79)

P 3 (iii). ARCHITECTURAL DETAILS OF SHALIMAR GARDENS: Gateway E (no.80)

P 4. THE PAVILION AND MARBLE CASCADE. Photo postcard, c. 1930. Photo by B.N. Kapur, Photogoods dealer, Lahore. (RS/90)

P 5. AN AERIAL VIEW OF THE GARDENS. Photograph, c.1920.

P 6. THE MIDDLE TERRACE. Photo postcard, c. 1920. (RS/92)

BIBLIOGRAPHY

Aijazuddin, F. S.,

Sikh Portraits by European Artists (London, 1979).

Aitchison College (Lahore, 1986)

Lahore: Illustrated Views of the 19th Century (Ahmedabad/Lahore, 1991).

Historical Images of Pakistan (Lahore, 1992).

Rare Maps of Pakistan (Lahore, 2000).

Automobile Association of Northern India: Handbook (Lahore, 1934).

Baqir, M., *Lahore past and present* (Lahore, 1952).

Bence-Jones, M., *Palaces of the Raj* (London, 1973)

Berridge, P. S. A., *Couplings to the Khyber* (Newton Abbot, 1969).

Bruce, J. F., *A History of the University of the Punjab* (Lahore, 1933).

Cell, J.W., *Hailey: A Study in British Imperialism, 1872-1969* (Cambridge, 1992).

Chaghatai, Dr. A.,

The Badshahi Masjid (Lahore, 1972).

The Wazir Khan's Mosque, Lahore (Lahore, 1975).

De Silva, R. K., *Early Prints of Ceylon (Sri Lanka) 1800-1900*, (London, 1985).

Eastwick, E. B., *Handbook of the Punjab, Western Rajputana, Kashmir, and Upper Sindh* (London, 1883).

Elmslie, G. R., *Thirty-Five Years in the Punjab* (Edinburgh, 1908).

Garrett. H. L. O., *The Punjab a hundred years ago, as described by V. Jacquemont (1831) and A. Soltykoff (1842) (Lahore, 1935).*

Gazetteer of the Lahore District (General Editor: Sir Denzil Ibbetson):

1883-84 (1884; Sang-e-Meel Reprint, 1989).

1893-94 (Lahore, 1894).

1916 (Lahore, 1916).

Goulding, H. R., *Old Lahore* (Lahore, 1924).

Hardinge, C. S., *Recollections of India* (London, 1847).

Honigberger, J. M., *Thirty-Five Years in the East* (London, 1852).

Hugel, C., *Travels in Kashmir and the Punjab, containing a particular account of the government and character of the Sikhs* (London, 1845).

India: Photographs and Drawings of Historical Buildings. 100 Plates reproduced by W. Griggs from the collection in the late office of Curator of Ancient Monuments in India. (London, 1896).

Journal of the Panjab Historical Society (Calcutta, 1911-1921).

Kausar, S., Brand, M. and Wescoat Jr, J. L., *Shalamar Garden, Lahore* (Karachi, 1990).

Kerr, I. J., *Building the Railways of the Raj 1850-1900* (Delhi, 1995).

Khan, M. Waliullah, *Lahore and its important monuments* (Karachi, 1961; revised edition 1964).

Khosla, B. P.,
The "City Guide" Lahore (Lahore, 1932).
The "City Guide" Lahore (Lahore, 1942).

Lahore Directory 1914.

Latif, S. M.,
History of the Panjab (Calcutta, 1891)
Lahore: its history, architectural remains and antiquities (Lahore, 1892)

Lee, H., *Brothers in the Raj* (Karachi, 2002).

Login, L., *Sir John Login and Duleep Singh* (London, 1890).

Lucas, C. J. (Ed.), *James Ricalton's Photographic Travelogue of Imperial India* (Lewiston, New York, 1970).

Malik, M. B. K., *Hundred Years of Pakistan Railways* (Karachi, 1962).

Master Plan for Greater Lahore (Lahore, 1973).

Mumtaz, K. K., *Architecture in Pakistan* (1985).

Qadeer, M. A., *Lahore: Urban Development in the Third World* (Lahore, 1983).

Scholberg, H., *The District Gazetteers of British India: A Bibliography* (Zug, Switzerland, 1970).

Stratton, A. W., *Letters from India* (London, 1908).

Thompson, J. P., "The Tomb of the Emperor Jehangir", *Journal of the Panjab Historical Society* (1911), Vol.1, No.1, pp. 12-30.

Thornton, T. H., and Kipling, J. L., *Lahore* (Lahore, 1876).

Vogel, J. Ph., "Historical Notes on the Lahore Fort", *Journal of the Panjab Historical Society* (1911), Vol. I, No.1, pp. 38-55.

"The Shalimar Bagh of Lahore in 1712", *Journal of the Panjab Historical Society* (1914), Vol. II, No.2, pp. 170-171.

Wilson, H. (Ed.), *Travels in the Himalayan Provinces of Hindustan and the Panjab from 1819-1825 by William Moorcroft and George Trebeck* (London, 1841; OUP reprint, Karachi 1979).

INDEX

E

F

G

H

I

J

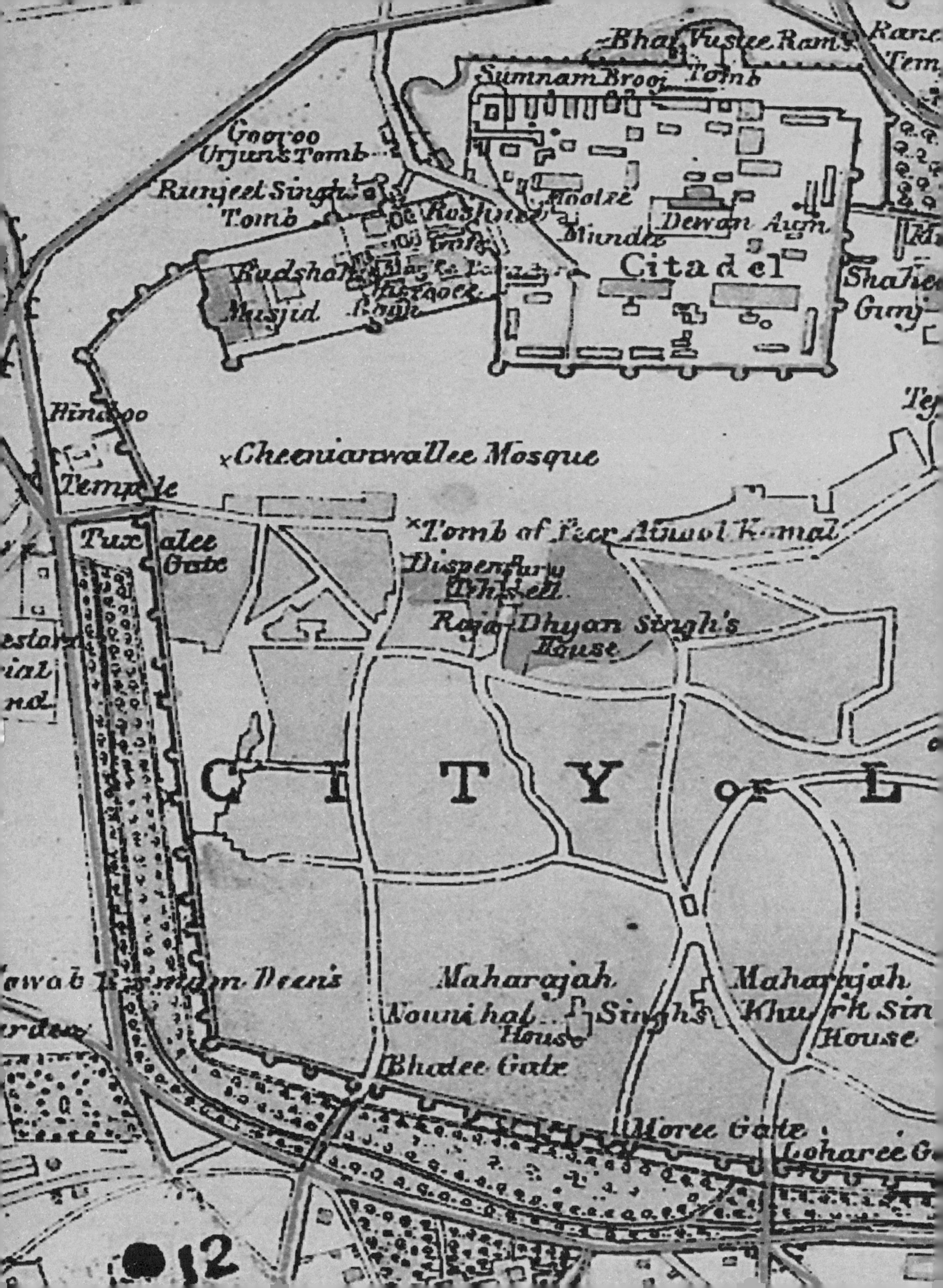
Bhai Vustee Ram's
Sumnam Brooj
Tomb
Gooroo Urjun's Tomb
Runjeet Singh's Tomb
Dewan Aum
Citadel
Budshahee Musjid
Hindoo Temple
Cheeniaonwallee Mosque
Tuxalee Gate
Dispensary
Tehseel
Raja Dhyan Singh's House
CITY of
Maharajah Nounihal Singh's House
Maharajah
House
Bhatee Gate
Moree Gate
12